The
Fast Forward
MBA in Finance

W9-AWM-104

The Fast Forward MBA in Finance

JOHN A. TRACY

John Wiley & Sons, Inc.

New York • Chichester • Brisbane • Toronto • Singapore

This text is printed on acid-free paper.

Copyright © 1996 by John A. Tracy
Published by John Wiley & Sons, Inc.

All rights reserved. Published simultaneously in Canada.

Reproduction or translation of any part of this work beyond
that permitted by Section 107 or 108 of the 1976 United
States Copyright Act without the permission of the copyright
owner is unlawful. Requests for permission or further
information should be addressed to the Permissions
Department, John Wiley & Sons, Inc.

This publication is designed to provide accurate and
authoritative information in regard to the subject matter. It is
sold with the understanding that the publisher is not engaged
in rendering legal, accounting, or other professional services.
If legal advice or other expert assistance is required, the
services of a competent professional person should be sought.

ISBN 0-471-10930-4

Printed in the United States of America

10 9 8 7 6 5 4 3 2

for
Richard and Robert, my dog track buddies,
who have helped me more than they know.

CONTENTS

This book is written for business managers, as well as for bankers, consultants, lawyers, and other business professionals who need a solid and practical understanding of how business makes profit, the cash flow from profit, the capital needed to support profit-making operations, and the cost of capital. Business managers and professionals don't have time to wade through a 600-plus page tome; they need a practical guide that gets to the point directly with clear and convincing examples.

In broad terms, this book explains the tools of the trade for analyzing accounting and financial information. *Financial statements* are the primary sources of such information. Therefore, financial statements are the best framework to explain and demonstrate how managers analyze accounting and financial information to make decisions and to keep control. Surprisingly, most books of this ilk do not use the financial statements framework. My book offers many advantages in this respect.

This book explains and clearly demonstrates those indispensable analysis techniques that street-smart business managers use to:

- Make profit.
- Control the capital invested in assets needed for making profit and to decide on the sources of capital for these asset investments.
- Generate cash flow from profit.

The threefold orientation of this book fits hand in glove with the three basic financial statements of every business: the profit report (income statement), the financial condition report (balance sheet), and the cash flow report (cash flow statement). These three "financials" are the center of gravity for all businesses.

This book puts much more emphasis on cash flow than typical books in this basic area of management skills. As a matter of fact, cash flow is put on an equal footing with profit. Business managers never can ignore the cash flow consequences of their decisions. Higher profit may mean lower cash flow; managers must clearly understand why, as well as the cash flow timing of their profit.

The book begins with a four-chapter review of financial statements, which are explained from the manager's point of view, in contrast with the generally accepted accounting principles (GAAP) point of view. GAAP are not wrong of course; externally reported financial statements must be prepared following these accounting standards. GAAP provide the bedrock rules for measuring profit. Business managers obviously need to know how much profit the business is earning.

But, to carry out their decision-making and control functions, managers need more information than is reported in the external financial statements of a business. GAAP are the point of departure for preparing the more informative financial statements and other accounting reports needed by business managers.

The "failing" of GAAP is *not* that these accounting rules are wrong for measuring profit, nor are they wrong for presenting the financial condition of a business—not at all. It's just that GAAP do not deal with all the types of information needed by managers. In fact, much of this management information is very confidential and would never be included in an external financial report open to public view.

Let me strongly suggest that you personalize every example in the book. Take the example as your own business; imagine that you are the principal owner or the top-level manager of the business, and that you will the reap the gains of every decision or suffer the consequences, as the case may be.

This book never would have happened without the initial push by John Mahaney, to whom I express my heartfelt appreciation. As usual, the editors at John Wiley were superb. Many thanks to Janet Coleman and all the others at 605 Third Avenue. I would like to mention that John Wiley & Sons has been my publisher for more than 20 years, and I'm very proud of our long relationship.

John A. Tracy
Boulder, Colorado
February 1996

The
Fast Forward
MBA in Finance

PART 1

Financial Statements for Managers

CHAPTER 1

Getting Down to Business

Every business has three primary financial tasks that determine the success or failure of the enterprise and by which its managers are judged:

- *Profit*—achieving profit goals through making sales and controlling expenses
- *Cash flow*—generating cash flow from profit and other sources and putting the cash to good use
- *Financial health*—deciding on the financial structure of the entity and controlling the financial condition and solvency of the business

To continue in existence for any period of time, a business has to make profit, generate cash flow, and stay solvent.

Accomplishing these financial objectives depends on doing all the other management functions well. Business managers are paid to develop new products and services, expand markets, improve productivity, anticipate changes, adapt to new technology, think out clear strategies, hire and motivate people, make tough choices, solve problems, and arbitrate conflicts of interests between different constituencies of business (customers who want lower prices versus employees who want higher wages, for example); and managers are expected to act ethically, comply with a myriad of laws, be responsible members of society, and not harm our natural environment—all the while making profit, generating cash flow, and avoiding insolvency.

ACCOUNTING SYSTEM OVERVIEW

The bedrock financial information of a business is found in its financial statements. Financial statements are prepared from the accounting database and records of the business, which in turn depend on its accounting system. The accounting database and records should be complete, accurate, and up to date; these are very tough demands that require a very good accounting system. Figure 1.1 presents an overview of the accounting system. Notice the Janus, or two-faced, nature of the accounting system that looks in two different directions, inside and outside. There is a certain amount of tension between the internal and the external demands on the accounting system.

THE INTERNAL FUNCTIONS

In addition to the day-to-day operational demands—preparing payroll checks, paying bills on time, sending out invoices to customers, and so on—please notice the other two main *internal* functions of the accounting system shown in Figure 1.1, which are the preparation of management control reports and the preparation of internal financial statements. Management control requires specific attention to a very large number of details; quite literally thousands of things can go wrong. Management decision making, in contrast, focuses attention on relatively few key factors. Decision making looks at the forest, not the trees. Thus, for planning and decision-making purposes, managers need financial statements that are condensed and global in nature—that present the big picture.

In passing, it should be mentioned that accounting information seldom comprises the whole set of information needed in decision making and control. Managers use many, many other sources of information: competitors' sales prices, delivery problems with suppliers, employee morale, and so on. Nonaccounting data comes from a wide diversity of sources: shopping the competition, sales force reports, market research studies, personnel department records, and so on. For example, customer files are very important and usually include both accounting data (past sales history) and nonaccounting data (sales reps assigned to each customer).

THE EXTERNAL FUNCTIONS

In addition to their internal functions within the business organization, accountants have two primary *external* responsibilities: the preparation of tax returns and external financial reports (see Figure 1.1 again). Accountants have to stay abreast of changing accounting standards to prepare external financial reports. State and federal income taxes, payroll taxes, property taxes, and sales taxes are governed by exceedingly complex and constantly changing laws, rules, and forms. Accountants have their hands full just keeping up with tax regulations and forms. Income tax accounting is beyond the scope of this book.

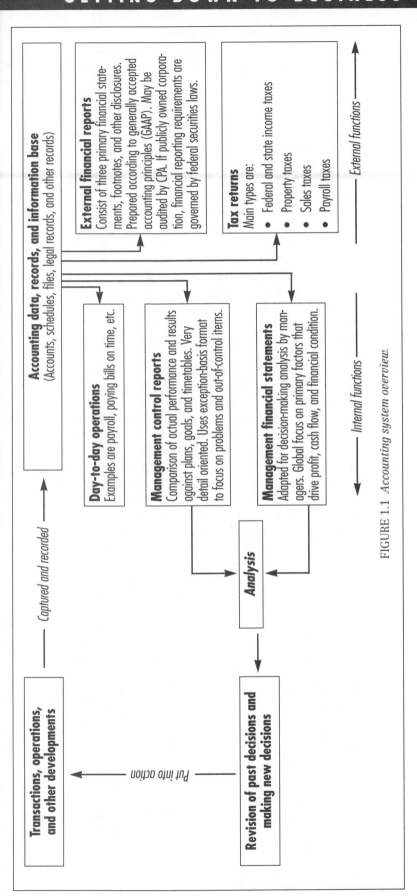

FIGURE 1.1 Accounting system overview.

External functions

Internal functions

Accounting data, records, and information base
(Accounts, schedules, files, legal records, and other records)

External financial reports
Consist of three primary financial statements, footnotes, and other disclosures. Prepared according to generally accepted accounting principles (GAAP). May be audited by CPA. If publicly owned corporation, financial reporting requirements are governed by federal securities laws.

Tax returns
Main types are:
- Federal and state income taxes
- Property taxes
- Sales taxes
- Payroll taxes

Day-to-day operations
Examples are payroll, paying bills on time, etc.

Management control reports
Comparison of actual performance and results against plans, goals, and timetables. Very detail oriented. Uses exception-basis format to focus on problems and out-of-control items.

Management financial statements
Adapted for decision-making analysis by managers. Global focus on primary factors that drive profit, cash flow, and financial condition.

Analysis

Captured and recorded

Transactions, operations, and other developments

Put into action

Revision of past decisions and making new decisions

External Financial Reports

In the next chapter I give an overview of external financial reports. Please bear in mind that this book does not examine in any great detail the *external* financial reports of business.* Instead, internal financial statements are the focus of attention and are developed in Chapters 3 and 4. Only brief comments about external financial reports of particular importance to managers are mentioned here.

External financial reports include footnotes that are integral addenda to the financial statements. Footnotes are needed because the external financial report is directed to the *outside* investors and creditors of the business who are not directly involved in the day-to-day affairs of the business. Managers should already know most of the information disclosed in footnotes. If managers prefer to have footnotes included with their internal financial statements, then the footnotes should be included—probably in much more detail and covering more sensitive matters than footnotes presented in external financial reports.

The financial statements included in the annual external financial reports sent to the creditors and shareholders of a business must conform with *generally accepted accounting principles* (GAAP). These are the authoritative guidelines, rules, and standards that govern financial reporting to creditors and external investors in the business. The main purpose of having the financial statements audited by an independent CPA firm is to test whether the statements have been prepared according to GAAP. If there are material departures from these ground rules of financial statement accounting and disclosure, the CPA auditor says so in the audit opinion on the statements.

As we shall see in the following chapter, the hard core of an external financial report consists of three primary financial statements. One summarizes the profit-making operations of the business for the period, one summarizes the cash inflows and outflows for the same period, and one presents the assets of the business at the end of the period, which are balanced by the claims against and sources of the assets.

The three primary financial statements do not come with built-in analysis. Rather the financial statements provide an organized source of information. It's up to the users to extract the vital signals and messages from the statements. Chapters 3 and 4 explain that managers need much more information than is reported in the external financial statements.

For example, suppose you're about ready to lower sales prices 10 percent because you think sales volume will increase more than enough to make this a smart

---

* Without too much modesty, I can recommend my book, *How to Read a Financial Report,* 4th ed. (New York: John Wiley & Sons, 1994).

move. You'd better know which profit and cash flow analysis tools to use to test the impacts of this move on your business. The external financial statements do not provide the information you need.

A WORD ABOUT ACCOUNTING METHODS

GAAP have been developed to standardize accounting methods for measuring net income (bottom-line profit), for presenting financial condition and cash flow information, and to provide financial disclosure standards for reporting to creditors and external investors. Over the years, GAAP have come a long way but have not yet resulted in complete uniformity and consistency from one business to the next, or even among companies in the same industry. Businesses can choose from among different but equally acceptable accounting methods, which can make significant differences in the profit (net income) reported for the year and in the asset, liability, and owners' equity values reported in the balance sheet.

Profit depends on how it's measured, i.e., on which accounting methods have been selected. I'm reminded of the old baseball joke here: There's an argument between the batter and the catcher about whether the pitch was a ball or a strike. Back and forth the two go, until finally the umpire settles it by saying, "It ain't nothing until I call it." Likewise, someone has to decide how to "call" profit for the period; profit depends on how the "strike zone" is determined and this depends largely on which particular accounting methods are selected to measure profit.

External financial reports are the primary means of communication to fulfill the *stewardship* function of management—that is, to render a periodic accounting of what has been done with the capital entrusted to management. The creditors and shareowners of the business are the sources of, as well as have the claims on, the assets of the business. Therefore, they are entitled to a periodic accounting by their stewards (*agents* is the popular term these days, in place of *stewards*).

Please keep in mind that managers have a fiduciary responsibility to the outside world. They are responsible for the fairness of their financial statements. There's no doubt that top management has the primary responsibility for the financial statements—this cannot be shifted or off-loaded on the CPA auditors of the financial report. Nor can legal counsel to the business be blamed if top management issues misleading financial statements.

Because external financial reports are public in nature, disclosure is limited, especially in the income statement (the profit performance report of the business). Disclosure standards permit the business to withhold information that creditors and external investors probably would like to know. The theory of this, I believe, is that such disclosure would reveal too much information and cause the business to lose some of its competitive advantages. The internal income statement (or management profit report) presented in Chapter 3 contains expense information that the business wouldn't want to reveal in its external financial report to the ouside world.

Publicly owned corporations are required to include a *management discussion and analysis* (MD&A) section in their annual financial reports to stockholders, which deals with the broad factors and main reasons for the company's profit performance. Generally speaking, these sections are not too specific and deal with broad issues and developments over the year.

END POINT

This book analyzes how to make profit, so it seems a good idea, in conclusion, to say a few words in defense of the profit motive. Profit stimulates innovation; it's the reward for taking risks; it's the return on capital invested in business; it's compensation for hard work and long hours; it motivates efficiency; it weeds out products and services no longer in demand; it keeps pressure on companies to maintain their quality of customer service and products.

In short, the profit system delivers the highest standard of living in the world. Despite all this, it's no secret that many in government, the church, and society at large have a deep-seated distrust toward our profit-motivated, free enterprise, and open market system— and not entirely without reason.

It would be naive to ignore the abuses and failings of the profit system and not to take notice of the ruthless "profit at any cost" behavior of some unscrupulous business managers. Unfortunately, you don't have to look very far to find examples of dishonest advertising, selling unsafe products, employees cheated out of their pensions, unsafe working conditions, or the deliberate violation of laws and regulations, to say nothing of other illegal activities.

Too many companies travel the low moral and ethical road. A form of Gresham's Law* seems to be at work. Dirty practices tend to drive out clean practices,

---

* You may recall that Sir Thomas Gresham was a sixteenth-century economist who is generally credited with the important observation or law that if there are two types of money circulating in the economy, the one that is perceived as more dear or of higher quality will be kept back and spent last; the cheaper or lower-quality money will be offered first in economic exchange. Thus, the cheaper form of money will drive out the higher-quality money. Even though we have only one currency in the American economy, you may have noticed that most of us tend to pass the currency that is in the worst shape first, and we hold back the bills that are in better condition.

the result being a sinking to the lowest level of tolerable behavior. Which is very sad. No wonder that profit is a dirty word to so many and business gets bad press. Ethical standards should be above and ahead of what the law requires.

Many businesses have adopted a formal code of ethics for all employees in the organization. It goes without saying that managers should set the example for full-faith compliance with the code of ethics. If managers cut corners, what do they expect employees to do? If managers pay only lip service to the code of ethics, employees will not take the code seriously.

External Financial Statements— What the World Knows about Your Company

Financial statements are the most basic touchstone and benchmark of every business. Separate financial statements are prepared to present a company's achievements for each of the three financial imperatives of business: making profit (the *income statement*), generating cash flow (the *cash flow statement*), and maintaining financial health (the *balance sheet*). An external financial report consists of these three primary statements plus other disclosures and comments by the business.

MEASURING PROFIT: THE INCOME STATEMENT

Of course, the principal financial motive of business is to make profit—fairly and honestly, as emphasized in Chapter 1. The income statement quite naturally occupies center stage. It reports the profit performance of the business for the latest period:

$$\text{Sales revenue} - \text{expenses} = \text{profit}$$

The income statement (Figure 2.1) shows how profitable a business is by summarizing the sales revenue and expenses of the business for the period. The bottom line of this statement is the profit or loss for the period. The bottom line, or profit, is also called *net income* or *net earnings.*

The measurement of sales revenue and expenses is neither obvious nor clear-cut, though many seem to believe that it's just a matter of good bookkeeping. In fact, many difficult accounting estimates, judgments, and choices have to be made in measuring revenue and expenses. Some accounting methods are quite arbitrary, such as depreciation expense. It goes without saying that accountants should be objective

INCOME STATEMENT FOR YEAR

Sales revenue	$ 6,019,040
Cost-of-goods-sold expense	(3,912,376)
Gross margin	$ 2,106,664
Operating expenses	(1,523,288)
Depreciation expense	(112,792)
Operating earnings	$ 470,584
Interest expense	(76,650)
Earnings before income tax	$ 393,934
Income tax expense	(133,938)
Net income	$ 259,996

CASH FLOW STATEMENT FOR YEAR

Cash flows from operating activities

Net income		$ 259,996
Changes in operating assets and liabilities:		
Accounts receivable	$ (96,404)	
Inventory	(150,481)	
Prepaid expenses	(24,341)	
Accounts payable	58,318	
Accrued expenses	40,283	
Income tax payable	1,720	
Depreciation expense	112,792	(58,113)
Cash flow from profit-making operations		$ 201,883

Cash flows from investing activities

Purchases of property, plant, and equipment		(389,400)

Cash flows from financing activities

Short-term debt increase	$ 50,000	
Long-term borrowings	75,000	
Capital stock issue	100,000	
Cash dividends to stockholders	(93,750)	131,250
Decrease in cash during year		$ (56,267)

The content, format, and terminology shown here for the three primary financial statements are typical for external financial reports. The statements are supplemented with one or more pages of footnotes as well as additional disclosures, and are accompanied by a transmittal letter from the president or chief executive officer of the company. The financial report may be audited by an independent CPA firm who includes its opinion on the financial report.

FIGURE 2.1 *External financial statements example.*

BALANCE SHEET AT YEAR-END

Assets	This year	Last year	Increases (Decreases)
Cash	$ 256,663	$ 312,930	$ (56,267)
Accounts receivable	578,754	482,350	$ 96,404
Inventory	978,094	827,613	$ 150,481
Prepaid expenses	117,176	92,835	$ 24,341
Total current assets	$1,930,687	$ 1,715,728	
Property, plant, and equipment	1,986,450	1,597,050	$ 389,400
Accumulated depreciation	(452,140)	(339,348)	$ (112,792)
Net of depreciation	$1,534,310	$ 1,257,702	
Total assets	$3,464,997	$ 2,973,430	

Liabilities and Owners' Equity

	This year	Last year	Increases (Decreases)
Accounts payable	$ 388,834	$ 330,516	$ 58,318
Accrued expenses	188,539	148,256	$ 40,283
Income tax payable	13,394	11,674	$ 1,720
Short-term notes payable	425,000	375,000	$ 50,000
Total current liabilities	$1,015,767	$ 865,446	
Long-term notes payable	550,000	475,000	$ 75,000
Total liabilities	$1,565,767	$ 1,340,446	
Owners' equity:			
Capital stock	725,000	625,000	$ 100,000
Retained earnings	1,174,230	1,007,984	$ 166,246
Total	$1,899,230	$ 1,632,984	
Total liabilities and owners' equity	$3,464,997	$ 2,973,430	

Compare these changes in assets, liabilities, and owners' equity with the amounts reported in the cash flow statement. *Note:* The $166,246 net change in Retained Earnings equals net income less cash dividends.

FIGURE 2.1 (*Continued*)

and unbiased in measuring profit (or loss) and should be free of any pressures to exaggerate or understate profit. However, sometimes top management lays a heavy hand on the accounting methods used to measure sales revenue and expenses.

The income statement reports the sales revenue and expenses of the business. To a very large extent, these profit-making operations determine the balance sheet of the business. In other words, the income statement is the main determinant of the balance sheet. The income statement as primary driver results from the financial nature and effects of sales revenue and expenses, which are summarized as follows:

Income statement	Balance sheet
Sales revenue $\longrightarrow$	+ asset or − liability
Expense $\longrightarrow$	− asset or + liability

Sales revenue increases an asset or decreases a liability. A cash sale increases cash immediately; a credit sale first increases accounts receivable, which are collected later and converted into cash. Though not too common, some companies, such as magazine publishers, collect cash *before* delivering the product. As the product is delivered, they decrease the liability that was recorded previously for the advance payments from customers. In other words, they do not record sales revenue until they deliver the product, even though the cash was received before this time.

Expenses decrease an asset or increase a liability. An expense, such as employee salaries, can decrease cash. The cost-of-goods-sold expense decreases the inventory asset account; when products are sold, their cost is removed from the asset account and charged to expense. Many expenses are recorded by first increasing the accounts payable liability, which is paid later. More expenses than you might imagine are recorded by increasing liabilities. Depreciation expense is unusual; it decreases the recorded amount, or *book value,* of the long-term operating assets of the business.

The relationships and interconnections of sales revenue and expenses with their corresponding assets and liabilities are measured by *operating ratios.* This very important tool of analysis is explained in Chapter 5.

 ## MEASURING CASH FLOW: THE CASH FLOW STATEMENT

Cash flow from profit + other sources of cash
− uses of cash = change in cash

 Profit does not automatically generate cash flow of an equal amount during the period. Over the long run, profit generates cash flow, but there may be a serious lag before profit is converted into cash.

The cash flow statement (Figure 2.1) is a "where got, where gone" summary of cash, that all-important lubricant of business activity. It is important to understand that cash flow for the year is different from bottom-line profit, or net income, for the year.

Cash flow from profit is an internal, or self-generated, source of cash. A business also uses other, external, sources of cash from borrowing and from owners investing capital into the business from time to time. These external sources of cash are reported so the reader can compare how much cash the business secured from its internal versus its external sources. (A company may also sell some of its operating assets that normally are not held for sale, such as a building.)

The cash flow statement reports the uses of cash, which generally fall into three major categories: cash dividends (distributions) of profit to owners, reduction of debt, and capital expenditures, which are outlays for new, long-term operating assets.

MEASURING FINANCIAL HEALTH: THE BALANCE SHEET

Assets = liabilities + owners' equity

The balance sheet (Figure 2.1) measures the organization's financial health. It presents the assets, liabilities, and owners' equity accounts of the business. Assets are the economic resources being used by the business. The business must raise the capital needed to invest in its assets. Basically, capital comes from two sources: liabilities and owners' equity. So the natural equation of the balance sheet is: Assets = liabilities + owners' equity.

The balance sheet is fundamentally different compared with the two other statements. Both the income statement and cash flow statement summarize *flows* during a period of time—revenue and expense flows in the income statement, and cash inflows and outflows in the cash flow statement. Both come down to a bottom line: net income in the income statement, and the net increase or decrease in cash in the cash flow statement. The third financial statement has no bottom line—it has *balance* instead.

The balance sheet is a *position* statement that summarizes the entity's financial condition or situation at a particular moment in time. The financial position of a business changes day to day because there is a constant stream of activities and transactions going on. The balance sheet is prepared at midnight on the last day of business for the profit (net income) measurement period that is reported in the income statement.

The balance sheet reports three basic components of information. First, it shows how the company's *assets* are deployed. In other words, it shows the distribution of the company's economic resources—how much in cash, how much in inventory, and so on. Second, this financial statement reports the *liabilities* of the business—how much is owed to creditors for inventory purchases and unpaid expenses, how much is owed to lenders on which interest must be paid, and other types of liabilities.

Third, the balance sheet shows the breakdown of *owners' equity*—how much capital has been invested by the owners over the years and how much profit (net income) has been retained in the business. Retained earnings are internally generated capital, in contrast to the external sources of capital, that is, capital invested by the owners and liabilities.

The balance sheet is carefully studied and analyzed by the creditors and equity stakeholders in the business. First of all, they are interested in the financial health of the business and whether the business can continue as a going concern, avoiding insolvency and the threat of bankruptcy. Second, they are interested in the capital efficiency of the business, which refers to how well the business is doing with the capital used to operate the enterprise.

END POINT

This chapter introduces an example of external financial statements for a business, which are stripped of the footnotes, supporting statements and schedules, and supplementary disclosure that is included in external financial reports. The chapter provides a useful though minimal review of the essential character and structure of the three primary financial statements of business.

If this were a book on externally reported financial statements, we would delve into many other aspects of the accounting methods and practices for preparing financial statements and their other disclosures. Basically, we would stand in the shoes of the creditors and stockholders of the business and attack financial statements from their perspective.

In contrast, starting in the next chapter this book takes a much different direction. We will stand in the shoes of the managers of the business and look at financial statements from their perspective. First and foremost, business managers are decision makers, and they need financial statements for their decision-making analysis. Externally reported financial statements provide no more than the skeleton of information needed by managers. We need to put much more muscle and bone on the financial statements for managers.

3

Income Statement for Managers

Managers have to keep on top of the unending stream of changes in today's business environment. Few factors remain constant very long. Managers need to quickly assess the profit and other financial impacts of these changes. Deciding the best response to changes is never easy, but one thing is clear. Managers need certain types of information for their profit-making decision analysis.

KEY CONCEPT   INFORMATION FOR MANAGERS

Is the external income statement (see Figure 2.1) adequate for management analysis? This question reminds me of a recent television ad for Hertz car rental in which one character keeps answering "not exactly." To demonstrate the type of information needed for profit-making analysis, consider the following decision situation.

Suppose you have done some market research and are of the opinion that if you were to reduce sales prices 5 percent, sales volume would increase 20 percent. Would this be a good move? Of course, the prediction of a 20 percent sales volume increase is critical. This is a large jump in sales volume and it may or may not materialize. In any case, does the external income statement provide enough information to analyze this decision? No, it doesn't.

DANGER! The main limitation of the external profit report (income statement) is that it doesn't include enough information about how expenses would react to the 20 percent sales volume increase and to the increase in total sales revenue. Expense behavior is a rock-bottom type of information that managers have to analyze before moving ahead with such a major decision.

Moreover, managers should look beyond the profit dimension; they should carefully identify the changes such a decision would cause in the financial condition and cash flow of the business or that segment of the business for which they have management responsibility.* For all they know, there might be dire consequences for cash flow or financial condition, even if profit should increase.

Figure 3.1 presents the internal income statement or profit report that discloses the basic types of expense behavior information needed by managers. This is the same company example for which external financial statements were introduced in Chapter 2 (also see Figure 2.1). Notice that the bottom-line profit number (net income) is exactly the same. In other words, the profit accounting methods are the same here as before—sales revenue, total expenses, and bottom-line net income are the same as before. I mention this point for a reason.

Contrary to what seems to be a popular misconception, companies do not keep two sets of books. Profit is measured and recorded by one set of methods, which are the same for both internal and external financial statements. A manager may ask the accounting staff to prepare an analysis of what profit would be if alternative accounting methods were used, such as a different inventory and cost-of-goods-sold expense method or a different depreciation expense method. But only one set of numbers is recorded and booked. There is not a "true" or "real" profit figure secreted away someplace that only managers know, although this seems to be a misconception held by many.

Figure 3.1 includes notes that explain key items in the profit report. These should help to answer questions you might have and to clarify aspects about the item that you may not be entirely certain about. Internal reports do not usually include such explanatory notes; the assumption is that the users (managers) know all this material. However, such notes are not unheard of. Some businesses include them to remind users of the official definitions and classifications adopted by the company. But this is not common.

 ## GROSS MARGIN: THE FIRST LINE OF PROFIT

The cost-of-goods-sold expense is the first expense deducted from sales revenue; the remainder is called

---

* Many departments and other organizational units have no direct profit responsibility, though they may have either revenue responsibility, such as a sales territory, or cost responsibility, such as the purchasing or the data processing department. Accordingly, only revenue is reported to a revenue center and only costs are reported to a cost center.

The discussion in this chapter refers to a manager who has profit responsibility for an autonomous segment (division, subsidiary, etc.) of the business or for the entire business. In some organizations, profit centers are isolated from any further financial responsibility. The discussion in this chapter takes the broader view, which includes financial condition and cash flow. Clearly, someone in the organization has to be responsible for these financial issues; profit is not the whole picture.

gross margin (or, sometimes, *gross profit*). Cost of goods sold is the cost of the products sold to customers. Cost of goods sold is usually the largest expense for companies that sell products, typically 50 to 60 percent or more of sales revenue (and is as much as 85 percent for some high-volume retailers). So you don't see gross margins of more than 40 to 50 percent too often. However, there are some interesting exceptions.

The cosmetics industry has very high gross profit margins, and Coca-Cola's gross profit recently has been over 60 percent. A full-service restaurant, as a rough rule of thumb, should keep its food costs at one-third of its sales revenue, leaving a two-thirds gross margin to cover all its other expenses and to yield a satisfactory bottom-line profit. Apple Computer made very high gross margins until it adopted a much more aggressive sales price strategy on its personal computers to get a larger market share. This cut deeply into its traditional high profit margins.

A general rule is the lower the gross margin percent, the higher the inventory turnover. The interval of time from acquisition of the product to the sale of the product is one inventory turnover. High turnover is five or more turns a year, or maybe six or seven turns a year, depending on who you talk with. Food supermarkets, for example, have very high inventory turnover—their products do not stay on the shelves very long. Even taking into account the holding period in their warehouses before the products get on their shelves in the stores, their inventory turnover is very high, thus, supermarkets can work on fairly thin gross margins of 20 percent, give or take a little.

In contrast, a retail furniture store may hold an item in inventory for more than six months on average before it is sold, so it needs fairly high gross margin percents. In this business example, the company's gross margin is 35 percent of sales revenue,* which is in the typical range for many businesses.

Cost of goods sold is a *variable* expense; it moves more or less in lockstep with changes in sales volume. If sales volume were to increase 10 percent, then this expense should increase 10 percent, assuming unit product costs remained constant over time. But unit product costs—whether the company is a retailer who purchases the products its sells or a producer who manufactures the products it sells—do not remain constant over time. Unit product costs may drift steadily upward over time with inflation, or unit product costs

---

* Calculated as follows: $2,106,664 gross margin ÷ $6,019,040 sales revenue = 35.0%. So the cost-of-goods-sold expense equals 65.0 percent of sales revenue. Percent means per hundred. So, 35 percent means 35 per hundred, and 120 percent means 120 per hundred. (I bring this up because many of my students seem not to understand percents as well as they should.)

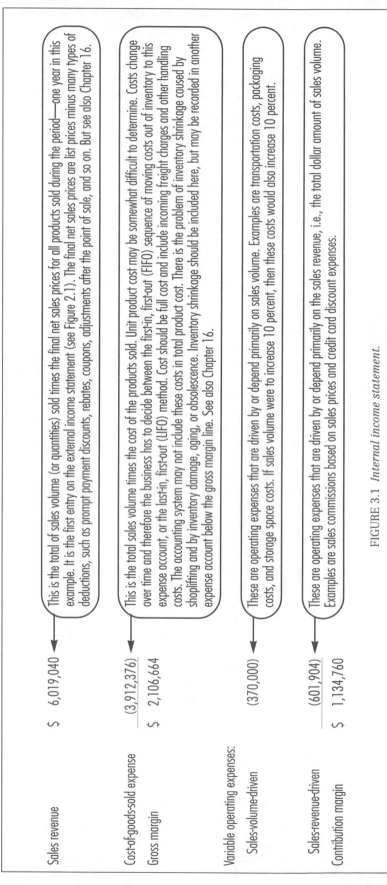

FIGURE 3.1 *Internal income statement.*

These are operating expenses that are relatively fixed and nonvariable for the period. These costs would be more or less the same, even if sales volume had been higher or lower. Examples are employees that are paid fixed salaries, rent, property taxes, and insurance.

Depreciation is listed separately because it is such an unusual expense—one of a kind, quite literally. It is a fraction of the total original cost of the company's fixed assets (except land) that is allocated to this period. Keep in mind that this expense depends on the useful life estimates of the assets and whether the company uses a fast (accelerated) method of allocation or the straight-line method.

Interest expense depends on the amount of short-term and long-term debt outstanding during the year and the interest rates on each issue of debt.

In this company example, income tax is the 34 percent corporate rate on taxable income, and the company's accounting methods are the same for tax and financial reporting.

The bottom-line profit for the period. This is the bottom line on the external income statement as well (see Figure 2.1).

Fixed expenses:	
Operating expenses	(551,384)
Depreciation expense	(112,792)
Operating earnings	$ 470,584
Interest expense	(76,650)
Earnings before income tax	$ 393,934
Income tax expense	(133,938)
Net income	$ 259,996

FIGURE 3.1 (Continued)

can take sharp nosedives because of technological improvements or competitive pressures.

VARIABLE OPERATING EXPENSES

The next step in the internal (management) income statement is to deduct *variable* operating expenses from gross margin. In Figure 3.1 variable operating expenses are divided into two types: those that vary with sales volume and those that vary with total sales dollars. *Variable* means that the expense varies with sales activity, either sales volume or sales revenue. Delivery expense, for example, varies with sales volume, that is, the quantity sold and shipped. On the other hand, commissions paid to salespersons are normally a percentage of sales revenue, that is, the number of dollars involved.

Deducting all variable operating expenses from gross margin gives the second profit line, which is labeled *contribution margin*. *Contribution* means that it contributes or helps toward the coverage of fixed expenses. *Margin* means it is the difference remaining after deducting cost-of-goods-sold expense and variable operating expenses from sales revenue.

Contribution margin should be large enough to cover the company's fixed operating expenses, its interest expense, and its income tax expense, and still leave a residual amount of profit (net income). In short, there are a lot of further demands on the intermediate measure of profit called contribution margin. Even if a business earns a reasonably good total contribution margin (sales revenue less all variable expenses), it still isn't necessarily out of the woods, because it has fixed operating expenses as well as interest and income tax.

The basic reason for striking a profit measure here—that is, for deducting all variable expenses from sales revenue to calculate the contribution margin—is to provide for an easy comparison and computation of what percentage of sales revenue the business keeps after deducting the variable expenses of generating the sales revenue. In this example, contribution margin is approximately 19 percent of sales revenue: $1,134,760 contribution margin ÷ $6,019,040 sales revenue = 19%.

In rough terms, if sales revenue were to increase, say, $100,000, the company's contribution margin would increase about $19,000, or 19 percent of the sales revenue increase.* Contribution margin would increase, but not fixed operating expenses. This is a key point: The contribution margin is an important

---

* It makes a difference whether the sales revenue increase is due to sales volume increases or sales price increases. This key point is explained in Chapters 9 and 10.

line of demarcation between the variable profit factors above the line and the fixed expenses below the line.

FIXED EXPENSES

KEY CONCEPT

Virtually every business has fixed operating expenses, as well as fixed depreciation expense. Notice in Figure 3.1 that the company's fixed operating expenses were $551,384 for the year, and its depreciation expense was $112,792. *Fixed* means that these operating costs remain, for all practical purposes, the same amount for the year over a very fairly broad range of sales activity—whether sales had been, say, 20 to 30 percent higher or lower than the actual sales level for the period.

Examples of such fixed costs are employees on fixed salaries, office rent, annual property taxes, many types of insurance, and the CPA audit fee. Once spent, advertising is a fixed cost. Generally speaking, these cost commitments are decided in advance and, once decided on, cannot be changed over the short run. The longer the time horizon, on the other hand, the more these costs can be adjusted up or down.

For instance, persons on fixed salaries can be laid off, but they may be entitled to several months or perhaps one or more years of severance pay. Leases may be not renewed, but you have to wait till the end of the lease. Most fixed operating expenses are cash based, which means that cash is paid out at or near the time the expense is recorded—though it must be mentioned that some of these costs have to be prepaid (such as insurance) and many are paid after being recorded (such as the CPA audit fee).

Depreciation expense is also a fixed amount for the year, but it is quite different and therefore is separated from other fixed operating expenses. Depreciation depends on the choice of accounting methods adopted to measure this expense—whether the level, straight-line method or a quicker accelerated method is used. Other fixed operating expenses are not so heavily dependent on the choice of accounting methods compared with depreciation.

Depreciation is a write-down of the book (recorded) value of long-term or fixed operating assets, except that the cost of land is not depreciated. For this reason, depreciation sometimes is referred to as "only a book entry." This has misleading implications, however. These operating assets do wear out over time and are eventually put on the junk heap. A Boeing 727 might fly 25 or even 35 years, but sooner or later the aircraft will be retired. Depreciation is a real expense but its unique nature requires that it be reported separately—not only in the income statement but also in the cash flow statement, which is discussed in the next chapter.

In passing, it should be noted that other assets are occasionally written-down, though not according to any predetermined schedule like depreciation. For example, inventory may have to be written-down, or marked down, if the products cannot be sold or will have to be sold below cost. Inventory also has to be written-down to recognize shrinkage due to shoplifting and employee theft. Accounts receivable may have to be written-down if they are not fully collectible. (Inventory loss and bad debts are discussed again in later chapters.)

Managers definitely should know where such write-downs are being reported in the profit report. For instance, are inventory knockdowns included in cost-of-goods-sold expense? Are receivable write-offs in fixed operating expenses? Managers have to know what all is included in the basic accounts in their internal profit report (Figure 3.1). Such write-downs are generally fixed in amount and would not be reported as variable expenses—although, if a certain percentage of inventory shrinkage is normal, then it should be included with the variable cost-of-goods-sold expense. The theory of putting it here is that to sell 100 units of product, the business may have to buy, say, 105 units as a general rule, because 5 units are stolen or damaged, or have become unsalable.

FROM OPERATING EARNINGS (EBIT) TO THE BOTTOM LINE

Deducting fixed expenses takes us down to the profit line labeled "operating earnings." This is sometimes labeled "earnings before interest and tax" (EBIT) instead. Interest expense is shown as one item in the internal profit report (see Figure 3.1 again). Alternatively, interest on short-term debt could be separated from interest on long-term debt. For instance, interest rates could be substantially different between the two and management might be considering restructuring of the company's debt. Interest expense should include loan origination fees and points paid by the business.

The last expense shown in the internal profit report is income tax expense. Only one total amount is reported, though the state income tax amount could be separated from the federal amount. Only federal income tax is included in this example. Income tax is complicated by many factors. In the examples throughout the book, a flat income tax rate based on the present tax law is used for the company.

END POINT

The internal profit report to managers should separate expenses into variable and fixed, and variable expenses should be further separated into those that vary with sales volume versus those that vary with sales revenue dollars. The central importance of the internal income statement cannot be overstated. This financial statement provides the measure of profit—actually, several measures of different profits on the way to the final, bottom-line profit. These key figures are the foundation of information for the tools of analysis explained in later chapters.

The sales revenue and expenses summarized in the income statement not only determine profit. These profit-making transactions are also the primary determinants of the balance sheet, which is examined in the next chapter.

CHAPTER

Financial Condition and Cash Flow Statements for Managers

Suppose someone unfamiliar with the balance sheet asks: Where does the balance sheet come from? What determines the financial condition of a business? What gives the balance sheet its shape, and what determines the dollar values reported in this financial statement? The answer is that the cumulative financial effects of three basic types of transactions are reported in the balance sheet, also called the *statement of financial condition.*

WHERE DOES THE BALANCE SHEET COME FROM?

First and foremost, this financial statement depends directly on sales revenue and expenses, or the profit-making operations of the business, summarized in its income statement. The balance sheet is prepared at the close of business on the last day of the profit measurement period. Sales revenue and expenses cause increases and decreases in certain assets and liabilities. The balance sheet summarizes all the assets and liabilities of the business.

Second, the business must raise capital to finance the investments in its assets. This capital comes from two main sources: debt and equity. Managers must convince lenders to loan money to the company, and managers must convince shareholders to invest their money in the company. The several basic differences between debt and equity are discussed in this chapter.

Both sources of capital demand to be compensated for the use of their capital. Interest is paid on debt and reported in the income statement as an expense. In contrast, no charge or expense of equity capital is reported in the income statement. Instead, bottom-line profit is the net earnings on equity capital. Shareholders may or may not be paid part of net income (profit) as a cash dividend. Dividends, if any, are reported in the cash flow statement.

Third, the business makes investments in long-term assets needed in its operations. These investments are called *capital expenditures* to emphasize the capital commitments in these long-term economic resources. The balance sheet reports the investments in the plant, equipment, and other long-lived assets of the business. Summing up, the balance sheet results from three basic types of transactions (see Figure 4.1).

Sales revenue and expenses pass through the income statement on their way to the balance sheet. The second and third types of transactions that drive the balance sheet do not pass through the income statement because they are not sales revenue and expenses. Rather, these financing and investing types of transactions pass through the cash flow statement.

BALANCE SHEET FOR MANAGERS

Figure 4.2 presents the company's internal balance sheet, which is arranged in a format for management use. You may want to take a moment here to read the notes attached to the main items in the balance sheet. Or you can use the notes as a convenient reference later in the chapter and throughout the book.

This is the same company example first introduced in Chapter 2. See Figure 2.1 for the company's external financial statements. In comparing the internal balance sheet presented here with the external statement presented earlier (Figure 2.1), you'll notice some changes. These rearrangements are for management interpretation and provide a better source of information for demonstrating the tools of analysis explained in the book.

The company's operating assets are listed first in Figure 4.2, and then its operating liabilities are immediately deducted to get a very key figure: *net operating*

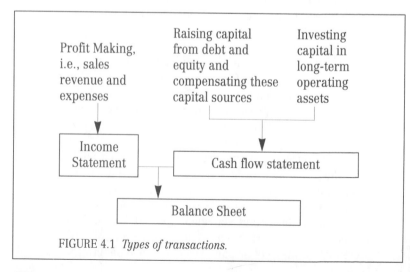

FIGURE 4.1 *Types of transactions.*

assets. This is the amount of capital the business must raise from interest-bearing debt and owners' equity sources. In brief, this management-based format is organized as shown in Figure 4.3.

In the process of making profit, a business generates certain short-term, non-interest-bearing liabilities that are part and parcel of carrying out its profit-making transactions. A good example is when the business buys inventory on credit. This purchase causes an accounts payable liability, which will be paid in a month or so, perhaps sooner. These are sometimes called *spontaneous* liabilities because they are caused by transactions that are not designed to borrow money or to raise capital.

Accounts payable are called *trade credit;* these sources of credit do not charge interest (unless the business is very late in paying the bill). The business does not borrow money from its suppliers like it does from a bank. The business convinces its suppliers to sell products to the business on the strength of its credit reputation and good name. The business has the use of the inventory for the month or so before the accounts payable liability has to be paid. Holding inventory beyond this time, which is typical, means that the business has to secure capital from its longer-term debt or equity sources.*

OPERATING ASSETS AND LIABILITIES

Several different operating assets are needed to carry on the profit-making operations of a business. And several different kinds of operating liabilities are generated as a normal part of its profit-making transactions. Certain assets have to be in place before sales and expense transactions can be carried on. For example, inventory has to be purchased or manufactured before it can be offered for sale to customers. Several expenses have to be prepaid, such as insurance premiums and office supplies.

Other operating assets and liabilities are the result of sales revenue and expense transactions. For example, accounts receivable are the result of making sales on credit. Accounts payable are the result of buying inventory on credit and not paying expenses until sometime after they are recorded as expenses.

---

* In external financial statements, short-term notes payable and the short-term (one year or less) portion of long-term debt are included with the company's short-term operating liabilities to determine a subtotal called current liabilities (see Figure 2.1). Total current liabilities are compared with total current assets as a rough measure of the company's short-term solvency, or debt-paying ability. Notice in the new format here that all interest-bearing debt, both short-term and long-term, is included in debt, and operating liabilities do not include short-term debt. By the way, current assets less current liabilities is called working capital, to draw a distinction between the more liquid capital of the business versus the less liquid capital that is invested in the company's long-term operating assets.

FIGURE 4.2 *Internal balance sheet.*

| | At end of | |
	This year	Last year
Operating assets		
Cash	$256,663	$312,930
Accounts receivable	578,754	482,350
Inventory	978,094	827,613
Prepaid expenses	117,176	92,835
Property, plant, and equipment at original cost	1,986,450	1,597,050
Less accumulated Depreciation	(452,140)	(339,348)
Total operating assets	$3,464,997	$2,973,430
Operating liabilities		
Accounts payable:		
Inventory	$300,952	$268,300
Operating expenses	87,882	62,216
Total accounts payable	$388,834	$330,516

Callout annotations:

Cash is usually in one or more checking accounts; however, some coin and currency is held by many retailers. Cash equivalents such as highly marketable, short-term securities may be included in the cash amount.

These are the three basic short-term operating assets whose turnover is generally one to three months, or perhaps 5 or 6 months for some businesses.

These are long-term operating assets whose useful lives range from 3 to 5 years all the way to 30 or more years for buildings. Their cost (except land) is depreciated over their useful life estimates.

This is the cumulative portion of the original cost of the assets that has been charged to depreciation expense since the date of acquisition.

These are non-interest-bearing, short-term liabilities that arise from two operating sources: (1) the purchase of inventory on credit, and (2) the acquisition of services and other items charged to expense that are not paid for immediately. In short, these are unpaid bills.

These are expenses that have been recorded, not from a purchase as such, but rather to match all expenses for the period against sales revenue to measure profit for the period. A primary example is accrued vacation and sick pay and other employee fringe benefits that haven't been paid by the year-end.

Usually not all the income tax for the year has been paid by year-end. This is the unpaid portion, usually due within 2 or 3 months.

These are interest-bearing liabilities from borrowing. Short-term means one year or less; long-term can be from 2 to 20 or more years. Footnotes disclose maturity dates for the long-term notes or bonds issued by the company.

Owners' equity arises from two sources: (1) capital invested by the owners for which they receive shares of stock (if the business is a corporation); and (2) profit earned but not paid out as a dividend, which is retained in the business.

Accrued expenses:		
Operations	175,764	137,900
Interest	12,775	10,356
Total accrued expenses	$188,539	$148,256
Income tax payable	$13,394	$11,674
Total operating liabilities	$590,767	$490,446
Net operating assets	$2,874,230	$2,482,984
Sources of capital		
Short-term notes payable	$425,000	$375,000
Long-term notes payable	550,000	475,000
Total interest-bearing debt	$975,000	$850,000
Capital stock	725,000	625,000
Retained earnings	1,174,230	1,007,984
Total stockholders' equity	$1,899,230	$1,632,984
Total debt and owners' equity	$2,874,230	$2,482,984

FIGURE 4.2 (*Continued*)

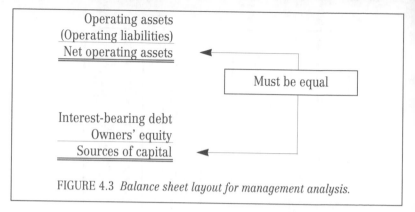

FIGURE 4.3 *Balance sheet layout for management analysis.*

In Figure 4.2 notice that accounts payable are separated into two parts: the amount from inventory purchases on credit and the amount from operating expenses bought on credit. Both are due in the short run, usually not much longer than a month, give or take a week or so. Accrued expenses are also separated into two parts: the amount from operating expenses and unpaid interest. These separations are needed to explain the analysis tools discussed in the next chapter, which are called *operating ratios*. Also, from the management point of view, each separate liability balance is the result of different decisions and policies.

Operating assets don't earn interest income and operating liabilities don't require interest expense, though there are minor exceptions. For example, temporary excess cash balances may be invested for short periods in highly liquid and very safe securities (such as short-term U.S. government issues) to earn some interest income on surplus cash instead of letting it lie fallow. Customers who don't pay their receivables on time may be penalized with an interest charge if they delay too long beyond the normal credit period.

Likewise, if the business delays too long beyond the credit period extended by its vendors and suppliers before paying its accounts payable, the company may be charged an interest penalty for late payment. Putting aside these minor exceptions, operating assets don't earn interest income and operating liabilities don't bear interest expense.

 Managers should know which particular operating assets and liabilities are needed. They should also know how large each operating asset and liability should be relative to sales revenue and the expenses of the business. For instance, managers should know how large the accounts receivable balance should be relative to total credit sales for the period, given the normal credit terms of the business and the history of its customers regarding late payment.*

---

* The analysis tool for this is called an operating ratio; the entire next chapter is devoted to operating ratios.

In summary, every business needs a portfolio of operating assets and liabilities that are essential for making profit. To carry on its sales revenue and expense activities, the company in this example uses $3,464,997 total operating assets at the end of its most recent year. This total consists of cash, accounts receivable, inventory, prepaid expenses, and long-term depreciable assets (property, plant, and equipment).

The company's total operating liabilities are $590,767 at the end of the most recent year, consisting of accounts payable, accrued expenses, and income tax payable (see Figure 4.2 again). The amount of operating liabilities is deducted from total operating assets, giving net operating assets of $2,874,230; this is the amount of capital the company had to raise.

SOURCES OF CAPITAL (TO FINANCE NET OPERATING ASSETS)

As just explained, the company has almost $3 million invested in its net operating assets to carry on its profit-making operations. Where did this capital come from? The company tapped two basic sources, each divided into two parts: (1a) short-term debt of $425,000 and (1b) long-term debt of $550,000, for total debt of $975,000; (2a) paid-in capital from stockholders of $725,000 and (2b) retained earnings of $1,174,230, for total owners' (stockholders') capital of $1,899,230. Collectively, these capital sources are referred to as the *capitalization* or *capital structure* of the business.

We could ask here whether the company is using the optimal capital structure. Perhaps the company should have carried more debt. Maybe the company could have gotten by on a smaller cash balance—say $100,000 less—which means that $100,000 less debt or owners' equity capital would have been needed. Perhaps the business should have kept its accounts receivable and inventory balances lower, which would have reduced the need for capital.

In any case, this basic question comes down to a few fundamental choices, which include debt versus equity, issuing capital stock versus retained earnings, and a lean versus a larger working cash balance. The analysis tools explained in this book are helpful for deciding these questions. Here, we'll review the essential features of and differences between debt and equity.

Debt may be very short term, usually meaning 6 months or less, or very long term, which means 20 years or more. (A recent *New York Times* article commented on the increasing trend of debt issues with 50-year maturities and mentioned one issue with a 999-year maturity date.) The term *debt* means *interest-bearing* in almost all cases. Interest rates can be fixed over the life of the debt contract or subject to change, usually at the lender's option.

A key feature is whether debt principal must be *amortized* or not. In addition to paying interest, the business (which is the borrower or debtor) may have to make payments to reduce the principal balance of the debt, instead of waiting until the final maturity date to pay off all the principal amount at one time. For example, a business loan may call for equal quarterly amounts over five years. Each quarterly payment amount is fixed to pay interest and to pay down part of the principal balance so that at the end of the five years the loan principal will be paid off. Alternatively, the business may negotiate a *term* loan. Nothing is paid on the principal during the life of a term loan; the entire amount borrowed (the principal) is paid at the maturity date of the loan.

Debt may or may not be secured with collateral. Debt instruments such as bonds may have very restrictive covenants (conditions) or may be quite liberal and nonbinding on the business. Some debt is convertible into equity stock shares, though generally this feature is limited to publicly held corporations whose stock shares are actively traded. The debt of a business may be a private loan, or debt securities may be issued that are actively traded on a bond market.

Equity capital may be supplied by just one person who operates the business as a sole proprietor; the business is not organized as a separate legal entity. Or the business may be legally organized as a partnership of two or more persons, which is a separate entity. Most businesses, including even relatively small ones, are organized as corporations, which are legal entities separate from their owners. A corporation is a legal type of entity that limits the liability of the owners (the stockholders). The corporate form is a practical way to organize equity ownership over a large number of investors.

There are literally millions of corporations in the American economy. Other countries around the globe have the equivalent of corporations, although the names of these organizations, as well as their legal and political features, differ somewhat from country to country. Corporations issue stock shares, which are the units of equity ownership in the corporation. A corporation may issue only one class of stock shares, called *common stock* or *capital stock*. Or a corporation may issue both preferred and common stock shares. A corporation may issue both voting and nonvoting classes of stock shares.

Debt bears an explicit and legally contracted rate of interest. Equity capital does not.* Nevertheless, equity capital has an imputed or implicit cost. Management must earn a satisfactory rate on the equity capital of

---

* Preferred stock shares carry a stated rate of cash dividend per period, but the actual payment of the dividend is contingent on the corporation earning enough net income and having enough cash on hand to pay the dividend.

the business to justify the use of this capital. Failure to do so reduces the value of the equity and makes it more difficult to attract additional equity capital (if and when needed).

Equity capital assumes the risk of business failure and poor performance. On the optimistic side, equity has no limits on its participation in the success of the business. Continued growth can lead to continued growth in cash dividends. The market value of the equity shares has no theoretical upper limit. The lower limit is zero (the shares become worthless)—although shares could be *assessable,* which means the corporation has the right to assess shareholders and make them contribute additional capital into the organization. Almost all corporate stock shares are issued as nonassessable shares, although one can't be too careful about this.

CASH FLOW STATEMENT FOR MANAGERS

Figure 4.4 presents the internal cash flow statement for managers. The main difference here is the explanatory notes, which you can read now or use as a convenient reference later. Otherwise, there is only one change in the format as compared with the external financial report format: operating cash flow before depreciation expense is calculated, which is $89,091—quite a bit less than the net income of $259,996. Next, depreciation is added to the $89,091 to determine cash flow from profit (or profit-making operations).

Cash Flow from Profit (Operating Activities)

Net income almost never equals cash flow from net income for the period. Profit is not money in the bank. As my youngest son the CPA asks: "If we're in the black, where's the green?" Cash flow does not equal net income for two quite different reasons. First, almost every business needs certain operating assets and certain operating liabilities to make sales or that result from its expenses. Cash goes through these assets and liabilities *before* or *after* the sales revenue or expense is recorded and, as the result, cash flow is different from net income.

For a simple example, consider a new business that makes $1,000,000 sales in its first year. So the top line in its income statement reports $1,000,000 sales revenue for the year. The company sells all its products on credit; at the end of the year it has $120,000 in accounts receivable, which are uncollected at year-end. Now suppose the company had no expenses (which is done only to illustrate the point here). Suppose also that the company had no operating assets other than cash and accounts receivable. The company's financial statements would be as follows:

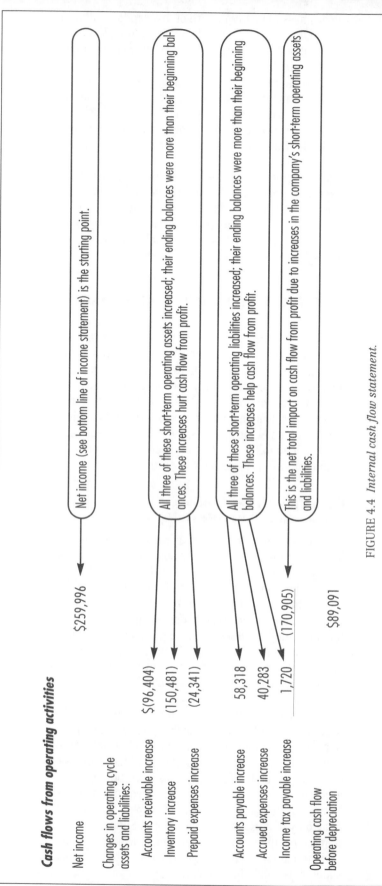

Cash flows from operating activities

Net income	$259,996

Net income (see bottom line of income statement) is the starting point.

Changes in operating cycle assets and liabilities:

Accounts receivable increase	$(96,404)
Inventory increase	(150,481)
Prepaid expenses increase	(24,341)

All three of these short-term operating assets increased; their ending balances were more than their beginning balances. These increases hurt cash flow from profit.

Accounts payable increase	58,318
Accrued expenses increase	40,283
Income tax payable increase	1,720
	(170,905)

All three of these short-term operating liabilities increased; their ending balances were more than their beginning balances. These increases help cash flow from profit.

This is the net total impact on cash flow from profit due to increases in the company's short-term operating assets and liabilities.

Operating cash flow before depreciation	$89,091

FIGURE 4.4 Internal cash flow statement.

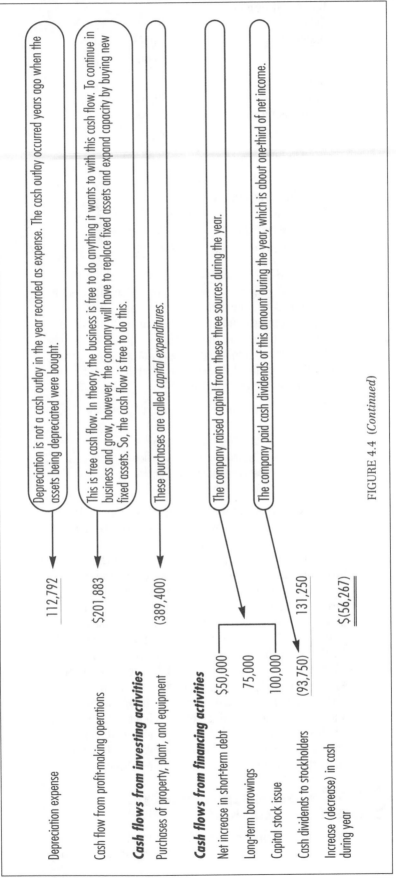

Depreciation expense		112,792

Depreciation is not a cash outlay in the year recorded as expense. The cash outlay occurred years ago when the assets being depreciated were bought.

Cash flow from profit-making operations		$201,883

This is free cash flow. In theory, the business is free to do anything it wants to with this cash flow. To continue in business and grow, however, the company will have to replace fixed assets and expand capacity by buying new fixed assets. So, the cash flow is free to do this.

Cash flows from investing activities

Purchases of property, plant, and equipment		(389,400)

These purchases are called *capital expenditures.*

Cash flows from financing activities

Net increase in short-term debt	$50,000	
Long-term borrowings	75,000	
Capital stock issue	100,000	131,250
Cash dividends to stockholders	(93,750)	
Increase (decrease) in cash during year		$(56,267)

The company raised capital from these three sources during the year.

The company paid cash dividends of this amount during the year, which is about one-third of net income.

FIGURE 4.4 (*Continued*)

Income statement

Sales revenue	$1,000,000
Expenses	none
Net income	$1,000,000

Balance sheet

Cash	$ 880,000
Accounts receivable	120,000
Total assets	$1,000,000
Total liabilities and owners' equity	$1,000,000

Cash flow statement

Net income	$1,000,000
Accounts receivable	(120,000)
Cash flow from profit	$ 880,000

Even though the company earned $1,000,000 profit (net income), only $880,000 was converted into cash by year-end because the company's accounts receivable increased from ground zero at the start of the year to $120,000 at the end of the year.

Although this simple example is not wholly realistic, it sets the stage for the basic rules that determine cash flow from net income (profit):

Start with net income, then adjust net income as follows:

$$\text{Operating asset} + \;=\; \text{cash flow} -$$
$$\text{Operating asset} - \;=\; \text{Cash flow} +$$
$$\text{Operating liability} + \;=\; \text{Cash flow} +$$
$$\text{Operating liability} - \;=\; \text{Cash flow} -$$

Cash flow from profit moves opposite to changes in operating assets and moves in the same direction as changes in operating liabilities.

The beginning balances of accounts receivable, inventory, and prepaid expenses are compared with their ending balances. In our company example, all three increase, as you can see in Figure 4.2, the company's internal balance sheet. Likewise, the start-of-year versus end-of-year comparison indicates increases for the three short-term operating liabilities. The net effect of all six is to decrease cash flow from profit by $170,905 (see Figure 4.4, the cash flow statement).

The cash flow impacts of changes in operating assets and liabilities are explained often in later chapters. You will become more and more comfortable with cash flow analysis as we move through the book. Like learning to enjoy the taste of olives, it takes some getting used to.

KEY CONCEPT   Depreciation: More Than an Add-Back

Depreciation expense is added to net income, following the adjustment for changes in the operating assets and liabilities. When depreciable assets are bought or constructed, the business invests cash in these long-lived operating assets, which are called *property, plant, and equipment* in the balance sheet, or *fixed assets* for short. As the business uses its fixed assets, it does not have to pay for them again, of course. If you paid cash for a new car, you don't have to pay again for the car as you drive it. The costs of a company's fixed assets can be thought of as a long-term prepaid expenses, which are gradually used up over the assets' useful economic lives.

The depreciation expense for the year is a real expense but is unique because it was paid for in previous years—going back many years for some fixed assets. The depreciation expense is not a cash outlay in the year recorded. The cash outlay occurred years earlier. If, on the other hand, the company had rented the assets instead of buying them, the rent expense would be a cash outlay in the period during which the expense is recorded.

As you can see in Figure 4.4, the amount of depreciation expense is added to net income; it is one of the two basic adjustments to determine cash flow from profit (the other is for the changes in the short-term operating assets and liabilities). The rules previously given for cash flow from profit apply to depreciation as well. A decrease in an operating asset is cash flow increase—the difference is that fixed assets are long-term operating assets, whereas accounts receivable, inventory, and prepaid expenses are short-term operating assets.

A company may invest in other types of long-term operating assets that are intangible, such as the purchase of patents that have several years of useful life to the business. The cost of intangibles is amortized,* which means charged off over the predicted economic useful life of the asset, just like depreciation. Amortization expense is also added back to net income.

There is another reason to give depreciation expense special attention in the cash flow statement. Suppose you tell me that your business made a profit for the year. I assume that you mean you made net income after deducting all expenses, including depreciation. Is this correct? Yes, I'm sure you mean this.

Suppose your accountant recorded $112,792 depreciation expense for the year. Therefore, your sales prices were set high enough to recoup some of the capital

---

* Unfortunately, the word *amortize* has two somewhat different meanings. When applied to a debt payoff schedule, it refers to payments made to reduce the principal balance of the debt, such as mortgage loan payments. The loan balance is said to be amortized, or gradually paid off over the life of the loan. The gradual charging off of the cost of an intangible asset is also called amortization of the cost, which means the gradual charging off of the cost over its predicted economic useful life.

invested in your fixed assets in prior years. It's like a taxicab owner setting fares high enough to recover the cost of the cab. Every time the taxi driver collects a fare, it's as if a small time-share in the cab is sold to the passenger. Likewise, your business sold off $112,792 of fixed assets to your customers. You converted this much of the original cost of the fixed assets into cash during the year.

Other Cash Sources and Uses

Please refer to the cash flow statement again (Figure 4.4). Notice that after adding back depreciation, the company's cash flow from profit is $201,883. This figure has come to be known as *free cash flow*. Well, nothing is free, as you know. What this term means is that this much cash was available for management use. There are always competing demands on the cash. Generally, free cash flow is allocated among four basic alternative uses:

1. Replace and/or expand fixed assets.

2. Add to the working cash balance.

3. Pay cash dividends from net income.

4. Reduce debt and/or equity.

The remainder of the cash flow statement answers what management decided to do with its free cash flow. The information is put into two categories: investing activities and financing activities. Under investing activities, you see that the company used all its free cash flow and then some for the purchase of new fixed assets (see Figure 4.4). The business spent $187,517 more than its free cash flow for its capital expenditures: $389,400 capital expenditures – $201,883 cash flow from profit-making operations = $187,517 excess. The obvious question is: Where did the business get the $187,517?

The other information in the cash flow statement answers this question. The company went to its debt and equity sources for $225,000 additional capital: $50,000 increase in short-term debt, $75,000 increase in long-term term debt, and $100,000 from increase in capital stock. The company paid $93,750 cash dividends, which reduced the cash brought into the business: $225,000 new capital – $93,750 cash dividend = $131,250.

The net effect of the new capital minus the cash dividend was to provide only $131,250 for capital expenditures, which is $56,267 short of the amount spent on the purchase of new fixed assets. The company allowed its cash balance to drop by $56,267, which you can see on the bottom line of Figure 4.4. Does this leave the company with an adequate working cash balance? We shall return to this question several times in later chapters.

END POINT

This chapter introduces the other two internal financial statements that serve as the foundation for explaining management analysis in later chapters: (1) the statement of financial condition at the end of the most recent period for which an income statement has been prepared, called the balance sheet; and (2) the cash flow statement, which summarizes the cash inflows and cash outflows for the period. The layout of the internal, management balance sheet is noticeably different compared with the external balance sheet shown in Figure 2.1. The internal and external cash flow statements are not so different.

Each asset, liability, and owners' equity reported on the balance sheet is like a piece in a puzzle; putting the pieces together gives a good picture of the financial health and position of the business at a moment in time. This financial statement is a freeze-frame from the videotape of the company's operations that are in constant motion.

The cash flow statement is the new kid on the block; it was not required in external financial reports until 1987. The statement begins with determination of cash flow from profit; this is internal, self-generated cash of the business. Other sources of cash are external, or from outside the business. The internal and external sources of cash should be compared. The uses of cash reported in this statement are very important decisions, reflecting whether the business is building for the future, holding the status quo, or downsizing.

PART 2

Management Analysis

Operating Ratios:
Indispensable Benchmarks

Figure 5.1 shows the lines of connection between sales revenue and expenses in the income statement and assets and liabilities in the balance sheet. This chapter explains how the profit-making operations of the business—its sales revenue and expenses—determine the operating assets and liabilities of the business. Figure 5.1 displays the vital links between making profit and the assets and liabilities needed for it, as well as the result of making profit.

CONNECTIONS BETWEEN THE INCOME STATEMENT AND THE BALANCE SHEET

Before discussing each connection, please notice that the company's operating liabilities are deducted from its assets to determine the company's net operating assets of $2,874,230. As discussed in Chapter 4, operating liabilities are different from the other liabilities of the company. In contrast to the interest-bearing debt of a company, the operating liabilities are *non-interest-bearing*—they are not the result of borrowing money. Rather, these liabilities are the outcome of the company's profit-making activities.

In round terms, the business has about three million dollars' capital invested in its net operating assets, which is supplied by its debt and equity capital. Both sources of capital have a cost. Cost of capital is extraordinarily important and is discussed in the next chapter. First, this chapter examines which and how much in operating assets and liabilities are needed to carry on profit-making activities.

 OPERATING RATIOS AND RELATIONSHIPS

The relative size comparison between sales revenue and each expense and its corresponding asset or liabil-

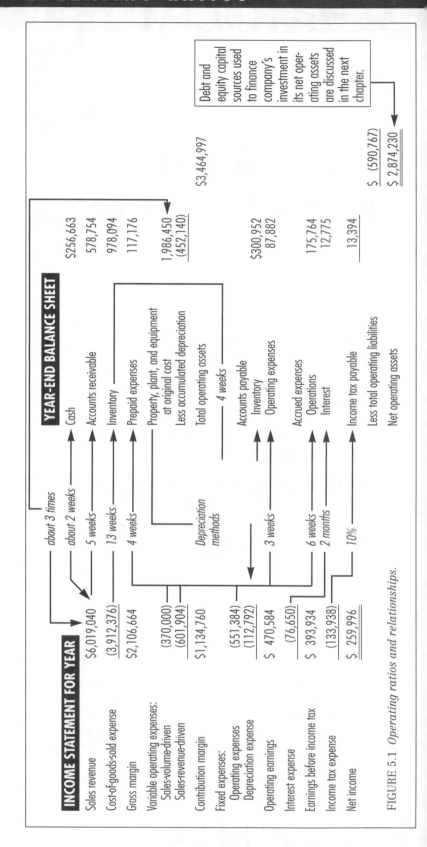

FIGURE 5.1 *Operating ratios and relationships.*

The figure contains the following elements:

INCOME STATEMENT FOR YEAR

Sales revenue	$6,019,040
Cost-of-goods-sold expense	(3,912,376)
Gross margin	$2,106,664
Variable operating expenses:	
Sales-volume-driven	(370,000)
Sales-revenue-driven	(601,904)
Contribution margin	$1,134,760
Fixed expenses:	
Operating expenses	(551,384)
Depreciation expense	(112,792)
Operating earnings	$ 470,584
Interest expense	(76,650)
Earnings before income tax	$ 393,934
Income tax expense	(133,938)
Net income	$ 259,996

YEAR-END BALANCE SHEET

Cash	$256,663
Accounts receivable	578,754
Inventory	978,094
Prepaid expenses	117,176
Property, plant, and equipment at original cost	1,986,450
Less accumulated depreciation	(452,140)
Total operating assets	$3,464,997
Accounts payable	
Inventory	$300,952
Operating expenses	87,882
Accrued expenses	
Operations	175,764
Interest	12,775
Income tax payable	13,394
Less total operating liabilities	$ (590,767)
Net operating assets	$ 2,874,230

Connecting labels between the statements: *about 3 times*, *about 2 weeks*, *5 weeks*, *13 weeks*, *4 weeks*, *Depreciation methods*, *4 weeks*, *3 weeks*, *6 weeks*, *2 months*, *10%*.

Debt and equity capital sources used to finance company's investment in its net operating assets are discussed in the next chapter.

ity is measured by an *operating ratio*. The term *ratio* means that the relationship or connection between the two is fairly definite and measurable. Other relationships between revenue and expenses and their corresponding asset or liability are not precisely measurable. This chapter presents a comprehensive, though compact, summary of the operating ratios and relationships that determine the shape of a company's balance sheet and the amounts of its operating assets and liabilities.*

Each operating ratio or relationship is discussed in three parts:

Ratio (or relationship) definition

Formula for ratio (or relationship)

Calculation for company example

We do *not* start with the cash account, which you might think would be the logical place to begin. Cash will be discussed last, once we have gone through all the other operating assets and liabilities. Cash is a buffer or slack variable, for which there is no standard or prescribed operating ratio. Cash balances depend on management's policies and attitudes, as well as the financial stresses and strains of the business at any moment in time. You'll notice from Figure 5.1 that cash equals about two weeks of annual sales revenue—but, more on this later.

 ACCOUNTS RECEIVABLE ← SALES REVENUE
CONCEPT

Receivable/revenue ratio

Weeks of annual sales revenue in ending accounts receivable

$5/52 \times \$6,019,040 = \$578,754$

The ending balance of accounts receivable is the amount of uncollected sales revenue at year-end—sales made on credit that have not yet been turned into cash receipts but will be early next year. The time it takes to collect receivables depends on the credit period offered to customers. In this example, the average collection period is five weeks, and all sales are made on credit.

Thus, the last five weeks of annual sale revenue is not collected yet at year-end. The ending balance of accounts receivable equals five weeks of annual sales revenue. In summary, the receivables/revenue operating ratio is 5/52,[†] so

---

* Operating ratios are also explained in my book, *How to Read a Financial Report,* 4th ed. (New York: John Wiley & Sons, 1994).
[†] This operating ratio should be based on the most recent sales. In other words, the last five weeks of credit sales would be the ending balance of accounts receivable. If sales follow seasonal fluctuations, the last five weeks of the year could be the seasonal peak, so the ending balance of accounts receivable would also be at its peak.

$578,754 ending accounts receivable =
5/52 × $6,019,040 annual sales revenue

In this company example, this key operating asset ratio assumes that all sales are made on credit and that sales are uniform during the year. If not, the ratio would be adjusted for seasonal patterns. It is based on the normal credit terms of the company and adjusted to reflect actual collection experience of the company.

The flip of the receivable/revenue ratio is computed as follows—

$6,019,040 annual sales revenue
÷ $578,754 ending accounts receivable = 10.4 times

This ratio is called the *accounts receivable turnover* ratio. Annual sales revenue is 10.4 times the ending balance of accounts receivable. This is correct, of course; however, the direction of cause and effect is reversed. Sales revenue causes accounts receivable, not the other way around. It is preferable for management analysis to focus on how many weeks of sales are in ending accounts receivable.

 ## INVENTORY ← COST-OF-GOODS-SOLD EXPENSE

> Inventory/cost-of-goods-sold ratio
>
> Weeks of annual cost of goods sold in ending inventory
>
> **13/52** × $3,912,376 = $978,094

Virtually all companies that sell products carry an inventory, or a stock of products, for some period of time before the products are sold and delivered to customers. The holding period depends on the business, of course. Supermarkets have short holding periods; retail furniture stores have fairly long holding periods. In this company example, the ending inventory asset balance equals 13 weeks of its annual cost-of-goods-sold expense. In short, the inventory/cost-of-goods-sold operating ratio is 13/52:

$978,094 ending inventory = 13/52 × $3,912,376 annual
cost of goods sold

This operating ratio is a *cost-to-cost* ratio. Inventory is carried at cost until sold and then charged to the cost-of-goods-sold expense. This operating ratio is based on the company's normal holding period averaged across all products.

 Generally speaking, inventory should not be held longer than necessary. Holding inventory is subject to several risks and requires several costs. Products may become obsolete, or they may be stolen, damaged, or even misplaced. Products have to be stored, they usually have to be insured, they may have to be guarded, and a certain amount of capital is invested in inventory. Inventory control is very important and is discussed later in the book.

The flip of the inventory/cost-of-goods-sold ratio is computed as follows:

$$\$3,912,376 \text{ annual cost of goods sold} \div \$978,094 \text{ ending inventory} = 4.0 \text{ times}$$

This is called the *inventory turnover* ratio; annual cost of goods sold is 4.0 times the ending balance of inventory. I think it preferable for management analysis to focus on how many weeks of sales are in ending inventory. This is the standard practice in the auto and other industries.

PREPAID EXPENSES ← OPERATING EXPENSES (EXCEPT DEPRECIATION)

Prepaids/operating expenses ratio

Weeks of annual operating expenses in ending prepaid expenses

4/52 × $1,523,288 = $117,176

Every business prepays several expenses. Two examples: Fire insurance must be prepaid for six months or more, and several weeks of office supplies or shipping materials are bought. These costs are not charged to expenses until the items are used or the costs are allocated over the period of benefit. Such paid-in-advance costs are recorded in the prepaid expenses asset account, until the time that this asset account is reduced and an expense account is charged for the cost of the items used up.

The ending balance of the company's prepaid expenses equals four weeks of its total operating expenses, excluding depreciation. In the income statement in Figure 5.1, operating expenses are in three different categories: (1) sales-volume-driven variable operating expenses, (2) sales-revenue-driven variable operating expenses, and (3) fixed operating expenses. The sum of these three expenses is $1,523,288 for the year. So the prepaids/operating expenses ratio is 4/52 and the ending balance of prepaid expenses is computed as follows:

$$\$117,176 \text{ ending prepaid expenses} = 4/52 \times \$1,523,288 \text{ annual operating expenses}$$

All businesses have these prepaids, though the relative size of their prepaid expenses to total operating expenses varies from industry to industry. Seldom would prepaid expenses be very large compared with accounts receivable and inventory. But prepaids cannot be ignored. Last, notice that the cost-of-sales expense (i.e., cost-of-goods-sold expense) is not included in this operating ratio. Inventory can be thought of as "pre-paid" cost-of-goods-sold expense, to draw a rough comparison here.

 **SALES REVENUE ↔ PROPERTY, PLANT, AND EQUIPMENT**

Sales/fixed assets relationship

Annual sales revenue ÷ fixed assets

$6,019,040 ÷ $1,986,450 = about **3 times**

Property, plant, and equipment is the broad asset account title that includes land, buildings, and other real estate improvements, machinery, manufacturing and other equipment, tools, furniture, shelving, vehicles, and so on. These assets provide *capacity* to carry on the activities of the business—so many square feet of space, so many employee hours, and so on.

The size of these so-called *fixed* assets relative to annual sales revenue depends on whether the industry is capital intensive or not, that is, whether it requires many such assets or not. Generally speaking, manufacturers need a lot more fixed assets than retailers. The average production line worker may use $500,000, $1,000,000, or more of machinery and equipment, to say nothing of the building space needed. A supermarket employee would not need so much, of course.

 There simply is no rule of thumb that can be applied across industries; even within the same line of business, the relative size of these long-term operating assets varies depending on when the business acquired its fixed assets. These assets are recorded at original cost and are not written-up in value, even though replacement costs for similar assets may be much higher. The older the assets, the older the cost.

In this company example, the original cost of these fixed assets is almost $2.0 million. Annual sales are a little over $6.0 million, which is about three times the original cost of its fixed operating assets. These long-term operating assets are depreciated, so the book value of the assets (original cost less accumulated depreciation) is considerably less than the original cost of the assets, which further complicates this operating relationship.

 **DEPRECIATION EXPENSE ← PROPERTY, PLANT, AND EQUIPMENT**

Depreciation/fixed asset relationship

Annual depreciation expense ÷ fixed assets cost

$112,792 ÷ $1,986,450 = about **6%**

All fixed assets, except for land, are charged to depreciation expense each year over some arbitrary life estimates according to some arbitrary allocation method, heavily influenced by what is allowed for federal income tax purposes. The annual depreciation expense is added to the accumulated depreciation account, which is deducted from the original cost of the fixed assets. By and large, depreciation expensing is very conservative and driven by tax considerations. The result is that depreciation is charged off too fast, causing book values to be too low.

Managers should take control over the depreciation decision or at least be fully aware of the depreciation lives and methods decided on. The depreciation decision has major impacts on the financial statements—on profit measurement and financial condition. Also, depreciation is quite different from other expenses, from the cash flow point of view. We'll have much more to say about depreciation as we move along.

In this company example, depreciation expense for the year is only about 6 percent of the original cost of its fixed assets. This is because the company has a large amount invested in a building which is being depreciated over 39 years, which is only about 2.5 percent of cost per year. Its other fixed assets have much shorter useful life estimates and are being depreciated over three, five, or seven years. There is no standard ratio for how large the annual depreciation expense should be relative to the cost of fixed assets.

KEY CONCEPT — ACCOUNTS PAYABLE: INVENTORY ← INVENTORY

Payable/inventory ratio

Weeks of inventory in ending accounts payable

4/13 × $978,094 = $300,952

Most businesses buy inventory on credit (or, if a manufacturer, the company buys its raw materials on credit). At any one time, not all of its inventory purchases have been paid for; there is still a balance owing to the suppliers of its products. Trade credit terms vary from industry to industry, as you probably know. In this company example, the year-end balance of accounts payable from inventory purchases equals four weeks of ending inventory cost; the payable/inventory operation ratio is 4/13. The ending accounts payable from inventory purchases is computed as follows:

$300,952 accounts payable: inventory =
4/13 × $978,094 ending inventory

Recall that inventory is held 13 weeks, so the first 9 weeks of the inventory was paid for by year-end, but the remaining 4 weeks of inventory is still unpaid at year-end. The unpaid balance is recorded in the accounts payable liability account. This operating ratio is based on the normal credit terms offered by the suppliers to a company.

ACCOUNTS PAYABLE: OPERATING EXPENSES ← OPERATING EXPENSES (EXCEPT DEPRECIATION)

Payable/operating expenses ratio

Weeks of annual operating expenses in ending accounts payable

$3/52 \times \$1,523,288 = \$87,882$

Many services and items charged to expense, such as the professional fees charged by lawyers and CPAs, are bought on credit. Some items recorded in prepaid expenses, such as office and packing supplies, are bought on credit. Telephone and other utility services are bought on credit. These unpaids for expenses that have been already recognized or for items already booked in the prepaid expenses account are recorded in the accounts payable liability account. These items are quite different from inventory purchases, so they are put in a separate account in the internal balance sheet (see Figure 5.1 again).

In this company example, the ending balance of accounts payable from operating expenses equals three weeks of annual total operating expenses; the payable/operating expenses operating ratio is 3/52. The ending accounts payable from operating expenses is computed as follows:

$$\$87,882 \text{ accounts payable: operating expenses} = 3/52 \times \$1,523,288 \text{ annual operating expenses}$$

This operating ratio is based on the average credit terms offered by the vendors of these expenses.

ACCRUED EXPENSES: OPERATING EXPENSES ← OPERATING EXPENSES (EXCEPT DEPRECIATION)

Accrueds/operating expenses ratio

Weeks of annual operating expenses in ending accrued expenses liability

$6/52 \times \$1,523,288 = \$175,764$

In my experience, managers and business professionals do not appreciate the rather large size of accruals of various operating expenses. Many operating expenses are *not* on a pay-as-you-go basis. For example, accumulated vacation and sick leave benefits are not paid until the employees actually take their vacations or sick days. At year-end the company calculates profit-sharing bonuses and other profit-sharing amounts, which should be recorded as expense in the period just ended even though they will not be paid until some time later.

Product warranty and guarantee costs should be accrued and charged to expense so that these follow-up costs are recognized in the same year the sales revenue is recorded—to get a correct matching of sales revenue and expenses to measure profit. In summary, there are a surprising number of expense accruals that should be recorded.

Accruals are quite different from accounts payable. For one thing, an account payable is based on an actual invoice received by the vendor, whereas accruals have no such hard document to serve as evidence of the liability. Accruals depend much more on the good-faith estimates of the accountants and others making these calculations. So, the accrued expenses from operating expenses are shown as a separate line item in the income statement (see Figure 5.1 again).

In this company example, the ending balance of this accrued liability equals six weeks of annual total operating expenses, so the accrueds/operating expenses ratio is 6/52. The ending balance of accrued expenses from operating expenses is computed as follows:

$$\$175{,}764 \text{ accrued expenses: operations} =$$
$$6/52 \times \$1{,}523{,}288 \text{ annual operating expenses}$$

This operating ratio is based on the types of accruals that the company records, such as accrued vacation and sick pay for employees, accrued property taxes, and accrued warranty and guarantee costs on products. It takes into account the average time between when each expense is recorded and when it is eventually paid out in cash, which can be quite a long time for some items but rather short for others.

 ## ACCRUED EXPENSES: INTEREST ← INTEREST EXPENSE

Accrueds/interest expense ratio

Months of annual interest expense in ending accrued expenses liability

$2/12 \times \$76{,}650 = \$12{,}775$

Interest expense grows or accrues day by day but is paid at the end of periodic intervals. At the end of each accounting year, the accountant records any unpaid interest in this liability account, so that the full amount of the interest for the year is recognized as expense for the year. In this example, two months, or one-sixth of its annual interest expense, is unpaid at year-end, so this operating ratio is 2/12. The ending balance in accrued expenses from unpaid interest expense is computed as follows:

$$\$12{,}775 \text{ accrued expenses: interest} =$$
$$2/12 \times \$76{,}650 \text{ annual interest expense}$$

There is no standard or rule of thumb for this operating ratio; it varies from company to company. A lot depends on the particular due dates for interest payments.

INCOME TAX PAYABLE ← INCOME TAX EXPENSE

Tax payable/income tax ratio

Percent of annual income tax expense in ending tax payable liability

10% × $133,938 = $13,394

Assuming the code is strictly observed, the federal corporate tax law requires that virtually all of the estimated income tax for the year has been paid by the end of the year. In this example, however, 10 percent is unpaid at year-end, which is not unrealistic:

$$\$13,394 \text{ income tax payable} =$$
$$10\% \times \$133,938 \text{ income tax expense for year}$$

Although a 10 percent unpaid income tax operating ratio would not be unusual, there are many technical reasons why the year-end unpaid income tax might be more than 10 percent, or perhaps less. It would be unusual for this liability to be a large percentage of the annual income tax expense—though sometimes a business is in an unusual tax situation.

SALES REVENUE ↔ CASH

Cash/sales relationship

Ending cash balance ÷ annual sales revenue

$256,663 ÷ $6,019,040 = about **2 weeks**

We have now walked through all the operating assets and operating liabilities of the company; it's time to return to the cash account. In this example, the company's year-end cash balance is a little more than two weeks of annual sales revenue.

$$\$256,663 \text{ ending cash balance}$$
$$\div \$6,019,040 \text{ annual sales revenue} = 2+ \text{ weeks}$$

The cash/sales operating ratio is about two weeks.

There's no doubt that every business needs to keep enough cash in its checking account (or on hand in currency and coin for cash-based businesses such as grocery stores and gambling casinos). But precisely how much? Every business manager would worry if cash were too low to meet the next payroll. Some liabilities can be put off for days or even weeks, but employees have to be paid on time.

Beyond a minimal amount of working cash balance to meet the payroll and to provide at least a bare-bones margin of safety, it is not clear how much additional cash balance a business should carry.

It's somewhat like your friends: Some may have only $5 to $10 in walking-around money on them; others could reach in their billfolds or purses and pull out $500.

Clearly, excess cash balances should be avoided. For one thing, capital has a cost and excess cash is an unproductive asset not paying its way towards meeting the company's cost of capital on its net operating assets. For another thing, excess cash balances can cause managers to get lax in controlling expenses. If the money is there in the bank, waiting only for a check to be written, it is more of an incentive to make unnecessary expenditures or not to scrutinize expenditures as closely as needed. Also, excess cash balances can lead to greater opportunities for fraud and embezzlement.

Yet having a large cash balance is a tremendous advantage in some situations. The business may be able to drive a hard bargain with a major vendor by paying cash up front rather than asking for the normal credit terms. There are many such reasons for holding a cash balance over and above what's really needed to meet the payroll and to provide for a safety buffer for the normal lags and leads in the cash receipts and cash disbursements of the company. Frankly, if this were my business, I think I would want more like three or even four weeks' cash balance. But, two weeks of cash is probably workable.

The company may be able to go to its external sources of capital—that is, debt and owners' equity—for additional money. Or maybe not. The company may be borrowed up to its limit, and its stockholders may not be willing or able to put any more money into the business. I wanted to use an example with enough, but not too much, cash because this should heighten your attention to the cash flow analysis discussed in later chapters.

An executive of a leading company said he kept the company's cash balance "lean and mean" to keep its managers on their toes. There's probably a lot of truth in this. But if too much time and effort goes into managing day-to-day cash flow, more important factors may not get managed well.

SALES REVENUE ↔ ASSETS

Asset turnover ratio

Annual sales/net operating assets

$6,019,040 ÷ $2,874,230 = **2.09 times**

There is one other ratio that should be mentioned in passing, called the *asset turnover ratio*. It is computed as follows:

$6,019,040 annual sales revenue
÷ $2,874,230 net operating assets = 2.09 times*

The asset turnover ratio is a very gross ratio. It is a macro-level or composite average of the several more specific operating ratios and relationships that have been discussed in this chapter. For decision making and control, managers have to focus on the specific operating ratios. One particular ratio may be out of control, but the other operating ratios may be satisfactory.

SOLVENCY RATIOS

KEY CONCEPT
The term *solvency* means the ability of the business to pay its liabilities on time (or to be more realistic, before the creditors get really mad and threaten legal action). Two ratios are widely used to gauge the short-term solvency of business: the *current* ratio and the *quick* (or *acid test*) ratio. In contrast to the operating ratios previously explained, these solvency ratios are composite ratios; two or more items are grouped into one number to calculate each ratio.

The company's current ratio is computed as follows (see Figure 2.1 for data): $1,930,687 current assets ÷ $1,015,767 current liabilities = 1.9 current ratio. In other words, the company has $1.90 of current assets for every $1.00 of current liabilities at year-end. The quick ratio includes only cash, cash equivalents, and accounts receivable in the numerator; it is computed as follows for the company: ($256,663 cash + $578,754 accounts receivable) ÷ $1,015,767 current liabilities = 0.82 quick ratio. The idea is that cash and accounts receivable are quicker sources of money for paying current liabilities. Rules of thumb call for a current ratio of 2.0 or better and a quick ratio of 1.0 or better—but these are questionable guidelines for many businesses.

Notice that both solvency ratios are based on information from the *external* balance sheet. Managers have access to operating ratios and other detailed information they need to judge whether or not the company will be able to pay its liabilities as they come due over the next week, next month, next quarter, or next year. Detailed cash flow budgets can be prepared that plot when cash will be received and when liabilities have to be paid. Alternatively, the business may simply

---

* To determine this ratio, sales revenue may be divided by total assets before deducting operating liabilities. In this example: $6,019,040 sales revenue ÷ $3,464,997 total assets = 1.7 times. I include this version of the asset turnover ratio because you may see it in your work and reading. I don't like it. Operating liabilities should be deducted to measure the *net* operating assets of the business—this is the amount that has to be financed from debt and equity sources on which cost of capital is based.

keep a relatively large cash balance to serve as a buffer against delays in cash receipts and/or other unexpected developments.

END POINT

The operating assets and liabilities discussed in this chapter are basic for a large range of businesses, across many different industries. However, some industries are relatively unique, and nonproduct, service-based businesses are quite different from the preceding example. For example, a commercial bank or other financial institution does not fit all aspects of the company example used in this chapter. For one thing, they do not have inventory, so the inventory/cost of goods sold operating ratio does not apply.

Nevertheless, every business—product-based or service-based, regulated or nonregulated, small or large, privately held or publicly owned—should develop operating ratios for its revenue and expenses that connect with its corresponding operating assets and liabilities. Without these essential benchmark ratios, it is very difficult to analyze the profit performance, financial condition, and cash flow effects of decisions—and managers would be without vital reference points for control.

6

Evaluating Business Investment Performance

T The previous chapter explains how making profit drives the balance sheet—how sales revenue and expenses determine the operating assets and liabilities of the business. Summing up: To carry on its profit-making operations, the business used $2,874,230 total net operating assets. The previous chapter looks at the operating side of the business. This chapter crosses over to the financial side and focuses on the sources of capital used to finance the net operating assets. The main concern of the chapter is how well the business has performed as an investor or *capital user.*

KEY CONCEPT

RETURN ON INVESTMENT (ROI)

The basic tool of analysis to evaluate capital investment performance is the ratio of earnings to capital. The earnings returned on the capital investment is expressed as a percent:

$$\text{Return} \div \text{investment} = \%$$

The term *return* means earnings, income, profit, or gain for the period; and the term *investment* means the amount of capital that was used during the period to generate the return.

The ratio of the two, quite naturally, is called *return on investment,* or ROI for short. For instance, if ROI were 10 percent for the year, the earnings (or profit, income, or gain) is 10 percent of the amount of capital that was invested to produce the earnings. ROI is the percent of growth in capital value—the improvement in wealth expressed as a percentage of the amount of capital started with. ROI neither indicates nor implies what was done with the earnings—whether they were spent on consumption or saved and added to the capital base next period.

ROI is a general and abstract concept—valid, to be sure, but rather vague until a particular type of capital investment is in mind. For business, the concept is defined as follows, going from the general concept of ROI to what it means for business:

ROI in general   *ROI for business*

$$\frac{\text{Return}}{\text{Investment}} \quad \begin{array}{c}\longrightarrow\\\longrightarrow\end{array} \quad \frac{\text{Profit}}{\text{Sources of capital}}$$

Business capital investment analysis uses, not one, but two fundamental ROI ratios.

Figure 6.1 presents in condensed format the operating and financial sides of the company example. The information is taken from the earlier exhibits that present the financial statements for the company; the data should be fairly familiar to you by now. The two sides of the business are coupled together to focus on the two key investment performance, or ROI, ratios. The two capital investment performance ratios are *return on assets* (ROA) and *return on equity* (ROE).

Return on assets (ROA) is defined as follows (see Figure 6.1 for data):

ROA = operating profit ÷ net operating assets
16.4% = $470,584 ÷ $2,874,230*

ROA is the before cost of capital return on investment for the business. It's the rate or percent that the company made on the total capital invested in its net operating assets before the cost of interest on debt capital and before the "cost" of equity capital is taken into account. ROA is the critical point of departure for capital investment analysis of business.

Return on equity (ROE) takes a narrower point of view: that of the equity owners in the business. This investment performance ratio excludes debt capital (which is included in the ROA) and looks only at the equity sources of capital. ROE is computed as follows (see Figure 6.1):

ROE = net income ÷ owners' equity
13.7% = $259,996 ÷ $1,899,230†

To achieve a satisfactory ROE, the business must start with a satisfactory ROA; this is why both ratios are important to understand.

The interest rate on debt is the ROI to the lender, for instance, the bank that loans money to the business.

---

* The year-end amount of net operating assets is used to compute ROA. The theoretically more correct amount is the weighted average for the year. However, the ending balance is a clearer trail to follow and usually is good enough for this type of analysis.
† The year-end amount of owners' equity is used to compute ROE. The theoretically more correct amount is the weighted average for the year. As with ROA, the ending balance is a clearer trail to follow and usually is good enough for this type of analysis—unless there was a major infusion of equity capital during the latter part of the year.

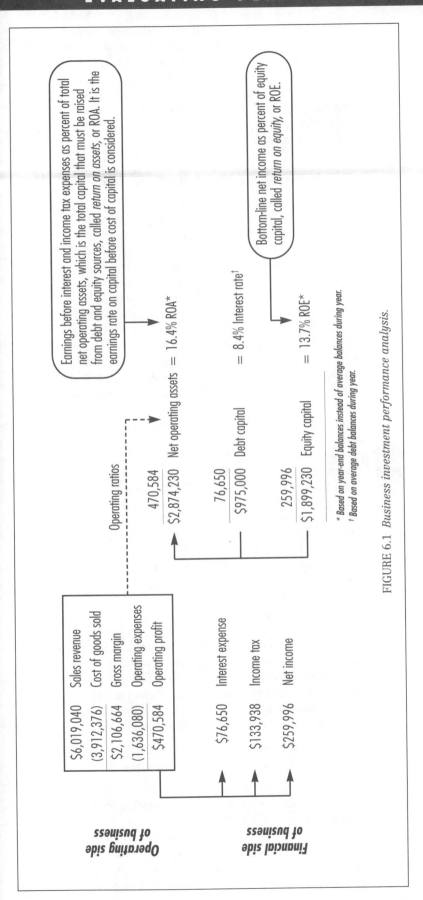

FIGURE 6.1 *Business investment performance analysis.*

Earnings before interest and income tax expenses as percent of total net operating assets, which is the total capital that must be raised from debt and equity sources, called *return on assets*, or ROA. It is the earnings rate on capital before cost of capital is considered.

Bottom-line net income as percent of equity capital, called *return on equity*, or ROE.

Operating ratios

470,584		
$2,874,230	Net operating assets	= 16.4% ROA*
76,650		
$975,000	Debt capital	= 8.4% Interest rate†
259,996		
$1,899,230	Equity capital	= 13.7% ROE*

* Based on year-end balances instead of average balances during year.
† Based on average debt balances during year.

Operating side of business

$6,019,040	Sales revenue
(3,912,376)	Cost of goods sold
$2,106,664	Gross margin
(1,636,080)	Operating expenses
$470,584	Operating profit

Financial side of business

$76,650	Interest expense
$133,938	Income tax
$259,996	Net income

Interest rates are an essential part of the debt contract with the lender, of course. For business capital investment analysis, different interest rates on different loans to the business are usually telescoped into one composite and overall average interest rate, which is done in this company example. As you can see in Figure 6.1, the company's average annual interest rate on all its debt is 8.4 percent.

THE PIVOTAL ROLE OF INCOME TAX

In a world without income taxes, operating profit would simply be divided between the two capital sources: interest on debt and the residual net income for the equity owners (stockholders). But in the real world, income tax takes out a share of operating profit—as you see in Figure 6.1. Since we are talking about return on capital investment, the following question might come to mind. Is income tax a return on government capital investment? Government does not invest *private* capital in business, of course. In a broader sense, however, government provides what could be called *public* capital. Government provides the public facilities (highways, schools, etc.), the political stability, the monetary system, the legal structure, and police protection. In brief, government provides the infrastructure for carrying on business activity.

The more relevant point about income tax is that under the United States income tax law (the Internal Revenue Code) interest paid by business is *deductible* to determine annual taxable income. Cash dividends paid to stockholders—even though these payments for the use of equity capital certainly can be viewed as substantially the same as interest payments for the use of debt capital—are *not* deductible to determine taxable income. This basic distinction has a significant impact on the amount of operating profit that has to be earned to cover the company's cost of capital.

To pay one dollar of interest on its debt, a business has to earn just one dollar of operating profit. A business does not have to earn anything additional to pay income tax. One dollar of operating profit used to pay one dollar of interest on debt results in no taxable income. In contrast, to make one dollar of after-tax net income, a business has to earn before-tax operating profit equal to:

$$\text{Operating profit needed to earn \$1.00 net income} = \frac{\$1.00}{(1 - \text{income tax rate})}$$

For example, if the income tax rate were 50 percent, a business would have to earn $2.00 operating profit to make $1.00 after-tax net income.

The current corporate income tax rate over a broad range of taxable income of business corporations is 34 percent, which is the rate used in this example. Applying the preceding formula, a business has to earn $1.52

(rounded) operating profit before income tax to yield $1.00 net income after tax. Income tax will take the other $.52 ($1.52 taxable income × 34% tax rate = $.52 income tax).*

Let's apply this discussion to the concrete facts of the company example (refer to Figure 6.1 as we go along). The company had to earn $76,650 operating profit to cover its cost of debt for the year. Now suppose, for the sake of making the point here, that the company's goal had been to make exactly 13.7 percent ROE. Given the amount of owners' equity at year-end, the 13.7 percent ROE would require $259,996 net income.

The company would have to earn $393,934 operating profit before income tax expense for its equity capital, which is computed as follows:

$$\text{Net income target} \div (1 - 34\% \text{ income tax rate})$$
$$\$259,996 \div .66 = \$393,934$$

In other words, the taxable income of the business (which is operating profit after deducting interest expense) would have to be $393,934—which it is, in fact, as you can check in Figure 3.1, the internal income statement.

To sum up, the company would have to earn $393,934 operating profit for its equity capital to achieve its 13.7 percent ROE goal, and earn another $76,650 to cover the interest on its debt capital—for total operating profit of $470,584. In Figure 6.1, notice that total operating profit for the year is exactly $470,584.

 THE NATURE OF RETURN ON EQUITY (ROE)

Net income is the compensation for the use of the owners' equity capital during the period. The company's equity owners put $725,000 in the business over the years, for which they received shares of capital stock. This is called *paid-in capital.* The stockholders could have invested this money elsewhere. Also, the company has reinvested a good amount of its annual profits in the business. In addition to the paid-in capital, the company's balance sheet (see Figure 4.2) reports that the company's accumulated retained earnings have grown to $1,174,230 at the most recent year-end. Total owners' equity capital is $1,899,230, which is the base for the ROE computation, as explained earlier.

The stockholders' equity capital is at risk; the business may or may not be able to earn enough net income on the invested capital. For that matter, the company could go belly up and declare bankruptcy.

---

* Presently, the federal income tax rate on taxable incomes from $75,000 to $10,000,000 is 34 percent. The income tax rate on taxable income over $18,333,333 is 35 percent. Tax rates are subject to change by Congress, of course.

Stockholders are paid last, after all debts and liabilities are settled, in a bankruptcy proceeding. There's no promise that cash dividends will be paid to the stockholders even when net income is earned.

Net income was $259,996 for the most recent year, but only $93,750 was distributed as cash dividends (Figure 4.4, the cash flow statement). The dividend payout decision is made by the corporation's board of directors. Not distributing net income as cash dividends means that the business does not have cash flow to pay dividends or the company needs the money for other purposes.

In any case, equity capital investment performance is not measured by how much is paid in dividends, but rather by the entire net income earned by the business. (The cash dividend yield is an important ratio in investment analysis by individuals and organizations who invest in stock shares—it is the most recent 12 months' cash dividends divided by the current market value of the stock.) ROE is the measure of the full yield, or the complete return on equity capital.*

Recall that ROE is 13.7 percent for the year—not bad but probably not all that good either. This comment raises the larger question regarding which yardstick is most relevant. It's a variation on the old theme: relative to what? Theoretically, the $1,899,230 owners' equity in the business could be pulled out and invested somewhere else and would earn an ROI on the alternative investment. Should the company's ROE be compared with the ROI that could be earned on a riskless and highly liquid investment, say short-term U.S. government securities? Surely not. ROE should be compared with a *comparable* investment alternative that has the same risk and liquidity as stockholders' equity.

The earnings rate, or ROI, on the most relevant alternative or next-best investment is called the *opportunity cost of capital*. To avoid a prolonged discussion here, we'll simply assume the stockholders are not totally satisfied with the 13.7 percent ROE, which implies that their opportunity cost of capital is higher. The company will try to do better, as we shall see in examining its financial plan for next year. First, we need to examine another key tool for analyzing business capital investment performance.

---

* If there is more than one class of stock (e.g., both preferred and common stock), net income has to be divided between the classes, and the share for the common stock is used in computing its ROE. There may be more than one class of common stock, each having different priorities and claims on net income, so a separate ROE may have to be computed for each class. Also, we do not consider any change in market value of the stock shares here; net income is treated as the total increase of value to the equity shareholders. If the capital stock shares are traded in a public market, the change in market value during the year should be included in determining the total return on investment for the period.

KEY CONCEPT

FINANCIAL LEVERAGE

Let me draw your attention to an apparent puzzle at this point. The company made 16.4 percent ROA for the year (see Figure 6.1). The income tax rate is 34 percent. Deducting income tax from the 16.4 percent ROA gives an after-tax 10.8 percent ROA: 16.4% ROA $\times (1 - .34) = 10.8\%$. The company made 16.4 percent on its equity capital and gave up 34 percent for income tax; therefore, it would seem that the return on owners' equity should be 10.8 percent. But ROE is actually 13.7 percent, a significant improvement. The difference is due to *financial leverage.*

Financial leverage refers to borrowing money at an interest rate lower than can be earned on the debt capital. The equity capital base of the business is leveraged by using additional debt capital in place of equity capital. For this reason, financial leverage is also called *trading on the equity.* A favorable spread between the interest rate and the company's ROA produces a financial leverage gain that supplements earnings on equity capital, which improves ROE. In this example, the company's ROE benefits from financial leverage.

Figure 6.2 demonstrates financial leverage analysis for the company example. The layout follows closely that of Figure 6.1—except that total operating profit is divided between the company's two sources of capital. The 16.4 percent ROA rate is multiplied by the amount of debt capital to determine the operating profit earned on this much of the capital invested in the company's net operating assets, and, likewise, the ROA is multiplied by the amount of equity capital. Accordingly, $159,632 operating profit is allocated to debt capital and $310,952 to equity capital. Although $159,632 was earned on debt capital, the interest expense is only $76,650. Thus, there is a before-tax financial leverage gain of $82,982, as you can see in Figure 6.2.

The stockholders benefit from the $82,982 pre-tax financial leverage gain. The company earned $310,952 on the equity capital and in addition benefited from the $82,982 financial leverage gain from using debt capital. So the total pre-tax earnings for equity capital are $393,934, which is also the amount of taxable income. After-tax net income is $259,996, which yields the 13.7 percent ROE shown in Figure 6.2.

Leverage works to the advantage of the stockholders only if the company's ROA (its rate of operating profit before interest and income tax on total net operating assets) is more than its interest rate on debt. There must be a favorable spread to make financial leverage work to the advantage of ROE. In this example, the favorable spread is 8 points (1 point = 1.00%)—16.4% ROA less 8.4% interest rate = 8 points spread.

Financial leverage looks good, of course, but it has limits and certain disadvantages. Lenders will loan only

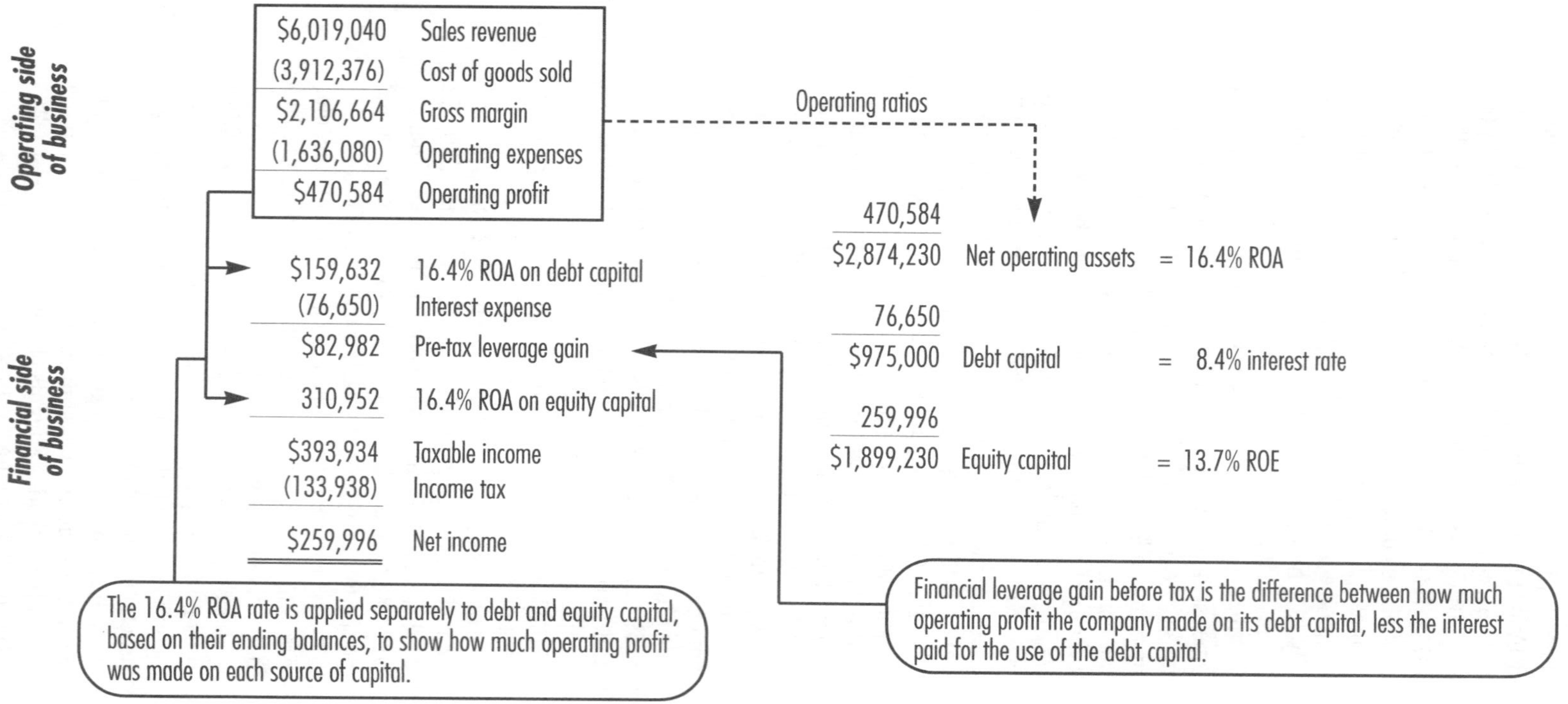
Operating side of business
$6,019,040 Sales revenue
(3,912,376) Cost of goods sold
$2,106,664 Gross margin
(1,636,080) Operating expenses
$470,584 Operating profit
Operating ratios
470,584 / $2,874,230 Net operating assets = 16.4% ROA
76,650 / $975,000 Debt capital = 8.4% interest rate
259,996 / $1,899,230 Equity capital = 13.7% ROE
Financial side of business
$159,632 16.4% ROA on debt capital
(76,650) Interest expense
$82,982 Pre-tax leverage gain
310,952 16.4% ROA on equity capital
$393,934 Taxable income
(133,938) Income tax
$259,996 Net income
The 16.4% ROA rate is applied separately to debt and equity capital, based on their ending balances, to show how much operating profit was made on each source of capital.
Financial leverage gain before tax is the difference between how much operating profit the company made on its debt capital, less the interest paid for the use of the debt capital.

FIGURE 6.2 *Financial leverage analysis.*

so much money to a business; once a business hits its borrowing capacity, new debt is either not available or interest rates become prohibitive. Any slippage in the spread between ROA and the interest rate has a magnifying effect on ROE. A lower ROA would not only reduce the earnings on equity capital but also would take away some of the leverage gain; there would be a twofold negative impact on ROE.

KEY CONCEPT **ACHIEVING ROE GOAL**

As previously mentioned, the 13.7 percent ROE for the year just ended may not be entirely satisfactory. The company probably would like to do better. Assume the company's objective for next year is to earn 15.0 percent ROE and that the company will continue to borrow money at an 8.4 percent annual interest rate. The company is planning on a debt-to-equity ratio of 1 to 2. Figure 4.2, the balance sheet, shows that total debt at the end of the most recent year is just under $1,000,000 ($975,000) and total stockholders' equity is just under $2,000,000 ($1,899,230), so the company is very close to a 1-to-2 debt-to-equity ratio. The income tax rate should remain at 34 percent, though with Congress in session this is subject to change.

The company is budgeting sales revenue to increase to $6,897,000 next year. Net operating assets are budgeted at $3,300,000 because the company expects its 2.09 asset turnover ratio to hold the same next year: $6,897,000 sales revenue ÷ 2.09 = $3,300,000 net operating assets. (See Chapter 5 for discussion of the asset turnover ratio.) Debt capital will be $1,100,000 and equity capital will be $2,200,000, based on the 1-to-2 debt-to-equity ratio assumed in the budget plan. The 15.0 percent ROE is the basic financial objective of the company for the coming year.

Setting the ROE goal is somewhat arbitrary. Should it have been set at 20.0 percent? Would 12.0 percent be acceptable? There is no official answer book on this question. Top management should set ROE goals that satisfy its equity capital sources. Many factors affect the ROE target rate, including interest rates, inflation rates, rates of return on comparative types of equity investments, and ROE earned by major competitors.

Net income will have to be $330,000 next year: 15.0% ROE × $2,200,000 stockholders' equity = $330,000. We can work our way back up to operating profit needed next year, starting with the net income goal. Figure 6.3 presents the company's financial plan for next year to achieve its 15.0 percent ROE target, which is based on the forecast sales revenue and the other budget assumptions just discussed.

Is this financial plan feasible? Well, clearly, this depends first and foremost on achieving sales goals. Sales revenue is budgeted to increase 14.6 percent, but

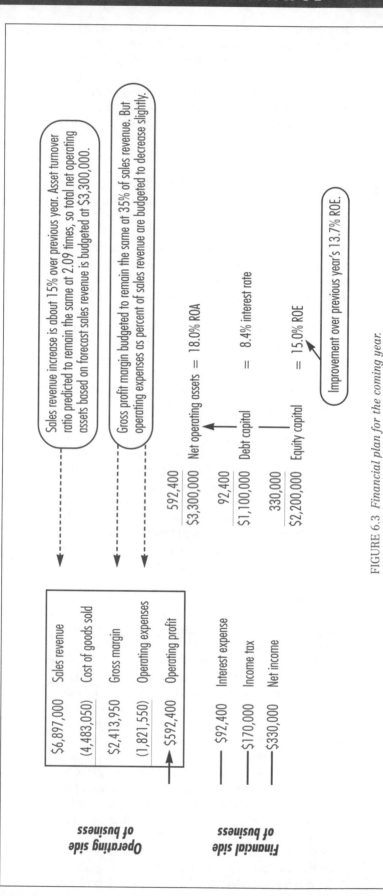

FIGURE 6.3 *Financial plan for the coming year.*

Sales revenue increase is about 15% over previous year. Asset turnover ratio predicted to remain the same at 2.09 times, so total net operating assets based on forecast sales revenue is budgeted at $3,300,000.

Gross profit margin budgeted to remain the same at 35% of sales revenue. But operating expenses as percent of sales revenue are budgeted to decrease slightly.

Improvement over previous year's 13.7% ROE.

	Net operating assets	=	18.0% ROA
592,400			
$3,300,000			
92,400	Debt capital	=	8.4% interest rate
$1,100,000			
330,000	Equity capital	=	15.0% ROE
$2,200,000			

Operating side of business

$6,897,000	Sales revenue
(4,483,050)	Cost of goods sold
$2,413,950	Gross margin
(1,821,550)	Operating expenses
$592,400	Operating profit

Financial side of business

$92,400	Interest expense
$170,000	Income tax
$330,000	Net income

nothing has been said regarding sales volume versus sales price increases. Operating profit is budgeted at 8.6 percent of sales revenue next year, compared with 7.8 percent for the year just ended. These points are critical.

The main thrust of the following chapters is to explain the tools of analysis used to gauge the impact of changes in the these key profit factors. For now, the financial plan is accepted as feasible. It serves as a good launch pad for the more in-depth analysis of the profit and capital investment factors that are explored in later chapters. The next chapter looks at the capital needs to finance the growth of the business.

END POINT

This chapter examines a business as an investment enterprise, or user of capital. The basic capital investment analysis tools are return-on-investment (ROI) ratios. Stockholders, being the suppliers of the equity capital to business, are primarily interested in return on equity (ROE), which is the ratio of net income divided by stockholders' equity. To earn a satisfactory ROE, a business must first earn a satisfactory return on assets (ROA), which is operating profit divided by total net operating assets. ROA also is the starting point in analyzing the effect of financial leverage on net income and ROE.

The main premise of this chapter is that every business must meet its cost-of-capital demands and objectives: interest on debt and net income for equity capital. The cost of capital changes over time. Interest rates fluctuate, income tax laws change, debt-to-equity ratios shift, and ROE goals change. So cost of capital is somewhat of a moveable feast. The basic concept and theory of COC is constant, but year-to-year calculations change. In developing the financial plan for one year ahead, such as we did in this chapter, cost-of-capital determinants can be predicted fairly accurately. But a 5- or 10-year financial plan is much more subject to forecast errors and revisions.

POSTSCRIPT
Income Tax: Not So Simple

The company example in this chapter, which is the centerpiece example used throughout the book, uses a 34 percent marginal income tax rate, which under the present Internal Revenue Code applies to corporations with taxable income between $75,000 and $10,000,000. (Even this statement is a little too simplistic.) Annual taxable income that is less or more than these amounts is subject to different rates. The assumption is that the company is organized as a corporation and is taxed as a "C" or regular corporation.

A corporation with 35 or fewer stockholders may elect to be treated as an "S" (for small) corporation. An S corporation pays no income tax itself; its annual taxable income is passed through to its individual stockholders in proportion to their percentage of share ownership. Business sole proprietorships and partnerships are also tax conduits; they are not subject to income tax as separate entities but pass their taxable income through to their owners, who have to include their shares of the entity's taxable income in their personal income tax returns.

Corporations may have *net loss carrybacks* or *net loss carryforwards* that reduce or eliminate taxable income in one year. There is also the alternative minimum tax to consider, to say nothing of a myriad of other provisions and options (loopholes) in the tax law. It's very difficult to generalize. The main point is that, in a given year in a given situation, the taxable income of the business may not result in the normal income tax.

Balance Sheet versus Other Values for Debt and Equity

Business capital investment analysis requires dollar values for debt and equity capital. The amounts usually used are the *book values* for debt and equity as reported in the company's most recent balance sheet—which are the values used in this chapter.

The book values of most debt instruments are equal to their maturity values, that is, the amounts due at maturity. Book values of debt are generally correct for capital investment analysis, and interest rates based on these maturity values are generally correct.* The book (maturity) value of debt may not be appropriate if the business is in financial distress, has defaulted on its debt payments, or is in bankruptcy proceedings. The capital investment performance of the business would not be the main concern in such a situation; the very survival of the company would be the main concern.

Book value of equity is used for calculating ROE, as explained in the chapter. Keep in mind that book value is *historical recorded* value. The book value of equity is the cumulative sum of paid-in capital amounts for capital stock (which may go back many years) plus the annual additions to retained earnings equal to net income less dividends paid each year (which also may

---

* There is one major exception. Debt may be sold with very heavy original issue discount, which means the amount received by the business at the time of borrowing is substantially less than the maturity value of the debt. The discount represents additional interest that will be paid eventually, and the effective interest rate is therefore higher than the rate based on maturity value. In these situations, the effective interest rate should be used; the debt's book value is equal to the original issue proceeds plus the cumulative amount of the discount that has been charged to interest expense since the issue date.

go back many years). The business may have bought back some of its own stock shares; if so, the cost of these *treasury stock* shares is deducted from the sum of paid-in capital and retained earnings. The book value of owners' equity capital is net of the treasury stock cost.

Private corporations have no ready market value information for their capital stock shares. These entities could estimate the market value of their owners' equity or have a formal appraisal done. But they seldom do. Thus, ROE is based on the book value of their owners' equity. Keep in mind, however, that this tends to inflate ROE because the historical book value of owners' equity may be low compared with any reasonable estimate of current value.

In their annual external financial reports, publicly owned corporations report ROE based on the book value of their equity capital—though this is not required to be disclosed. Stockholders in public corporations have market value information at their fingertips, by looking in the *Wall Street Journal,* the *New York Times, Barrons, Investor's Daily,* and many other sources of financial market information.

Instead of ROE, stockholders of publicly owned companies are more interested in two other ratios: the *earnings per share* (EPS) and the *price/earnings* ratio (P/E). EPS is net income divided by the number of common stock shares outstanding. The trend of EPS clearly has more impact on the market value of stock shares than ROE based on book value equity balances.

Stock investors closely watch the stock's P/E ratio, which is the current market price divided by EPS. In fact, P/E ratios are reported in the *Wall Street Journal,* whereas ROE ratios are not. There's no question that ROE (based on book value) takes a backseat to EPS and P/E ratios for investors in publicly owned corporations.

Capital Needs
of Growth

As discussed in the previous chapter, the company is planning on sales growth next year. From the cost-of-capital point of view, the basic test for growth is to protect ROE. A company should not seek growth at the expense of its ROE performance. Well, this is the theory at least. Without some growth, the very survival of the entity may be threatened. Short-term ROE performance may be sacrificed to keep the business alive.

GROWTH AND ROE

Growth causes an increase in net operating assets that are needed to support the higher level of sales revenue and expenses. It would be very unusual to achieve growth without higher levels of investment in operating assets. In short, sales growth means capital growth. The manager should make sure that sales growth will generate enough operating earnings growth to cover the cost of the additional capital resulting from the growth. Otherwise, ROE may head south. To prevent this, managers have to keep a sharp eye on the incremental change in the total capital invested in net operating assets.

PLANNING FOR GROWTH

Planning for the capital growth needed for sales growth can be done on various levels. One level looks only at the tips of the mountains. Only a skeleton income statement and balance sheet are prepared. Figure 7.1 illustrates this level of analysis, which lays out the financial plan of the business for the coming year in broad terms. The year just ended is the point of departure for next year. This plan is discussed in the previous chapter mainly from the ROE viewpoint. This chapter examines the capital growth needed to support this plan.

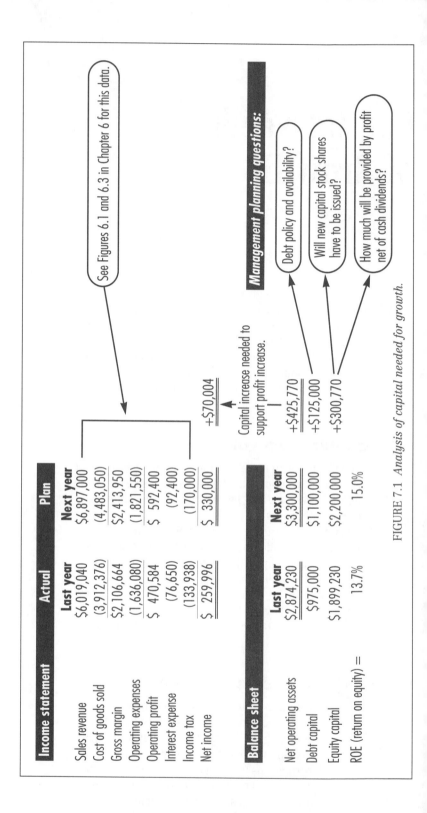

Income statement

	Actual Last year	Plan Next year
Sales revenue	$6,019,040	$6,897,000
Cost of goods sold	(3,912,376)	(4,483,050)
Gross margin	$2,106,664	$2,413,950
Operating expenses	(1,636,080)	(1,821,550)
Operating profit	$ 470,584	$ 592,400
Interest expense	(76,650)	(92,400)
Income tax	(133,938)	(170,000)
Net income	$ 259,996	$ 330,000

See Figures 6.1 and 6.3 in Chapter 6 for this data.

Balance sheet

	Last year	Next year
Net operating assets	$2,874,230	$3,300,000
Debt capital	$975,000	$1,100,000
Equity capital	$1,899,230	$2,200,000
ROE (return on equity) =	13.7%	15.0%

+$70,004

Capital increase needed to support profit increase.

+$425,770
+$125,000
+$300,770

Management planning questions:

Debt policy and availability?

Will new capital stock shares have to be issued?

How much will be provided by profit net of cash dividends?

FIGURE 7.1 Analysis of capital needed for growth.

The company is planning for sales revenue to grow to $6,897,000 next year. To determine the capital investment needed at the higher sales level, the company assumes that its asset turnover ratio (sales revenue divided by net operating assets) will be 2.09, the same as last year. In other words, $6,897,000 annual sales revenue divided by $3,300,000 net operating assets equals 2.09.

The business is planning that its ratio of debt to equity will remain at 1 to 2 next year, or one dollar of interest-bearing debt for every two dollars of equity capital. So one-third of the capital, or $1,100,000, is put into the debt slot, and two-thirds, or $2,200,000, in the equity slot, as you can see in Figure 7.1.

This level of analysis, although in fairly broad and general terms, is a valuable point of departure for more detailed planning. Even though rather condensed, this level of analysis is reasonably accurate. Some very important points need to be observed. Net income is forecast to increase $70,004, and this will require $425,770 more capital to make it happen. Notice that last year net operating assets were more than 11 times net income, and for next year they are planned at 10 times net income. It takes a lot of capital to generate net income.

In summary, Figure 7.1 reveals that $425,770 additional capital will be needed for the increase in net operating assets. Where will this additional capital come from? This is an extremely important question. Managers must plan for capital growth to support their profit growth. Given the assumptions in the financial plan, the company plans on increasing its debt $125,000 (from $975,000 to $1,100,000) and its stockholders' equity capital $300,770 (from $1,899,230 to $2,200,000).

Can the company borrow an additional $125,000? Will the lenders be willing? Steps should be taken now to line up this additional borrowing. Bankers don't like to be surprised or rushed into things like this. Indeed, a plan such as that shown in Figure 7.1 is a good "talking" document to convince lenders that a plan has been developed and how the additional debt fits into the capitalization of the business.

This plan also raises the critical question about the additional equity capital that will be needed. As you can see in Figure 7.1, stockholders' equity will have to increase $300,770. There are two sources of stockholders' equity: net income less cash dividends and additional capital investment by the stockholders. Net income will provide $330,000 additional capital; this is the very essence of profit, that is, an increase in the net operating assets of the business. But how much will be retained? In other words, how much in cash dividends will be paid, if any? It would seem that the company had better plan on little or no cash dividends next year.

So profit will provide all the additional equity capital needed.

There are several loose ends in the plan presented in Figure 7.1. It's not a bad starting point—indeed, it is a very useful first step—but many more detailed questions have to be addressed. For instance, how will cash flow and the cash balance be impacted by the sales and profit growth? What's needed is a more detailed *budget*.

DEVELOPING THE MASTER BUDGET

The rudimentary financial plan shown in Figure 7.1 sets the stage. Next, the manager would have to make his or her plans more specific. We won't get too complex here; we'll keep details straightforward. Assume the following:

Key Budgeting Assumptions

- Sales growth will come from volume (quantities sold); sales prices will be kept the same.

- During the year just ended, the company's fixed expenses (excluding depreciation) provided a good deal of unused capacity, such that the additional sales volume can be taken on with very little increase in the fixed operating costs.

- All operating ratios will remain the same.

- The increase in debt will be equally divided between long-term and short-term, and interest rates will remain the same.

- No cash dividends will be paid.

- Capital expenditures for new machinery and equipment will cost $435,000.

- Depreciation expense will increase to $141,792 because of the new fixed assets acquired.

- Tentatively, no cash dividends will be paid and so no new shares of capital stock will be issued.

Figure 7.2 shows the master budget for next year based on these assumptions. Of course, these are arbitrary assumptions to illustrate what a master budget looks like. But the assumptions are not unrealistic. Sure, some of the sales growth could be driven by higher sales prices as well as by sales volume increases. Fixed operating expenses could increase much more than in the example. For that matter, the company may be able to reduce its variable operating expenses; in this example, these two costs are held constant on a per-unit-sold or per-dollar-of-sales-revenue basis. Looking closely at each key assumption is precisely the job of managers.

INCOME STATEMENT FOR YEAR

	Last year	Next year	
Sales revenue	$6,019,040	$6,897,000	14.6% increase; all of increase due to sales volume increase; sales prices remain constant.
Cost-of-goods-sold expense	(3,912,376)	(4,483,050)	Also increases 14.6% because all of increase in sales revenue is due to sales volume increase.
Gross margin	$2,106,664	$2,413,950	Increases exactly 14.6% because all of increase in sales revenue is due to sales volume increase.
Variable operating expenses:			
Sales-volume-driven	(370,000)	(423,970)	Equals 10.0% of sales revenue, same as last year.
Sales-revenue-driven	(601,904)	(689,700)	Does not increase very much (which is unusual) because the company had a sizable amount of unused capacity last year.
Contribution margin	$1,134,760	$1,300,280	
Fixed expenses:			
Operating expenses	(551,384)	(566,088)	Increases because new machinery and equipment is acquired during the year.
Depreciation expense	(112,792)	(141,792)	
Operating earnings	$470,584	$592,400	Increases because of higher debt levels.
Interest expense	(76,650)	(92,400)	Increases because of higher taxable income.
Earnings before income tax	$393,934	$500,000	
Income tax expense	(133,938)	(170,000)	Increases about 27%, even though sales revenue increases only about 15%, a key point that is explained in later chapters.
Net income	$259,996	$330,000	
ROE (based on end-of-year stockholders' equity balances)	13.7%	14.8%	Slightly less than the 15.0% target ROE because year-end owners' equity is a little more than original plan in Figure 7.1.

FIGURE 7.2 Master budget for next year (page 1 of 3).

BALANCE SHEET AT END OF	Last year	Next year
Operating assets		
Cash	$ 256,663	$ 256,542
Accounts receivable	578,754	663,173
Inventory	978,094	1,120,763
Prepaid expenses	117,176	129,212
Property, plant, and equipment at original cost	1,986,450	2,421,450
Less accumulated Depreciation	(452,140)	(593,932)
Total operating assets	$3,464,997	$3,997,208
Operating liabilities		
Accounts payable:		
Inventory	300,952	344,850
Operating expenses	87,882	96,909
Total accounts payable	$ 388,834	$ 441,759
Accrued expenses:		
Operations	175,764	193,818
Interest	12,775	15,400
Total accrued expenses	$ 188,539	$ 209,218
Income tax payable	13,394	17,000
Total operating liabilities	590,767	667,977
Net operating assets	$2,874,230	$3,329,231

See cash flow statement for changes in these balances.

Sources of capital	Last year	Next year
Short-term notes payable	$425,000	$487,500
Long-term notes payable	550,000	612,500
Total interest-bearing debt	$975,000	$1,100,000
Capital stock	725,000	725,000
Retained earnings	1,174,230	1,504,231
Total stockholders' equity	$1,899,230	$2,229,231
Total debt and owners' equity	$2,874,230	$3,329,231

Increases by entire amount of net income because no cash dividends were paid.

FIGURE 7.2 Master budget for next year (page 2 of 3).

CASH FLOW STATEMENT FOR YEAR

	Last year	Next year
Cash flows from operating activities		
Net income	$ 259,996	$ 330,000
Changes in operating cycle assets and liabilities		
Accounts receivable increase	(96,404)	(84,419)
Inventory increase	(150,481)	(142,669)
Prepaid expenses increase	(24,341)	(12,036)
Accounts payable increase	58,318	52,925
Accrued expenses increase	40,283	20,679
Income tax payable increase	1,720	3,606
Operating cash flow before depreciation	$ 89,091	$ 168,087
Depreciation expense	112,792	141,792
Cash flow from profit-making operations	$ 201,883	$ 309,879
Cash Flows From Investing Activities		
Purchases of property, plant, and equipment	$(389,400)	$(435,000)
Cash flows from financing activities		
Net increase in short term debt	$ 50,000	$ 62,500
Long-term borrowings	75,000	62,500
Capital stock issue	100,000	0
Cash dividends to stockholders	(93,750)	0
Increase (decrease) in cash during year	$ (56,267)	$ (121)

Notice that capital expenditures are more than free cash flow both years.

FIGURE 7.2 *Master budget for next year (page 3 of 3).*

IS THE BUDGET FEASIBLE?

What does the master budget tell us? Well, the basic message is that, from the capital point of view, the plan seems feasible. In other words, if the company can achieve its sales revenue goal and if expenses can be controlled, then the sources of capital built into the plan will be enough to support the sales and profit growth.

This is an extremely important point, and should be carefully examined. Of course, the business will have to go out and borrow an additional $125,000 from its lenders, and it will have to convince its stockholders to accept no cash dividends on their equity in the business.

One alternative would be to pay, say, $100,000 in cash dividends and issue additional shares of capital stock for $100,000.* If this were a publicly owned corporation whose shares were actively traded, the strong increase in net income probably would be rewarded with an increase in its common stock market value. But private corporations do not have a market in which to test the value of their stock shares. Their stockholders may be impatient for cash dividends.

The other point of some interest revealed by the budget plan (Figure 7.2) is that cash is still not very large relative to annual sales revenue. Ending cash would be under two weeks of annual sales. This size cash balance may be uncomfortable to many managers. But, as mentioned before, there is no agreement on what a "proper" or "appropriate" cash balance should be.

The lower cash balance is one of several reasons why the end-of-year amount of the net operating assets amount of the business does not exactly equal $3,300,000, which was forecast in the original plan. Also, notice that the year-end owners' equity balance is a little more than originally planned on, so the ROE in Figure 7.2 is slightly below the original 15.0 percent goal.

CAPITAL TURNOVER ANALYSIS

The preceding discussion has focused on the marginal or incremental increase in capital needed to support sales and profit growth. In closing, we should not overlook the total capital and cash flows through the business. A business must keep in motion its *capital turnover cycle*. As inventory is sold, it is replaced with new inventory; as accounts receivable are col-

---

* You may logically ask why a company would pay $100,000 cash dividends in the same year it raises $100,000 by the issue of new stock shares. Wouldn't it be better to pay no dividends and avoid the issue of new shares? One possible reason is that the new shares may be issued to new stockholders; perhaps the present stockholders do not want to invest more capital in the business. Or perhaps the stock shares may be issued to key executives under an incentive compensation plan.

lected, they are replaced with new accounts receivable from new sales; as prepaid expenses are used up, new prepayments are made; as accounts payable are paid, they are replaced with new accounts payable; and so on, in like manner for accrued expenses and income tax payable.

The asset replacement cycle applies to the long-term, depreciable assets of the business as well: buildings, machinery, vehicles, equipment, and tools. Of course, the rollover cycle is much longer for these fixed assets—5, 10, 20, or more years—compared with the fairly short turnover cycles for accounts receivable (a month or so), inventory (two or three months), accounts payable (about a month), and so on.

Figure 7.3 summarizes the capital turnovers next year based on the budget plan. The presentation focuses on the capital recovery and reinvestment for each basic group of operating assets, and the payment and replacement of operating liabilities. We'll discuss the capital/cash cycle in the past tense, as of the end of next year, assuming everything goes according to plan.

The company's three short-term operating assets at the start of the year were converted into cash during the year. Accounts receivable were collected, inventory was sold, and prepaid expenses expired and were recovered through sales revenue. To continue in business, the business has to reinvest in these three assets; to grow, the company has to reinvest more than the amounts recovered, which you can see in Figure 7.3.

During the year, $141,792 depreciation expense was recorded. From the capital investment point of view, this means that $141,792 capital was recovered through sales revenue. The company converted this much of the original capital invested in its fixed assets into cash—by setting sales prices high enough to cover current operating expenses and also to recoup a portion of the original cost it invested in its fixed assets. Each year a business "sells" part of its fixed operating assets to its customers—not literally, of course, but in the sense that sales revenue includes an embedded charge for the use of the fixed assets.

The company carefully examined which fixed assets had to be replaced during the year and which new assets had to be acquired to provide more space, more processing capacity, and so on. In total, the company made $435,000 capital expenditures during the year, which is much more than its depreciation recovery for the year. Some of this difference was caused by inflation since the time the original assets were acquired that had to be replaced during the year.

During the early part of the year, the company paid the beginning balances of its three short-term operating liabilities: accounts payable, accrued expenses, and income tax. At the end of the year, these three operating liabilities had higher balances because of the sales

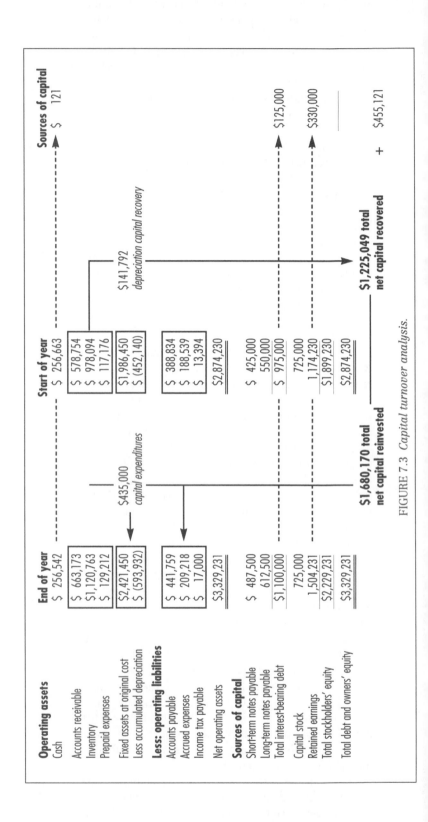

FIGURE 7.3 *Capital turnover analysis.*

Operating assets	End of year	Start of year	Sources of capital
Cash	$ 256,542	$ 256,663	$ 121
Accounts receivable	$ 663,173	$ 578,754	
Inventory	$1,120,763	$ 978,094	
Prepaid expenses	$ 129,212	$ 117,176	
Fixed assets at original cost	$2,421,450	$1,986,450	
Less accumulated depreciation	$ (593,932)	$ (452,140)	
			$141,792 depreciation capital recovery
Less: operating liabilities			
Accounts payable	$ 441,759	$ 388,834	
Accrued expenses	$ 209,218	$ 188,539	
Income tax payable	$ 17,000	$ 13,394	
Net operating assets	$3,329,231	$2,874,230	
Sources of capital			
Short-term notes payable	$ 487,500	$ 425,000	
Long-term notes payable	612,500	550,000	
Total interest-bearing debt	$1,100,000	$ 975,000	$125,000
Capital stock	725,000	725,000	
Retained earnings	1,504,231	1,174,230	
Total stockholders' equity	$2,229,231	$1,899,230	$330,000
Total debt and owners' equity	$3,329,231	$2,874,230	

$435,000 capital expenditures

$1,680,170 total net capital reinvested

$1,225,049 total net capital recovered

+ $455,121

growth. From the cash flow point of view, the rollover of these liabilities was a net positive amount because the unpaid (ending) amounts were more than the paid (beginning) amounts.

To sum up, the net capital recovered from the beginning balances of its operating assets and liabilities plus depreciation was $1,225,049, which you can see in Figure 7.3. The net capital reinvested in its operating assets was $1,680,170. Reinvested capital is $455,121 more than the capital recovered. This difference is supplied by additional borrowing of $125,000, plus the net income for the year of $330,000, and the small $121 decrease in cash—as you can see in the right-hand column of Figure 7.3.

Notice that the cash balance itself is a source of capital in this analysis. In other words, the company's cash can be used to supply part of the capital needed for investments in the operating assets. If the company decides that more cash is needed to operate the business, it will have to go to its sources of capital to provide for the increase in its cash balance. The proper or best level of cash balance is not a matter of settled opinion. Some companies keep very large working cash balances, and others barely have enough to get by day to day. There is no standard operating ratio for cash, in other words.

Figure 7.3 provides a good overview of the capital turnover flows for the year and the sources of capital to finance the growth of the business. It provides a good basis for review of the financial plan of the company by top management and by the corporation's board of directors. One of the basic responsibilities of top management and directors of a business corporation is to make such reviews of capital investment and financing strategies.

Basic questions include the following: Should the company have increased its debt? Is the business near its debt capacity and, if not, how much more debt could be taken on? Should the company have issued additional stock shares? Did the additional investment in its net operating assets yield a good return on the investment? Is the year-end cash balance too low for its level of operations? What are the short-term and longer-term solvency prospects of the business? These are very tough questions, and the capital turnover analysis summary shown in Figure 7.3 helps focus attention on the relevant figures.

END POINT

The central strategy of many businesses is growth. Growth means that more capital must be secured to finance the increase in net operating assets needed to support the higher sales level. Growth penalizes cash flow from profit to some extent, because growth causes the operating assets of the business to increase more than its operating liabilities. Thus, the business cannot look to its internal cash flow to supply all the capital needed and must go to outside sources of capital.

Planning for the capital needed and the sources for the additional capital is vital to keeping the momentum of the business going. The chapter explains three basic analysis tools that are most useful for planning the capital needs of growth: a summary-level analysis tool that keys on the asset turnover ratio, the more detailed and complete budgeted financial statements approach, and capital turnover analysis.

CHAPTER 8

Breaking Even
and Making Profit

As we have seen, the company in our example made
profit for the year just ended and earned a reasonably
satisfactory ROE for the year. How did they do that?
The answer is not as simple as it might appear.

KEY CONCEPT

HOW DID THEY DO THAT?

A business must earn sufficient operating profit
before interest and income tax to meet the company's
cost-of-capital requirements and objectives. How do successful companies do this year in and year out? The
answer is not just by making sales, but by keeping
enough of the sales revenue as operating profit. The
long-term sustainable success of any business rests on
the ability of its managers to produce operating profit.
Managers must know well the pathway to operating
profit and avoid detours along the way.

Operating profit, also called *operating earnings* or
earnings before interest and tax (EBIT), depends on
three primary factors: (1) *unit profit margin,* (2) *sales
volume,* and (3) *fixed expenses.* Unit profit margin
equals sales price minus both the product cost and the
variable expenses of selling each unit.

Managers must set sales prices and control product
costs and variable expenses; these key factors determine unit profit margins. Managers must also make
sales and generate sales volume, of course. Unit contribution profit margin times sales volume equals the total
contribution margin that is needed to overcome fixed
expenses and yield operating profit.

To simplify analysis, we assume that the company
sells just one product. Of course, most businesses sell a
variety of different products, and sales mix is very
important. But at this point we use the one product as
the stand-in or proxy average for all the products sold
by the company. The product serves as the common

denominator for all products. To measure overall sales activity, many industries use a common denominator, such as barrels for a brewery, tons for a steel mill, passenger miles for an airline, vehicles for a car and truck manufacturer, and so on.

Figure 8.1 presents the company's internal income statement again with some very important new information presented here for the first time. Annual sales volume is given, as well as the sales price, product cost per unit, and the variable operating expenses per unit. The company sells its product for $10.00, makes a gross margin of $3.50 per unit, and earns $1.89 contribution margin per unit. (Remember that contribution margin is profit after all variable expenses are deducted but before deducting fixed expenses.) These unit values are extremely important; they are the basis of the following analysis of how the company made its operating profit. First, however, we need to take a closer look at the company's fixed costs.

FIXED COSTS
Fixed Operating Expenses versus Depreciation Expense

In contrast to product cost (cost-of-goods-sold expense) and the variable operating expenses of sales, the other expenses of the business are fixed for the year. These costs do not vary with sales activity; they are relatively insensitive to changes in sales volume. Fixed expenses often are called *overhead*. Some fixed expenses are not flexible at all, such as rent, insurance premiums, and annual property taxes.

Some fixed expenses are flexible on the edge, such as total labor expense for the year. The business could switch to more part-time employees if sales volume were to drop off substantially. Conversely, overtime hours could be worked if sales volume surged unexpectedly. Another example of a fixed expense that is a little soft on the edge is when the business extends the hours that it is open, which nudges up the company's utility bill.

In this example, the company's fixed expenses are presented in two accounts: $551,384 operating expenses and $112,792 depreciation expense. Why this separation? Fixed operating expenses are recorded by decreasing cash, decreasing the prepaid expense asset account as items are used up, increasing the accounts payable liability account, or increasing the accrued expense liability account. Basically, these are cash-based expenses—cash is paid either directly or indirectly by first going through the prepaid expense account, or it is paid later after first going through one of the operating liability accounts. In other words, there is a cash outflow either at the time of recording the

Sales volume =   601,904 units

	Per unit	Totals
Sales revenue	$10.00	$6,019,040
Less: cost-of-goods-sold expense	6.50	3,912,376
Gross margin	$3.50	$2,106,664
Less: variable operating expenses		
Sales-volume-driven	0.61	370,000
Sales-revenue-driven	1.00	601,904
Contribution margin	$1.89	$1,134,760
Less: fixed costs		
Operating expenses		$551,384
Depreciation expense		112,792
Operating earnings		$470,584
Less: interest expense		76,650
Earnings before income tax		$393,934
Less: income tax expense		133,938
Net income		$259,996

These two expenses depend on the number of units sold. Whether the sales price had been higher or lower than $10.00 per unit, these two expense totals would have been the same for the actual 601,904 units sales volume.

These expenses vary with the total dollars of sales revenue and equal 10.0% of sales revenue in this example. Suppose that the sales price had been lower than $10.00. Total sales revenue for the 601,904 units sold would have been lower. Thus, these expenses would have been lower also.

This key amount is the profit per unit after deducting product cost (i.e., cost of goods sold) and other variable expenses from sales price—but before fixed costs, interest expense, and income tax expense are considered. Each unit sold provides this much contribution towards fixed expenses. Once fixed expenses are covered, the contribution margin per unit provides earnings before income tax.

Note: In previous income statement examples, expense amounts are presented in parentheses to emphasize that they are deductions. In this figure and several more to follow, expense amounts are presented without parentheses. Expenses are reported both ways in financial statements. In either case, expenses are deducted. This figure sets the stage for several subsequent figures that show increases and decreases of expenses due to changes in the basic profit factors. The increases and decreases are easier to follow if the original expense amount does not have parentheses around it.

FIGURE 8.1 Income statement including sales volume and unit values.

expense, or shortly before or shortly after recording the expense.

In sharp contrast, depreciation expense is a certain fraction of the original historical cost of the company's fixed assets (except land) that is charged off and allocated to expense in the year. The book value of fixed assets is decreased by the amount of the depreciation expense. In particular, the cash account is not decreased by recording depreciation expense. The cash outlay occurred when the fixed assets were bought some many years ago.

Total fixed operating expenses and depreciation expense would have been the same even if sales volume had been lower or higher than the actual sales volume. These costs would stay the same over the short run if sales revenue went down or up—well, within limits. For instance, if sales revenue were to decrease substantially, management may take action to decrease the company's fixed operating costs. Some employees on fixed salaries may be laid off, employees may be asked for salary givebacks, or fringe benefits may be reduced. In the following discussion, the fixed costs are just that—*fixed*.

Owner/Manager Salaries and Other Expenses

Suppose this business were a privately owned and closely held corporation whose top managers are also its major stockholders. Are the salaries of the owner/managers included in fixed operating expenses? Sure, salaries are included in this basic expense account. I bring this up because the salaries of owner/managers are not based on arm's-length bargaining.

The owner/managers can more or less set their own salaries. Their salaries may be artificially high or low and may not reflect an objective, competitive market-based salary. I don't mean to suggest anything illegal or unethical here. I just mean to make the point that the user of the financial statement has to keep this in mind: The fixed operating expenses may be padded a little or may perhaps be too skinny.

Also, the user should keep in mind whether or not personal expenses are being run through the business for income tax purposes. In my experience, owner/managers often charge to the business some of their own personal expenses, such as vacation trips and auto expenses, which are not deductible on their individual income tax returns. Last, I assume in this example that there is no skimming of sales revenue and no other type of fraud involving the business. Again, I must say that this is not unheard of. Some business owners/managers will use the business as a vehicle for fraud, as you may have read about.

What about Interest Expense?

As you can see in Figure 8.1, the company had $76,650 interest expense for the year. Is this a fixed expense? For relatively minor swings in the sales level, the answer is probably yes, it is a fixed expense. In other words, if the company had sold, say 5,000 or even 10,000 units less or more than it did last year, would its interest expense have been any less or more? Would the company have changed its interest-bearing debt to adjust to the lower or to the higher sales volume?

Probably not. Most businesses take on a certain level of debt and tend to stay with it, unless there are major upturns or downturns in their level of sales. (A business can adjust its short-term debt without too much trouble.) In the following analysis, we will assume that, for all practical purposes, the annual interest expense is fixed—unless we are talking about a major change in the sales level.

KEY CONCEPT — COMPUTING OPERATING PROFIT

We now compute the company's operating profit (earnings before interest and income tax), even though the operating profit number is already presented in the company's income statement (see Figure 8.1). The purpose is to lay the groundwork for the analysis that follows. The first way to compute operating profit is probably the most intuitive:

	$	1.89	Unit contribution margin*
×		601,904	Units sales volume
=	$	1,134,760	Total contribution margin
−		664,176	Total fixed expenses
=	$	470,584	Operating earnings

The linchpin in this computation is the multiplication of unit contribution profit margin times sales volume to get total contribution margin. Sales volume needs a good profit margin per unit to start with. Maybe you've heard the old joke: "A business loses a little on each sale but makes it up on volume."

KEY CONCEPT — THE BREAKEVEN HURDLE

Business managers worry a lot about fixed expenses—there's no operating profit until fixed expenses are overcome. The *breakeven point* is that

---

* Per-unit values are shown to two decimal places only, but in actual computations the number is carried out with as many digits of accuracy as needed for the computation. For example, the sales-volume-driven expense per unit is shown as $.61 but is actually $.614716 ($370,000 ÷ 601,904 units sold). The other unit values are not rounded off. With calculators and spreadsheet programs, this is not a problem.

sales volume which, multiplied by unit contribution profit margin, gives total contribution margin that is equal to total fixed expenses. Breakeven tells the manager the sales volume that has to be achieved just to cover fixed expenses for the period.

The following quotes from articles about Chrysler Corporation illustrate the importance of the breakeven point. By the way, notice that *vehicles* is the common denominator for its sales volume, even though Chrysler makes a wide variety of autos and trucks.

> *Chrysler's break-even point now stands at 1.8 million vehicles a year, far above the 1.1 million point that Mr. Iacocca vowed to maintain two years ago. The rise isn't entirely alarming—Chrysler sold about 2.3 million vehicles last year, partly because the acquisitions have added to its sales base—but the break-even point is higher than Chrysler would like it to be as it heads into the trough of the industry's sales cycle. (*The Wall Street Journal, *January 12, 1988, page 17.)*

> *Along with diversification came a top-heavy holding company structure that sent Chrysler's costs soaring. The company must now sell 1.9 million cars and trucks a year just to break even. That's far above the break-even point of 1.1 million vehicles in 1985 and a much bigger increase than can be justified by Chrysler's 1987 purchase of American Motors Corp. (*The Wall Street Journal, *September 17, 1990, page 1A.)*

Although showing their age a little, both of these articles are useful because they offer a breakeven estimate for a major, well-known business.

The operating profit breakeven point for the company example, that is, the sales volume level at which the company's operating profit before interest and income tax would be zero, is computed as follows:

 Computation of operating profit breakeven

Fixed expenses ÷ unit contribution margin
$664,176 ÷ $1.89
= 352,295 breakeven volume

In other words, if the company had sold only 352,295 units during the year, it would have earned an operating profit of zero, but would still have $76,650 interest expense to worry about.

To cover interest as well as other fixed expenses, the company's breakeven point is computed as follows:

 Computation of breakeven including interest expense as fixed expense

Fixed expenses ÷ unit contribution margin
$740,826 ÷ $1.89
= 392,952 breakeven volume

At this sales volume, the company's earnings-after-interest expense and before-income-tax expense would be zero. The company's taxable income would thus have been zero and its income tax would have been zero. Net income would have been zero. Figure 8.2 illustrates the breakeven sales volume scenario, which is a useful, though hypothetical, point of reference.

USING BREAKEVEN VOLUME TO COMPUTE PROFIT

A second way to compute profit (after interest expense, before income tax) begins with breakeven volume. Actual sales volume is compared with breakeven volume and profit is computed as follows:

 Excess over breakeven method to compute profit

Annual sales volume	601,904 units
Less: breakeven sales volume	392,952 units
Excess over breakeven volume	208,952 units
× Unit contribution margin	× $1.89
= Profit after interest expense	$393,934

The first 392,952 units sold during the year are assigned to covering fixed expenses; the total contribution margin from the first 392,952 units is treated as consumed by fixed expenses. The 208,952 units in excess of breakeven volume are viewed as the source of profit. In other words, sales volume is divided into two piles: the breakeven group and the profit group.

Profit is the same both ways, of course, although the method of getting there is different. The difference is a little deeper than meets the eye. It's more than an exercise with numbers; it concerns how managers think about making profit in the first place.

The first method of computing profit stresses the multiplication of unit contribution margin times sales volume to get total contribution margin for the period. Fixed expenses are not ignored but are deducted from total contribution margin to get down to profit. In contrast, the excess over breakeven method puts fixed expenses first and profit second—the business first has to get over its fixed expenses hump before it gets into the black.

One key point not to overlook is this: Fixed operating expenses provide *capacity*. Why would any rational manager commit to overhead expenses? These costs make available the capacity to carry on the sales activity of the business. Fixed expenses buy the space, equipment, and personnel to sell products. By committing to these costs, the business buys a certain amount of capacity.

Sales volume = 392,952 units

	Per unit	Totals
Sales revenue	$10.00	$3,929,519
Less: cost-of-goods-sold expense	6.50	2,554,188
Gross margin	$3.50	$1,375,332
Less: variable operating expenses		
Sales-volume-driven	0.61	241,554
Sales-revenue-driven	1.00	392,952
Contribution margin	$1.89	$740,826
Less: fixed costs		
Operating expenses		$551,384
Depreciation expense		112,792
Operating earnings		$76,650
Less: interest expense		76,650
Earnings before income tax		$0
Less: income tax expense		0
Net income		$0

The breakeven sales volume is computed by dividing the $740,826 total of the three fixed expenses ($551,384 fixed operating expenses + $112,792 depreciation expense + $76,650 interest expense) by the $1.88528 contribution margin per unit (which is rounded to $1.89 in the example). Interest is included as a fixed expense here; sometimes it is not clear in the discussion whether or not interest is included as a fixed expense. In this example, the breakeven sales volume is 208,952 units, or 35% less than the actual sales volume of 601,904 units, which is called the *margin of safety*.

In breakeven analysis, it is assumed that the contribution margin per unit remains the same—i.e., it is assumed that the per-unit-sales price, product cost, and variable operating expenses all remain the same. Also, it is assumed that fixed expenses remain the same. All these assumptions are subject to question, especially if the breakeven sales volume is substantially less than the actual sales volume as it is in this example. The breakeven sales volume is no more than a rough estimate and should not be taken as a precise measurement.

Note: *Pro forma means "as if" or "based on certain conditions or circumstances."*

FIGURE 8.2 *Pro forma income statement for breakeven sales volume (compare with Figure 8.1).*

The manager should estimate sales capacity, that is, the maximum sales volume that is possible from the fixed expenses of the business, and compare this capacity against actual sales volume. The business may have unused sales capacity. Sales could grow 10, 20, 30 percent before more space would have to be rented, more persons hired, or more equipment installed.

Estimating sales capacity may not be all that precise. But a reasonable, ballpark estimate can be made. You can start by asking whether a 10 percent sales volume increase would require any increase in total fixed expenses. Maybe not. This is especially important for planning ahead and analyzing the profit impact of changes.

THE THIRD WAY TO COMPUTE PROFIT

The excess over breakeven profit calculation method divides sales volume into two piles: (1) the breakeven quantity necessary to cover total fixed expenses and (2) the surplus over breakeven volume which provides profit. A third basic method of computing profit divides *every unit* sold into two parts: the fixed expenses part and the profit part.

The basic concept of the third method is that profit derives from spreading fixed expenses over a large enough sales volume so that the *average* fixed expenses per unit are less than the unit contribution margin. The fundamental thinking is that every unit sold has to do two things: (1) contribute its share to cover fixed expenses, and (2) provide a profit residual. The computation steps follow.

 Unit average method of computing profit

1. Compute the average fixed expenses per unit sold.
   Average fixed expenses per unit

   $$\$740,826 \div 601,904 \text{ units} = \$1.23$$

2. Compute the difference between the average fixed expenses per unit and the unit contribution margin, to determine the average profit per unit.
   Average profit per unit

Contribution margin per unit sold	$1.89
Less: average fixed expenses per unit	1.23
Average profit per unit	$ .66

3. Multiply the average profit per unit times sales volume to get total profit for the year.

$.66	×	601,904	=	$393,934
Average profit per unit		sales volume		Profit before income tax

This method spreads fixed expenses for the year over all units sold, which gives $1.23 per unit. Profit is viewed as the *spread* between this average cost and the $1.89 unit contribution margin. So the business makes $.66 profit per unit. Each unit sold is viewed on equal terms—sort of the "one unit, one vote" idea. Of course, profit for the year is the same as with the other two computation methods.

Suppose the business had sold only 392,952 units (which we already know is its breakeven volume). The average fixed expenses per unit sold would have been much higher. In fact, they would have been $1.89 per unit ($740,826 total fixed expenses ÷ 392,952 units = $1.89). This is exactly equal to the unit contribution margin. So the business would have made precisely zero profit per unit, and total profit would be zero.

MARGIN OF SAFETY

One purpose of breakeven analysis is to put a measure on the company's *margin of safety*. This refers to how far sales volume would have to drop before the business slips out of the black into the red, from profit to loss. Basically, the company has a fairly good margin of safety—its breakeven volume is 35 percent lower than its actual sales level for the year. (You can compare Figures 8.1 and 8.2 to see this.) Of course, this does not necessarily guarantee a profit next year. Sales could drop dramatically or expenses could get out of control. The following chapters explore what would happen based on changes in the factors that determine profit.

END POINT

Because of fixed expenses, a business has to worry about its breakeven point, computed by dividing total fixed expenses by the contribution profit margin per unit, which gives the sales volume at which the business would have exactly zero earnings after all expenses are deducted including interest. At breakeven the company has zero taxable income and, thus, no income tax. Its bottom-line net income is zero also. Of course, a company does not deliberately try to earn a zero profit.

This chapter examines closely the nature of fixed expenses, what all is included in this critical figure in the income statement, and why fixed expenses are not really 100 percent fixed and unchangeable but are treated as if they were over the short run for breakeven analysis.

The value of the breakeven tool is not to focus on the zero profit volume but to use the breakeven volume as a useful reference point for understanding how profit is made and to analyze why profit changes by a greater percentage than changes in sales volume—a key point in later chapters. Three different ways are explained to compute profit, each of which has its unique advantages. The manager may find one more useful than the others in a given situation or to explain the profit strategy of the business to others.

Sales Volume Changes

Business managers face constant change. All profit factors are subject to change, due both to external changes beyond the control of the business and changes initiated by the managers themselves. A large portion of management decisions are triggered by change. Indeed, managers are often characterized as "change agents."

THE BUSINESS ENVIRONMENT: CONSTANT CHANGE

Purchase costs of the products sold by the business may be increased by its suppliers; the company may raise wages for some or all of its employees, or wage rates might be actually reduced by employee givebacks or downsizing; the landlord may raise the rent; competitors may drop their sales prices and the business may follow them down. Managers may decide that they have to raise sales prices.

 One basic function of managers is to keep a close watch on all relevant changes and know how to deal with them. Changes set in motion a new round of profit-making decisions. In this chapter, we concentrate mainly on the profit and operating cash flow impact of sales *volume* changes. Sales volume, of course, is one of the most important determinants of operating profit and cash flow.

The preceding chapter explains breakeven analysis. Often, this is called *cost-volume-profit analysis* to indicate that we are not just interested in the breakeven point, but rather the broader picture of how profit behaves relative to changes in volume. In this chapter, we analyze how changes in sales volume impact profit performance and cash flow.

SALES VOLUME INCREASES

Business managers, quite naturally, are sales oriented. No sales, no business; it's as simple as that. As they say in marketing, "nothing happens until you sell it." Many businesses do not make it through their start-up phase because it's very difficult to build up and establish a sales base. Customers have to be won over. Once established, sales volume can never be taken for granted. Sales are vulnerable to competition, shifts in consumer preferences and spending decisions, and general economic conditions both domestically and globally.

Thinking more positively, sales volume growth is the most realistic way to increase profit. Sales price increases are met with some degree of customer resistance in most cases, as well as competitive response. Indeed, demand may be extremely sensitive to sales prices. Cost containment and expense control are important, to be sure, but are more of a defensive tactic and not a profit growth strategy as such.

Suppose the company in our example could increase its annual sales volume 10 percent at the same sales price—from 601,904 to 662,094 units, an increase of 60,190 units. Of course, there's no such thing as a free lunch. An experienced manager would ask: how could the business increase its sales volume? Would customers buy 10 percent more, without any increase in advertising, without any sales price incentives, without some product improvements or other inducements? Not too likely. Increasing sales volume usually requires some stimulant, such as more advertising.

Another question an experienced manager might ask is whether the business has enough *capacity* to handle 10 percent additional sales. It's always a good idea to run a capacity check whenever looking at sales volume increases. Fixed expenses may have to be increased to support the additional sales. However, we'll assume that the company has enough untapped capacity to take on 10 percent more sales volume without having to increase any of its fixed expenses.

The business makes $1.89 contribution margin per unit, as explained in the previous chapter. Selling 60,190 additional units would increase total contribution margin $113,476, computed as follows:

$1.89	$\times$	60,190	$=$	$113,476
Contribution margin per unit		Additional units		Contribution margin increase

Figure 9.1 shows the profit impact for the 10 percent higher sales volume scenario; notice in particular the changes caused by the higher sales volume. All of the unit values remain the same, as do fixed expenses. Total sales revenue, total product cost (cost of goods sold), and the two variable operating expenses all increase 10.0 percent. Thus, contribution margin

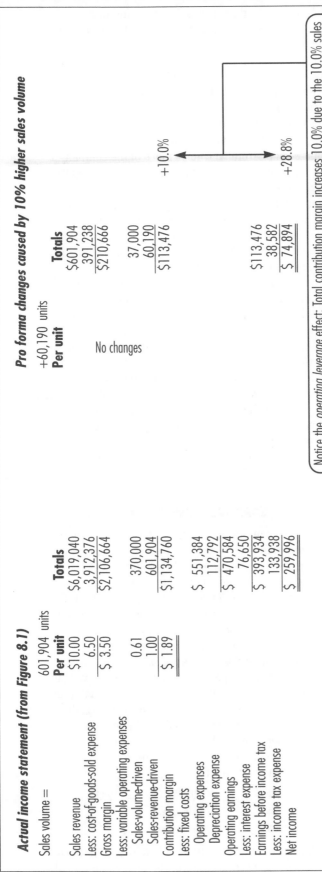

Actual income statement (from Figure 8.1)

Sales volume = 601,904 units

	Per unit	Totals
Sales revenue	$10.00	$6,019,040
Less: cost-of-goods-sold expense	6.50	3,912,376
Gross margin	$ 3.50	$2,106,664
Less: variable operating expenses		
Sales-volume-driven	0.61	370,000
Sales-revenue-driven	1.00	601,904
Contribution margin	$ 1.89	$1,134,760
Less: fixed costs		
Operating expenses		$ 551,384
Depreciation expense		112,792
Operating earnings		$ 470,584
Less: interest expense		76,650
Earnings before income tax		$ 393,934
Less: income tax expense		133,938
Net income		$ 259,996

Pro forma changes caused by 10% higher sales volume

+60,190 units

	Per unit	Totals
Sales revenue		$601,904
		391,238
		$210,666
	No changes	
		37,000
		60,190
		$113,476
		$113,476
		38,582
		$ 74,894

+10.0%

+28.8%

> Notice the *operating leverage* effect: Total contribution margin increases 10.0% due to the 10.0% sales volume increase. But bottom-line profit or net income increases 28.8% because fixed costs and interest expense do not increase in this example.

FIGURE 9.1 *Profit impact of 10 percent higher sales volume.*

(profit before fixed expenses, interest, and income taxes) would be 10.0 percent higher, which you can see in Figure 9.1.

Fixed operating expenses, depreciation, and interest do not increase at the higher sales volume level. As previously mentioned, the company has enough capacity (and enough capital) to take on an additional 10 percent sales volume without any increase in these expenses. Keep in mind that these assumptions should be made very carefully! One or more of the company's fixed expenses might have to be increased to support a higher sales volume.

For instance, the company might have to rent more retail floor space, or hire more salaried employees, or purchase additional equipment on which depreciation has to be recorded. And, at the higher level of sales, the company's investment in its net operating assets will be higher, which means more capital will be needed, which means more interest-bearing debt may have to be secured that would increase the interest expense. For now, however, the fixed expenses are held constant at the higher sales level, for purposes of analyzing the profit increase. Keeping fixed expenses constant at a moderately higher sales volume level is generally reasonable.

Net income would be $74,894 higher, a 28.8 percent profit increase. Just a minute here. How can only a 10.0 percent sales volume increase generate a 28.8 percent profit increase? The net income percent increase is 2.88 times the sales volume percent increase.

KEY CONCEPT   **OPERATING LEVERAGE**

This multiplier effect is referred to as *operating leverage*. In this example, a 10 percent sales volume increase causes almost a threefold percent increase in net income. To understand this leverage effect, recall the second way we computed profit in the previous chapter—the excess over breakeven method. This method divides annual sales into two piles or groups: the number of units needed to reach the breakeven point and the excess of sales volume over this number. The company sold 208,952 units over and above its breakeven volume (see Chapter 8). Each unit sold in excess of the breakeven volume earns $1.89 contribution profit margin, which can be thought of as pure profit because fixed expenses have already been covered by the breakeven sales volume.

Now please notice the following:

60,190	÷	208,952	=	28.8%
Additional units sold		Units in excess of breakeven		

The 10 percent additional units sold add 28.8 percent more units to the profit pile of units. This is the nub of operating leverage. Of course, you have to be in the leverage zone to make this happen; you have to be above your breakeven point. But if you are, then the profit swing is more than the sales volume swing.

Operating leverage means that profit percent changes are usually a multiple of sales volume percent changes. There's hardly ever a one percent–for–one percent relationship. This rule is based on fixed expenses remaining constant at the higher sales level. If the fixed expenses increased 10.0 percent right along with the sales volume increase—that is, if fixed operating expenses, depreciation, and interest all went up 10.0 percent as well—then taxable income, income tax expense, and net income would have gone up only 10.0 percent.

Operating leverage reflects that the business has not been fully using its capacity. When capacity is reached—and sooner or later it will be, with sales volume growth—fixed expenses will have to be increased to provide more capacity. If the company had already been selling at its maximum capacity, then its fixed expenses would have to have been increased. This points out the importance of knowing where you are presently relative to the company's capacity.

KEY CONCEPT — WHAT ABOUT CASH FLOW?

Managers should not overlook the impacts of the higher sales volume on the cash flow and financial condition of the business. The 28.8 percent profit increase is good, of course. But what would be the cash flow effects of this change?

Chapter 7 discusses growth and capital needs. Budgeted financial statements were prepared based on several critical assumptions about financing the capital needs of growth, such as whether cash dividends would be paid, new debt would be borrowed, or new capital stock shares would be issued. Such a full-blown set of budgeted financial statements is too much to repeat here.

However, we can at least look at the impact of sales volume growth on cash flow from profit. For this purpose, we keep the company's operating ratios the same. Figure 9.2 presents a *differential* cash flow statement—one that shows the differences that would be caused by the sales volume increase. This is only a partial cash flow analysis that extends down only to the cash flow from profit before depreciation.

A complete cash flow analysis requires that we make a complete set of assumptions about all sources and all uses of cash, as done in Chapter 7 in developing the master budget (Figure 7.2) for the company's financial plan for growth. Instead, we shall focus on changes in cash flow from profit before depreciation for the several different what-if scenarios that we will be analyz-

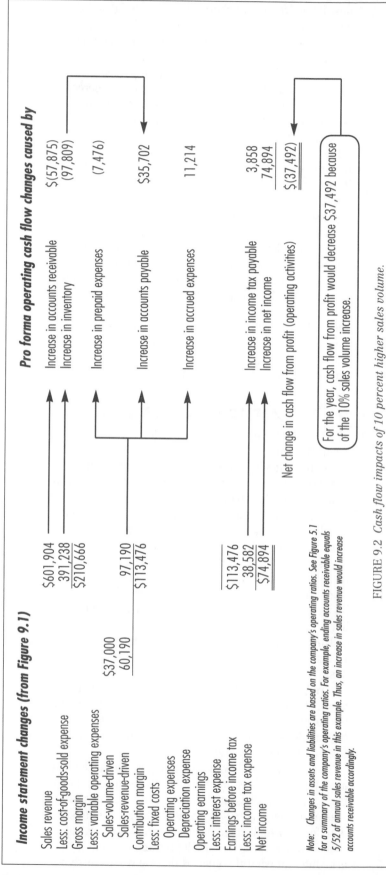

Income statement changes (from Figure 9.1)

Sales revenue		$601,904
Less: cost-of-goods-sold expense		391,238
Gross margin		$210,666
Less: variable operating expenses		
Sales-volume-driven	$37,000	
Sales-revenue-driven	60,190	97,190
Contribution margin		$113,476
Less: fixed costs		
Operating expenses		
Depreciation expense		
Operating earnings		
Less: interest expense		
Earnings before income tax		$113,476
Less: income tax expense		38,582
Net income		$74,894

Pro forma operating cash flow changes caused by

Increase in accounts receivable	$(57,875)
Increase in inventory	(97,809)
Increase in prepaid expenses	(7,476)
Increase in accounts payable	$35,702
Increase in accrued expenses	11,214
Increase in income tax payable	3,858
Increase in net income	74,894
Net change in cash flow from profit (operating activities)	$(37,492)

For the year, cash flow from profit would decrease $37,492 because of the 10% sales volume increase.

Note: Changes in assets and liabilities are based on the company's operating ratios. See Figure 5.1 for a summary of the company's operating ratios. For example, ending accounts receivable equals 5/52 of annual sales revenue in this example. Thus, an increase in sales revenue would increase accounts receivable accordingly.

FIGURE 9.2 Cash flow impacts of 10 percent higher sales volume.

ing in this and following chapters. The point of departure is the company's most recent year as reported in its financial statements (Figures 3.1, 4.2, and 4.4). For the scenario here, we ask: What if the sales volume had been 10 percent higher for the year?

From the balance sheet (Figure 4.2), we see that the company's year-end cash balance is $256,663, which is not that large. The company does not have a large cushion or reserve of cash to fall back on. If, for instance, a 10 percent higher sales volume would have caused cash flow from profit to have been substantially less for the year, then the company would have had to consider going to other sources of cash.

In this scenario (10 percent sales volume increase), we see from Figure 9.2 that cash flow from profit would be $37,492 *less* than in the original scenario. Thus, the company's ending cash balance would have been $37,492 less: $256,663 balance in the original example less $37,492 = $219,171. The company may have had to increase its debt or have issued additional capital stock shares to shore up its cash balance. A $219,171 cash balance at year-end may have been too low for comfort. In each of the what-if scenarios in this and the following chapters, the differences in cash flow from profit (before depreciation) are analyzed in the manner shown in Figure 9.2.

Why does cash flow from profit decrease $37,492 in the 10 percent sales volume increase scenario? The $601,904 sales revenue increase (see Figure 9.1) would cause ending accounts receivable to be $57,875 higher: $601,904 × 5/52 = $57,875 greater increase in accounts receivable. Recall that the company's receivable/sales operating ratio equals 5/52 of annual sales revenue. An increase in accounts receivable decreases cash flow from profit, as explained in Chapter 4.

From Figure 9.1 we see that the cost-of-goods-sold expense would increase $391,238. This increase would cause ending inventory to be $97,809 higher, which is equal to 13/52 times the cost-of-goods-sold expense increase. (The company's average inventory holding period is 13 weeks.) This inventory increase is based on the company's operating ratio, which we assume remains the same. However, cash flow may be hit by an even larger increase in inventory.

In the heat and pressure of a marketing campaign to increase sales volume, unbridled enthusiasm and overly optimistic sales quotas can lead to building up inventory to levels not justified by the actual sales growth. The sales staff doesn't want to be caught short of inventory that would delay delivery of products and cause lost sales. So ending inventory may be considerably above what would be needed for the actual sales volume increase. Or very liberal credit terms may be offered to customers, and the accounts receivable collection period may stretch out.

DANGER!

We will not go through all the detailed explanations for the other changes in operating assets and liabilities shown in Figure 9.2. Like the accounts receivable and inventory changes, the other changes are based on the operating ratios of the company, which are held constant. You can check each of the changes by applying the appropriate operating ratio to each of the changes in sales revenue and expenses shown in the comparative income statement (Figure 9.1).

To sum up, cash flow from profit would suffer from the sales volume increase, even though net income would increase. So the additional profit from the sales volume increase would need additional financing—either by drawing down the cash balance, increasing debt, or increasing capital stock (or cutting the cash dividend).

Cash flow analysis of sales volume changes draws management's attention to these important points. Furthermore, it reminds managers that a profit increase does not necessarily lead to an immediate cash flow increase and, indeed, may decrease cash flow in the short run, as it does in this scenario. Profit analysis without cash flow analysis is like putting on only one shoe. You have to wear both shoes to get where you're going.

SALES VOLUME DECREASES

Suppose the company had sold 10 percent less sales volume than it actually did. Its managers should be very concerned and probe into the reasons for the decrease. More competition? Are people switching to substitute products? Are hard times forcing customers to spend less? Is the location deteriorating? Has service to customers slipped? Are total quality management (TQM) techniques needed to correct the loss of sales?

Sales volume losses are one of the most serious problems confronting any business. Unless quickly reversed, the business has to make extremely wrenching decisions regarding how to downsize that would require laying off employees, selling off fixed assets, shutting down plants, and so on. The late economist Kenneth Boulding has called downsizing "the management of decline," which hits the nail on the head, I think. It's a very unpleasant task, to say the least.

The immediate (short-run) operating profit impact of a 10 percent sales volume decrease would depend heavily on whether the company could reduce its fixed expenses at the lower sales level. Assume not. Fixed operating expenses and depreciation expense remain the same. And assume interest expense would stay the same; total debt would not be decreased at the lower sales level, at least not in the short run.

Figure 9.3 shows the impact on profit performance at the 10 percent lower sales volume level. Bottom-line profit would decrease $74,894. This is what you would

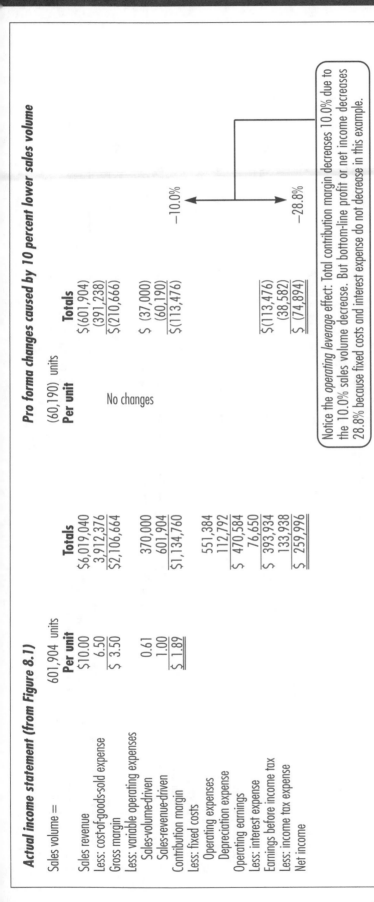

FIGURE 9.3 *Profit impact of 10 percent lower sales volume.*

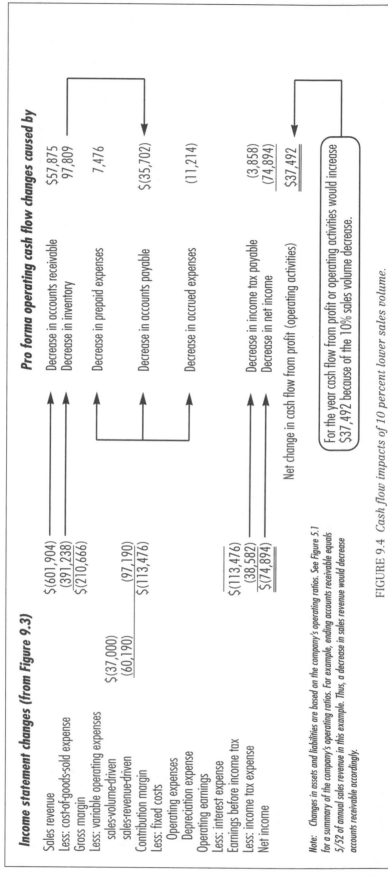

Income statement changes (from Figure 9.3)

Sales revenue		$(601,904)
Less: cost-of-goods-sold expense		(391,238)
Gross margin		$(210,666)
Less: variable operating expenses		
sales-volume-driven	$(37,000)	
sales-revenue-driven	(60,190)	(97,190)
Contribution margin		$(113,476)
Less: fixed costs		
Operating expenses		
Depreciation expense		
Operating earnings		
Less: interest expense		
Earnings before income tax		$(113,476)
Less: income tax expense		(38,582)
Net income		$(74,894)

Pro forma operating cash flow changes caused by

Decrease in accounts receivable	$57,875
Decrease in inventory	97,809
Decrease in prepaid expenses	7,476
Decrease in accounts payable	$(35,702)
Decrease in accrued expenses	(11,214)
Decrease in income tax payable	(3,858)
Decrease in net income	(74,894)
Net change in cash flow from profit (operating activities)	$37,492

> For the year cash flow from profit or operating activities would increase $37,492 because of the 10% sales volume decrease.

Note: Changes in assets and liabilities are based on the company's operating ratios. See Figure 5.1 for a summary of the company's operating ratios. For example, ending accounts receivable equals 5/52 of annual sales revenue in this example. Thus, a decrease in sales revenue would decrease accounts receivable accordingly.

FIGURE 9.4 Cash flow impacts of 10 percent lower sales volume.

expect because fixed expenses do not change. Notice that operating leverage compounds the felony—net income decreases 28.8 percent in this scenario caused by only a 10.0 percent drop in sales volume.

What about cash flow in this case? In the previous 10 percent growth case, cash flow from profit decreases $37,492. However, in the 10 percent decline case, operating cash flow *increases* $37,492, as presented in Figure 9.4.

The lower sales revenue and lower cost-of-goods-sold expense would lead to decreases in accounts receivable and inventory, assuming these two operating ratios remain the same. Basically, the cash flow impacts would be just the opposite between the two sales volume change cases. Few managers would accept the decrease in profit to gain the cash flow advantage.

END POINT

All profit factors are subject to change. Management neglect or ineptitude can lead to profit deterioration, sometimes very quickly. Increases in product cost, as well as increases in variable and fixed expenses, can do serious damage to profit performance. But managers may not be able to improve certain factors much.

Fixed expenses may already be cut to the bone. Product costs may be controlled by one vendor, or alternative vendors may offer virtually the same prices. Competition may put a fairly tight straitjacket on sales prices. Customers are sensitive to sales price increases. Sales volume is the key success factor for most businesses, which explains why managers are so concerned about market share. Market share is mentioned often in later chapters.

Sales Price and Cost Changes

Before we get going in this chapter, let me ask a basic question. Suppose you could have one or the other, but not both, which would you prefer: a 10 percent sales volume increase or a 10 percent sales price increase? In most cases, there's a huge difference between the two. This chapter contrasts the difference between sales volume and sales price changes. You may be surprised. In any case, you should be very certain about the differences!

SALES PRICE INCREASES

KEY CONCEPT

Setting sales prices is one of the most perplexing decisions facing business managers. Competition normally dictates the basic range of sales prices. But usually there is some room for deviation from your competitors' prices because of product differentiation, brand loyalty, location advantages, quality of service—to cite only a few of the many reasons that permit higher sales prices than the competition.

Fixed expenses are generally insensitive to sales price increases. In contrast, sales volume increases very well could require increases in fixed operating expenses, especially when the company's capacity is crowded. Very few fixed expenses are directly affected by raising sales prices, even if the company were operating at full capacity. Advertising (a fixed cost once spent) might be stepped up to persuade customers that the hike in sales prices is necessary or beneficial. Other than this, it's hard to find many fixed operating expenses that are tied directly to sales price increases.

So, with this in mind, let's consider the hypothetical case in which the company could have sold the same volume but at 10.0 percent higher sales prices. Figure 10.1 presents this scenario for our company example. Profit more than doubles; it increases 137.5 percent, as shown in the figure. Would this be realistic? Only to the extent that a 10 percent sales price increase would be realistic. In this situation, only one variable operating expense would increase: the one driven by sales revenue.

Notice that cost of goods sold does not increase because the volume sold remains the same. In the sales volume increase situation (previous chapter), the sales revenue increase is offset substantially by the increase in cost-of-goods-sold expense. In contrast here, in the sales price increase case, 90 percent of the $601,904 incremental sales revenue flows through to operating earnings (earnings before income tax).

Chapter 3 discusses the internal income statement for managers, and one key point there is that expenses should be classified and reported according to their behavior or what drives them.* Some operating expenses depend directly on the dollar amounts of sales and not the quantity of products sold. As total sales revenue (dollars) increases, these expenses increase directly in proportion.

Most retailers accept national credit cards, such as VISA, MasterCard, Discover, American Express, and Diners Club. The credit card charge slips are deposited daily with a local participating bank. The bank then discounts the total amount and credits the net balance in the business' checking account. Discount rates vary between 2 and 4 percent (sometimes lower or higher). In short, the business nets only 98 to 96 cents from the dollar on credit card sales. The credit card discount expense comes right off the top of the sales dollar.

Sales commissions are another common example of sales-revenue-dependent expenses. As you probably know, many retailers and other businesses pay their sales representatives on a commission basis, which usually is a certain percentage of the total sales amount, such as 5 or 10 percent. The salespersons may also receive a base salary, which would be the fixed floor of the expense; only the commission over and above the fixed base would be variable. (This requires the separation of the fixed part and the variable part in the management income statement.)

Many businesses extend short-term credit to their customers, especially in selling to other businesses. No matter how carefully customers are screened before extending credit, a few never pay their accounts owed to the business. Eventually, after making repeated collection efforts, the business ends up having to write off all or some of these receivables' balances as uncollectible. These losses are called *bad debts* and are a

---

* *Cost driver* is a popular term these days, which means that managers should identify which factors determine, push, or drive a particular cost. Identifying cost drivers is the key step in the method of cost analysis and allocation called *activity-based costing,* or ABC. More on this later.

Actual income statement (from Figure 8.1) **Pro forma changes caused by 10% higher sales price**

Sales volume = 601,904 units

	Per unit	Totals	Per unit (No change)	Totals
Sales revenue	$10.00	$6,019,040	$1.00	$601,904
Less: cost-of-goods-sold expense	6.50	3,912,376		
Gross margin	$3.50	$2,106,664	$1.00	$601,904
Less: variable operating expenses				
Sales-volume-driven	0.61	$370,000		
Sales-revenue-driven	1.00	601,904	0.10	60,190
Contribution margin	$1.89	$1,134,760	$0.90	$541,714
Less: fixed costs				
Operating expenses		$551,384		
Depreciation expense		112,792		
Operating earnings		$470,584		
Less: interest expense		76,650		
Earnings before income tax		$393,934		$541,714
Less: income tax expense		133,938		184,183
Net Income		$259,996		$357,531

+47.7%

+137.5%

Notice the *sales price leverage* effect: Total contribution margin increases 47.7% due to the 10.0% sales price increase. But bottom-line profit or net income increases 137.5% because fixed costs and interest expense do not increase in this example.

FIGURE 10.1 *Profit impact of 10 percent higher sales price.*

normal expense of doing business on credit. This expense depends on the sales amount, not sales volume (number of units sold).

Another example of an expense that varies with sales revenue is one you might not suspect: *rent.* Companies often sign lease agreements that call for rental amounts based on gross sales. There may be a base amount or fixed minimum monthly rent. In addition, there may be a variable amount equal to a percent of total sales revenue. This is common for retailers renting space in shopping centers. There are several other examples of expenses that vary with total sales revenue, such as franchise fees based on gross sales.

To sum up, sales revenue would increase 10.0 percent, but this would be offset by a 10.0 percent increase in the sales-revenue-driven expenses, yielding a net $541,714 increase in contribution margin, as shown in Figure 10.1. We assume that the company's fixed operating expenses, depreciation expense, and interest expense do not change at the higher sales price level. Thus, the contribution margin increases taxable income the same amount. Uncle Sam takes a 34 percent cut of the action, leaving $357,531 increase in bottom-line net income.

This produces a rather hefty 137.5 percent gain in net income; in other words, net income more than doubles. This could also be viewed as a type of leverage—or sales price leverage.* However, the main focus should be on the huge jump in the contribution margin per unit, which goes from $1.89 to $2.79, an increase of 47.7 percent. This is the key change. The company bumps its sales price by $1.00, but its revenue-driven operating expenses are 10 percent of sales revenue, so $.10 comes off the top, leaving a $.90 net sales price gain per unit. The 601,904 units sold times the $.90 gain in unit contribution margin equals $541,714, the increase in total contribution margin.

Frankly, a 10 percent increase in sales price with no increase in the product cost and no increase in the other expenses of the company is not too likely to happen. It is presented here to illustrate the powerful impacts of a sales price increase and to contrast it with a 10 percent increase in sales volume. So we also consider the cash flow impacts of a 10 percent sales price increase, which also differs, like day from night, from the sales volume increase case.

 **CASH FLOW AT HIGHER SALES PRICE**

Figure 10.2 presents the impacts on operating cash flow before depreciation; cash flow would increase

---

* Usually, the operating leverage concept refers only to sales *volume* changes, so the multiplier effect on profit caused by a sales price increase is not called operating leverage.

$323,861—a huge increase! Accounts receivable would increase because of the sales revenue increase. Variable operating expenses and income tax expense would cause relatively minor cash flow effects. Overall, the operating cash flow increase is nearly as much as the profit increase.

Indeed, the increase in cash flow from profit would more than double the cash balance of the company, which is $256,663 (from Figure 4.2). This big increase in the cash balance would raise questions about what to do with the excess cash: Increase cash dividends? Reduce debt? Retire some capital stock? Until these financial issues are resolved, we cannot prepare a balance sheet for the company. The double-barreled analysis of both profit and operating cash flow effects of sales price increases calls such questions to the attention of managers who have to make such decisions.

SALES PRICE
DECREASES

What goes up can go down. We now consider the 10 percent sales price decrease scenario. Managers hardly need to be reminded of the bad effects of decreasing sales prices, although they may not realize just how damaging sales price decreases can be. It takes a very large sales volume increase to offset sales price decreases, which we examine in the next chapter. At this point, I'll simply mention that a 10 percent sales volume increase does not even come close to offsetting a 10 percent sales price decrease.

Here, we analyze the damage done by a 10 percent sales price decrease, assuming sales volume remains the same. Figure 10.3 shows what a disaster this would be. The company would give up $601,904 off the top of its sales revenue, and only one operating expense would decrease. Earnings before income tax would decrease $541,714, which would push the company into a *net loss* before income tax. Notice the $184,183 income tax decrease is more than $133,938.

A business can use a taxable loss from one year to offset taxable income in another year. If tax has been paid in one or more prior years, the business is entitled to a refund. Deducting a taxable loss of one year against a taxable income of a prior year is called a *carryback*. (The business may have to take the loss forward and use it to offset taxable income in future years, which is called a *carryforward*.)

In this example, the company probably would carry back the taxable loss to the previous year's taxable income (assuming it had taxable income last year). Basically, the company can reclaim tax it paid based in the three previous years of taxable income. None of this refund would have been collected by the end of the

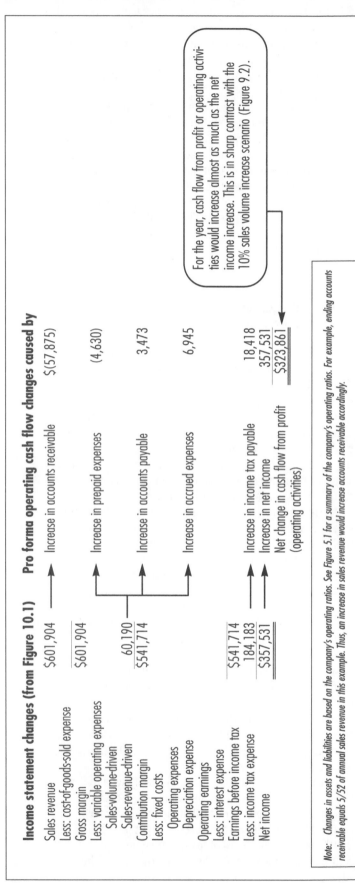

Income statement changes (from Figure 10.1)

Sales revenue	$601,904
Less: cost-of-goods-sold expense	
Gross margin	$601,904
Less: variable operating expenses	
Sales-volume-driven	
Sales-revenue-driven	60,190
Contribution margin	$541,714
Less: fixed costs	
Operating expenses	
Depreciation expense	
Operating earnings	
Less: interest expense	
Earnings before income tax	$541,714
Less: income tax expense	184,183
Net income	$357,531

Pro forma operating cash flow changes caused by

Increase in accounts receivable	$(57,875)
Increase in prepaid expenses	(4,630)
Increase in accounts payable	3,473
Increase in accrued expenses	6,945
Increase in income tax payable	18,418
Increase in net income	357,531
Net change in cash flow from profit (operating activities)	$323,861

For the year, cash flow from profit or operating activities would increase almost as much as the net income increase. This is in sharp contrast with the 10% sales volume increase scenario (Figure 9.2).

FIGURE 10.2 Cash flow impacts of 10 percent higher sales price.

Note: *Changes in assets and liabilities are based on the company's operating ratios. See Figure 5.1 for a summary of the company's operating ratios. For example, ending accounts receivable equals 5/52 of annual sales revenue in this example. Thus, an increase in sales revenue would increase accounts receivable accordingly.*

Actual income statement (from Figure 8.1)
Sales volume = 601,904 units

	Per unit	Totals
Sales revenue	$10.00	$6,019,040
Less: cost-of-goods-sold expense	6.50	3,912,376
Gross margin	$3.50	$2,106,664
Less: variable operating expenses		
Sales-volume-driven	0.61	370,000
Sales-revenue-driven	1.00	601,904
Contribution margin	$1.89	$1,134,760
Less: fixed costs		
Operating expenses		551,384
Depreciation expense		112,792
Operating earnings		$470,584
Less: interest expense		76,650
Earnings before income tax		$393,934
Less: income tax expense		133,938
Net income		$259,996

Pro forma changes caused by 10% lower sales price

	No change Per unit	Totals
	$(1.00)	$(601,904)
	$(1.00)	$(601,904)
	(0.10)	(60,190)
	$(0.90)	$(541,714)
		−47.7%
		$(541,714)
		(184,183)
		$(357,531)
		−137.5%

The business would not have any taxable income for the year; thus, all the $133,938 income tax shown for the actual income statement would be avoided. Also, it is assumed that the taxable loss in this situation would be a carryback and generate an income tax refund.

Notice the *sales price leverage* effect: Total contribution margin decreases 47.7% due to the 10.0% sales price decrease. But operating earnings before income tax would decrease 137.5% because fixed costs and interest expense do not decrease in this example.

FIGURE 10.3 Profit impact of 10 percent lower sales price.

year, so no cash flow is shown for income tax in Figure 10.4 that presents the impact on cash flow from profit for the 10 percent sales price decrease scenario.

Cash flow from profit would decrease $305,443, which is more than the company's cash balance! So, quite literally, a 10 percent sales price decrease would drive the company to the edge of insolvency. The company would have to cut its cash dividend, borrow money, or convince its stockholders to put more money into the business to finance the loss—not an easy task, to say the least.

CHANGES IN PRODUCT COST AND OPERATING EXPENSES

Changes in sales volume and sales prices usually have the biggest impact on profit. Product cost would rank as the next most-critical factor for most businesses (except for service businesses that do not sell products; see Chapter 14). A retailer needs smart, tough-nosed, sharp-penciled, aggressive purchasing tactics to control its product costs. On the other hand, this can be carried to an extreme.

I knew a purchasing agent who was a neighbor when I lived in California some years ago. George was a real tiger. For instance, he would return new calendars sent by vendors at the end of the year with a note saying, "Don't send me this calendar; give me a lower price." This may be overkill, though George eventually became general manager of the business.

Even with close monitoring and relentless control, the variable and fixed operating expenses of a business may increase. Salaries, rent, insurance, utility bills, audit and legal fees—virtually every operating expense—are subject to inflation. To illustrate this situation, let's consider the case in which sales prices and sales volume remain the same, but the company's product cost (cost of goods sold) and its variable and fixed operating expenses increase by 10 percent.

However, the depreciation expense remains unchanged since it is based on the original cost of fixed assets and, for convenience, we will hold interest expense constant. Figure 10.5 presents the impact on profit performance. As you can see, 10 percent increases in product cost and operating expenses would drop the company into the red. The company could ill afford to let its product cost and operating expenses get out of control by 10 percent.

The company could carry back its taxable loss and offset it against its taxable income last year (or prior years). This is the only good thing that can be said about this scenario. Although not shown here, the cash flow from profit would be almost as bad as in the 10 percent sales price decrease situation. The cash flow from profit decrease would be more than the com-

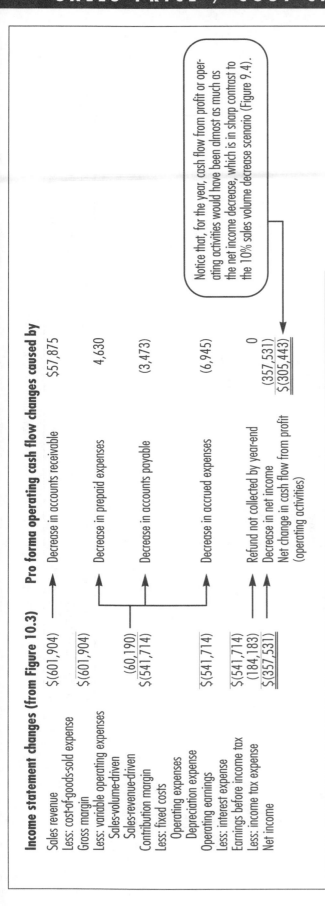

Income statement changes (from Figure 10.3)

Sales revenue	$(601,904)
Less: cost-of-goods-sold expense	
Gross margin	$(601,904)
Less: variable operating expenses	
Sales-volume-driven	
Sales-revenue-driven	(60,190)
Contribution margin	$(541,714)
Less: fixed costs	
Operating expenses	
Depreciation expense	
Operating earnings	$(541,714)
Less: interest expense	
Earnings before income tax	$(541,714)
Less: income tax expense	(184,183)
Net income	$(357,531)

Pro forma operating cash flow changes caused by

Decrease in accounts receivable	$57,875
Decrease in prepaid expenses	4,630
Decrease in accounts payable	(3,473)
Decrease in accrued expenses	(6,945)
Refund not collected by year-end	0
Decrease in net income	(357,531)
Net change in cash flow from profit (operating activities)	$(305,443)

Notice that, for the year, cash flow from profit or operating activities would have been almost as much as the net income decrease, which is in sharp contrast to the 10% sales volume decrease scenario (Figure 9.4).

FIGURE 10.4 Cash flow impacts of 10 percent lower sales price.

Note: Changes in assets and liabilities are based on the company's operating ratios. See Figure 5.1 for a summary of the company's operating ratios. For example, ending accounts receivable equals 5/52 of annual sales revenue in this example. Thus, a decrease in sales revenue would decrease accounts receivable accordingly.

Actual income statement (from Figure 8.1)

Sales volume = 601,904 units

Pro forma changes caused by 10 percent higher costs

	Per unit	Totals	Per unit	Totals
			No change	
Sales revenue	$10.00	$6,019,040		$391,238
Less: cost-of-goods-sold expense	6.50	3,912,376	$0.65	$(391,238)
Gross margin	$3.50	$2,106,664	$(0.65)	$(391,238)
Less: variable operating expenses				
Sales-volume-driven	0.61	370,000	0.06	37,000
Sales-revenue-driven	1.00	601,904	0.10	60,190
Contribution margin	$1.89	$1,134,760	$(0.81)	$(488,428)
Less: fixed costs				
Operating expenses		$551,384		$55,138
Depreciation expense		112,792		
Operating earnings		$470,584		$(543,566)
Less: interest expense		76,650		
Earnings before income tax		$393,934		$(543,566)
Less: income tax expense		133,938		(184,813)
Net income		$259,996		$(358,754)

−43.0%

The 10% cost inflation (except on depreciation and interest expense) means that the company would suffer a 43% drop in its contribution margin per unit and in total. It would be below its breakeven volume and experience a taxable loss, so it would escape any income tax and may be able to carry back its taxable loss to previous years and be entitled to an income tax refund on previously paid income tax, which is the assumption in this figure.

FIGURE 10.5 Profit impact of 10 percent higher product cost and operating expenses.

pany's cash balance. The company would have to raise money to subsidize its loss, which is not easy to do.

END POINT

If you had your choice, the best change would be a sales price increase, assuming all other profit factors remain the same. A sales price increase yields the largest profit increase and the best cash flow result—much better than a sales volume increase of equal magnitude. A sales volume increase is a distant second. Sales volume and sales prices are the "big two" factors. However, no profit factor can be overlooked.

The unit costs of the products sold by the business and virtually all its operating costs—both variable and fixed—can change for the worse. Such unfavorable cost shifts can cause devastating profit impacts unless they are counterbalanced with prompt increases in sales prices, which is a topic explored in the following two chapters.

CHAPTER 11

Price–Volume Trade-Offs

If a business raises sales prices, its sales volume may very well drop. If it decreases sales prices, its sales volume should increase, unless competitors lower their prices also. Higher sales prices may be in response to higher product costs. Spending more on fixed operating expenses, such as bigger advertising budgets, higher rent for larger stores, or more expensive furnishings, may increase sales volume.

INTRODUCTION

None of this is news to experienced business managers. The business world is one of *trade-offs* among profit factors. In other words, in most cases a change in one profit factor causes or is in response to a change in another factor.

Chapters 9 and 10 analyze changes one at a time; all other profit factors are held constant. In the real world of business, seldom can you change just one thing at a time. In this chapter, we analyze the *interaction effects* of changes in two or more profit factors.

TEN PERCENT SALES PRICE REDUCTION TO GENERATE TEN PERCENT VOLUME INCREASE

Suppose you're the sales manager of our example company. You are seriously considering decreasing sales prices 10 percent, which you predict would increase sales volume 10 percent. Of course, competition may follow you down, so the sales volume increase may not materialize. But you don't think they will. Your product is differentiated from the competition. (Brand names and product specifications are two types of differentiation.) There always has been some sales price spread between your products and the competition. A 10 percent price cut should not trigger price reductions by competition, in your opinion.

One reason for reducing sales prices is that the business is not selling up to its full capacity. This is not unusual; many businesses have some slack or untapped sales capacity provided by their fixed expenses. In this example, total fixed expenses provide enough space and personnel to handle perhaps a 20 to 25 percent larger sales volume. Spreading total fixed expenses over a larger number of units sold seems like a good idea. Rather than downsizing, which would require cutting fixed expenses, your first thought is to increase sales volume and thus take better advantage of the sales capacity provided by fixed expenses.

You're aware that sales volume may not respond to the reduction in sales price as much as you predict. On the other hand, sales volume may increase more than 10 percent. In any case, you plan to closely monitor the reaction of customers. There is a serious risk here. Suppose sales volume doesn't increase; you may not be able to reverse directions quickly. You may not be able to roll back the sales price decrease without losing customers, who may forget the sales price decrease and see only the reversal as a price increase.

Before you make the final decision, wouldn't it be a good idea to see what would happen to operating profit? Managers should run through a quick analysis of the consequences of the sales price decision before moving ahead. Otherwise, they are operating in the dark and hoping for the best, which may turn out to be the worst.

Figure 11.1 presents the analysis of your sales price reduction plan. Whoops! The sales price cut would be nothing short of a disaster. Assuming your sales volume prediction turns out to be correct, the sales price reduction strategy would wipe out operating profit and cause an operating loss. There would be a negative swing of $318,390—from $259,996 profit to $58,394 loss. The business would fall below its (new) breakeven point and slip into the red.

Why is there such a devastating impact on profit? First of all, notice that total sales revenue would *decrease* one percent, or $60,190. A simple example shows why. Suppose last period a business sold 100 units at a $100 sales price. This period it decreased sales price 10 percent and sales volume increased 10 percent:

Before:	100 units	¥	$100	= $10,000
After:	110 units	¥	$ 90	= $ 9,900
Difference:	+ 10 units	¥	-$ 10	= -$100

There would be a one percent sales revenue decrease: $-\$100/\$10,000 = -1\%$.

The worst effect, however, would be the increase in cost-of-goods-sold expense (see Figure 11.1 again).

Actual income statement (from Figure 8.1)

Sales volume = 601,904 units

Pro forma changes caused by 10% lower sales price and 10% higher volume

60,190 units

	Actual — Per unit	Actual — Totals	Pro forma — Per unit	Pro forma — Totals
Sales revenue	$10.00	$6,019,040	$(1.00)	$(60,190)
Less: cost-of-goods-sold expense	6.50	3,912,376		391,238
Gross margin	$3.50	$2,106,664	$(1.00)	$(451,428)
Less: variable operating expenses				
Sales-volume-driven	0.61	370,000		37,000
Sales-revenue-driven	1.00	601,904	(0.10)	(6,019)
Contribution margin	$1.89	$1,134,760	$(0.90)	$(482,409)
Less: fixed costs				
Operating expenses		551,384		
Depreciation expense		112,792		
Operating earnings		$470,584		$(482,409)
Less: interest expense		76,650		
Earnings before income tax		$393,934		$(482,409)
Less: income tax expense		133,938		(164,019)
Net income		$259,996		$(318,390)

−42.5%

> The company would give up almost half its contribution margin per unit—$.90 of $1.89—and increase its sales volume only 10%, with the result that total contribution margin would fall 42.5%! At the lower contribution margin per unit, the business would be below its breakeven volume and suffer a taxable loss, so it would escape any income tax and may be able to carry back its taxable loss to previous years and be entitled to an income tax refund on previously paid income tax, which is the assumption shown in this figure.

FIGURE 11.1 Profit impact of 10 percent lower sales price yielding 10 percent higher sales volume.

Cost-of-goods-sold expense would increase $391,238 (10 percent). Combining this with the sales revenue decrease, your gross margin would fall $451,428. Sales-volume-driven operating expenses would increase $37,000 (10 percent), though sales-revenue-driven expenses would drop slightly by $6,019 with the fall-off in sales revenue. Contribution margin would plunge $482,409, or 42.5%, which would cause the contribution to be less than the fixed expenses, resulting in a loss before income tax. What an unmitigated disaster! Why would things turn out so badly?

Look at the unit profit margin in your plan: It drops to only $.90 (rounded), which is a 47.7 percent drop. You can't give up almost half your unit contribution margin and make it back with a 10 percent sales volume increase. In fact, any such trade-off that lowers sales price on the one side with an equal percentage increase in sales volume on the other side pulls the rug out from under profit. Total sales revenue would go *down* and total expenses would go *up*.

Yet, frequently we see sales price reductions of 10 percent or more. What's going on? First of all, many sales price reductions are from the *list* price, such as sticker price on a new car, which no one takes seriously as the final price. List prices are only a point of departure for getting to the real price. Everyone wants a discount. I'm sure you've heard the saying, "I can get it for you wholesale."

The example uses the *real* price, or the sales revenue per unit actually received by the business. Can a business cut its real sales price 10 percent and increase profit? Sales volume would have to increase much more than 10 percent, which we'll look at shortly. Would a 10 percent sales price cut for a 10 percent sales volume increase trade-off *ever* be a smart move? It would seem not; we have settled this point in the previous analysis, haven't we? Well, there is one exception, which brings up an important point.

 **A SPECIAL CASE: SUNK PRODUCT COSTS**

Notice in Figure 11.1 that unit product cost remains the same at $6.50; there is no change in product cost per unit. This assumes that to have products for sale the business either has to buy (or make) them at this unit cost or, if already in inventory, the business has to pay this cost to replace units sold. This is the normal situation, of course, but it may not be true in certain unusual and nontypical cases.

A business may not replace the units sold; it may be at the end of the product's life cycle. For instance, the product may be in the process of being replaced with a newer model. In this situation, the historical, original accounting cost of inventory becomes a sunk cost. This means that the historical cost is like water over the dam; it can't be reversed.

Now, suppose the units held in inventory will not be replaced—the business is at the end of the line on these units and is selling off its remaining stock of the product. In this situation, the book value of the inventory (the recorded accounting cost) is not relevant. What the business paid in the past for the units should be disregarded.* For all practical purposes, the unit product cost can be set to zero for the units held in stock. The manager should ignore the recorded product cost and find the highest sales price that would move all the units out of inventory.

DECREASE IN CASH FLOW AT LOWER SALES PRICE AND HIGHER SALES VOLUME

What would happen to cash flow from profit in this price reduction scenario? It would be equally disastrous, as we can see in Figure 11.2, which presents the impact on operating cash flow caused by the lower sales prices coupled with the higher sales volume. Cash flow from profit (before depreciation) would decrease $377,338. This decrease is more than the company's cash balance ($256,663 from Figure 4.2), which means that the company would have had to go to other sources to provide enough cash to stay in business.

The loss for the year is the main reason for the negative impact on cash flow. The increase in inventory would also aggravate the cash flow problem, as you can see in Figure 11.2. You might also notice that cash flow due to income tax payable is zero because it is assumed here that the tax refund from the loss carryback would not have been received by the year-end. In short, the cash flow from profit before depreciation would be much worse from reducing sales prices 10 percent to gain only 10 percent more sales volume.

SALES VOLUME INCREASE NEEDED TO JUST KEEP EVEN

We should ask here how much sales volume increase would be needed to offset a 10 percent sales price cut? In other words, what level of sales volume would keep

---

* This means for decision-making purposes. The recorded cost of the inventory will, in fact, be charged off to expense and thus reduce the bottom line. What happens is two quite different things. First, the value of the inventory as it approaches the end of the life cycle declined and the company should have written down its inventory to the lower of cost or market (LCM). This write-down should reduce the inventory to a relevant cost for decision making. But, often, what happens is that the inventory is not written-down and remains on the books at original cost, which is charged to cost-of-goods-sold expense when the products are sold.

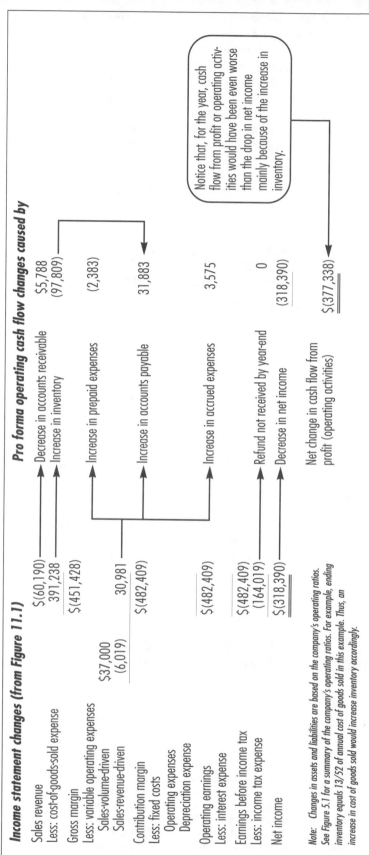

Income statement changes (from Figure 11.1)

Sales revenue		$(60,190)
Less: cost-of-goods-sold expense		391,238
Gross margin		$(451,428)
Less: variable operating expenses		
Sales-volume-driven	$37,000	
Sales-revenue-driven	(6,019)	30,981
Contribution margin		$(482,409)
Less: fixed costs		
Operating expenses		
Depreciation expense		
Operating earnings		$(482,409)
Less: interest expense		
Earnings before income tax		$(482,409)
Less: income tax expense		(164,019)
Net income		$(318,390)

Pro forma operating cash flow changes caused by

Decrease in accounts receivable	$5,788
Increase in inventory	(97,809)
Increase in prepaid expenses	(2,383)
Increase in accounts payable	31,883
Increase in accrued expenses	3,575
Refund not received by year-end	0
Decrease in net income	(318,390)
Net change in cash flow from profit (operating activities)	$(377,338)

Notice that, for the year, cash flow from profit or operating activities would have been even worse than the drop in net income mainly because of the increase in inventory.

Note: Changes in assets and liabilities are based on the company's operating ratios.

See Figure 5.1 for a summary of the company's operating ratios. For example, ending inventory equals 13/52 of annual cost of goods sold in this example. Thus, an increase in cost of goods sold would increase inventory accordingly.

FIGURE 11.2 Cash flow impacts of 10 percent lower sales price yielding 10 percent higher sales volume.

total contribution margin the same? This means we are holding, at least temporarily, the fixed expenses the same and that the additional sales volume could be taken on with no increase in these expenses. The sales volume needed to keep profit the same is computed as follows:

$1,134,760 contribution margin target ÷ $.99 unit
contribution margin = 1,151,709 units

Sales volume would have to reach over 1.1 million units!

In other words, sales volume at the lower sales price would have to about double over the present sales volume. Would this be possible? Doubtful, to say the least. Even if this many units could be sold, fixed expenses would have to be increased, probably by quite a large amount. And interest expense would increase because more debt would be used to finance the increase in operating assets needed to support the higher sales volume.

The moral of the story, basically, is that a 10 percent sales price cut usually takes such a big bite out of unit contribution margin that it would take a huge increase in sales volume to keep even (i.e., to earn the same profit as before the price cut). Managers should think long and hard before making sales price reductions.

The preceding analysis applies the sales price reduction to all sales for the entire year. However, many sales price reductions are limited to a relatively few items and are short-lived, perhaps for just a day or weekend. Furthermore, the sale may bring in customers who buy other items not on sale. Profit margin is sacrificed on selected items to make additional sales of other products at normal profit margins.

Indeed, many retailers seem to always have some products on sale virtually every day of the year. In this case, the normal profit margin is hard to pin down, since almost every product takes its turn at being on sale. In short, every product may have two profit margins: one when not on sale and one when on sale. The *average* profit margin for the year depends on how often the item goes on sale.

In any case, the same basic analysis as explained here also applies to short-term, limited sales price reductions. The manager should calculate, or at least estimate, how much additional sales volume would be needed on the sale items just to remain even with the profit that would have been earned at normal sales prices. What complicates the picture is sales of other products (not on sale) which would have not been made without the increase in sales traffic from the sale items. Clearly, the additional sales made at normal profit margins is a big factor to consider, though it may be very hard to estimate with any precision.

GIVING UP TEN PERCENT SALES VOLUME FOR TEN PERCENT SALES PRICE INCREASE

Suppose the president of the company is thinking of a 10 percent sales price *increase,* knowing that sales volume probably would decrease. In fact, the president predicts it will drop at least 10 percent. Sales managers generally are very opposed to giving up any sales volume, especially a loss of market share that could be very hard to recapture later. Any move that decreases sales volume has to be considered very carefully. But for the moment, let's put aside these warnings. Would a 10 percent sales price hike be a good move if sales volume dropped only 10 percent?

The profit analysis for this trade-off is shown in Figure 11.3. However, before you look at it, what did you expect? An increase in profit? That big? Notice that sales revenue actually decreases one percent, or $60,190—exactly the same effect as in the reverse situation discussed earlier. But in this scenario, cost of goods sold would decrease $391,238 (10 percent) and both variable operating expenses decrease. In short, the company would give up about $60,000 sales revenue to save over $440,000 expenses.

As before, the key to the analysis is unit contribution margin, which would increase $.90 because the sales price would increase $1.00 less the $.10 increase in the sales-revenue-driven expense. This is on a base of $1.89 unit contribution profit margin, which is an increase of 47.7 percent. Increasing the unit contribution profit margin per unit by almost 50 percent with only a 10 percent give-up in sales volume is a very good trade-off. Fixed expenses would remain the same; these costs certainly wouldn't go up with the decrease in sales volume. If anything, some of the company's fixed operating costs possibly could be reduced at the lower sales volume level.

The big jump in profit is based on the prediction that sales volume would drop only 10 percent. Now it might fall 15, 20, or 25 percent. Profit can be calculated for any particular sales volume decrease. No one knows how sales volume might respond to a 10 percent sales price increase. Sales may not decrease at all. The higher prices might enhance the prestige or premium image of the products and attract more of an upscale clientele who are quite willing to pay the higher price. Or sales may drop more than 25 percent because customers search for better prices elsewhere.

How much could sales volume fall and keep total contribution margin the same? This sales volume is computed as follows:

$1,134,760 contribution margin target ÷ $2.79 unit
contribution margin = 407,413 units

Actual income statement (from Figure 8.1)

Sales volume = 601,904 units

Pro forma changes caused by 10 percent higher sales price and 10 percent lower volume

−60,190 units

	Per unit	Totals	Per unit	Totals
Sales revenue	$10.00	$6,019,040	$1.00	$(60,190)
Less: cost-of-goods-sold expense	6.50	3,912,376		(391,238)
Gross margin	$3.50	$2,106,664	$1.00	$331,047
Less: variable operating expenses				
Sales-volume-driven	0.61	370,000		(37,000)
Sales-revenue-driven	1.00	601,904	0.10	(6,019)
Contribution margin	$1.89	$1,134,760	$0.90	$374,066
Less: fixed costs				
Operating expenses		551,384		
Depreciation expense		112,792		
Operating earnings		$470,584		$374,066
Less: interest expense		76,650		
Earnings before income tax		$393,934		$374,066
Less: income tax expense		133,938		127,183
Net income		$259,996		$246,884

+33.0%

The company would increase its contribution margin per unit by almost half—$.90 on $1.89—and lose only 10% of its sales volume, with the result that total contribution margin would increase 33%! Notice also that if fixed expenses do not increase, which they don't in this scenario, then bottom-line net income would almost double. The increase in net income is almost as much as the original amount of net income. This demonstrates the tremendous leverage power of improving the contribution profit margin per unit. Of course, sales volume may drop by more than 10% and giving up sales and market share may not be a smart long-run move by the business.

FIGURE 11.3 *Profit impact of 10 percent higher sales price resulting in 10 percent lower sales volume.*

Sales volume would have to drop to about 400,000 units, well below the 541,714 units or 10 percent decline in sales volume shown in Figure 11.3. Even if sales volume dropped to 500,000 units, the company's profit would be better at the 10 percent higher sales prices. Sales may not drop off this much, at least in the short run. And fixed operating expenses could probably be reduced at the lower sales level.

My guess is that, given their choice, the large majority of business managers would prefer keeping their market share and not giving up any sales volume, even though profit could be maximized in the higher-sales-price/lower-sales-volume situation. Protecting sales volume and market share is deeply ingrained in the thinking of most businesses.

Cash flow from profit would be an even better story. It would increase more than the profit increase because the cost-of-goods-sold expense would decrease, leading to a decrease of inventory. In other words, the higher profit would be made on a smaller inventory. (An incremental cash flow statement is not shown here.) The large increase in cash would raise questions about what to do with the excess cash balance, which would be a pleasant task for management to deal with.

DANGER! An earlier point deserves repeating. Any loss of market share is taken very seriously. By and large, you'll find that the successful company has built its success on getting and keeping a significant market share, so that it is a major player and dominant force in the marketplace.

True, some companies don't have very large market shares—they carve out relatively small niches and build their businesses on low sales volume at premium prices. The analysis presented here demonstrates the profit potential of this niche strategy, which is built on higher unit profit margins that more than make up for smaller sales volume.

END POINT

Seldom does one profit factor change without changing or being changed by one or more other profit factors. The joint interaction effects of the changes should be carefully analyzed before making final decisions or locking on a course of action that might be hard to reverse. Managers should keep their attention riveted on *unit contribution profit margin*. Profit performance is most responsive to changes in the unit profit margin, which this chapter demonstrates.

Basically, there are only two ways to improve unit contribution margin: Increase sales price or decrease product cost and/or other variable operating expenses per unit. The sales price is the most external or visible part of the business—the factor most exposed to customer reaction. In contrast, product cost and variable expenses are more internal and invisible. Customers may not be aware of these expense decreases, unless such cost savings show through in lower product quality or worse service.

Last, the importance of protecting sales volume and market share is mentioned several times in the chapter. Marketing managers know what they're talking about on this point, that's for sure. Recapturing lost market share is not easy. Once gone, customers may never return.

CHAPTER

12

Cost–Volume
Trade-Offs

It might seem simple enough. Suppose your unit product cost goes up. Then all you have to do is to raise the
sales price the same amount to keep the contribution
margin the same, true? Not true. Even if sales volume
were to remain the same at the higher sales price, the
sales revenue increase would cause some variable
expenses to increase. And sales volume may be affected
by the higher price, of course. It's more complicated
than it might first appear.

 **PRODUCT COST INCREASES:
WHICH KIND?**

There are two quite different reasons for product
cost increases. First is *inflation,* which can be of two
sorts. General inflation is widespread and drives up
costs throughout the economy, including the products
sold by the business. Or inflation may be localized on
particular products—for example, problems in the Middle East driving up oil and other energy costs, or floods
in the Midwest affecting corn and soybean prices. In
either situation, a product is the same but now costs
more per unit.

The second reason for higher product costs is quite
different from inflation. Increases in unit product costs
may reflect either quality or size improvements. In this
situation, the product itself is changed for the better.
Customers may be willing to pay more for the improved
product, with the result that the company would not
suffer a decrease in sales volume. Or if the sales price is
held the same on the improved product, then sales volume may increase.

 Customers tend to accept higher sales prices if they
perceive that the company is operating in a general
inflationary market environment. In their minds,
everything is going up. So, on a comparative basis, the

product does not cost more relative to price increases of other products they purchase. Sales volume may not be affected by higher sales prices in a market dominated by the inflation mentality. On the other hand, if customers' incomes are not rising in proportion with sales price increases, demand would likely decrease at the higher sales prices.

If competitors face the same general inflation of product costs, the company's sales volume may not suffer from passing along product cost increases in the form of higher sales prices—the competition would be doing the same thing. The exact demand sensitivity to sales price increases cannot be known except in hindsight. And, even then, it's hard to know for sure because many factors change simultaneously in the real world.

DANGER! Whenever sales prices are increased due to increases in product costs—whether because of general or specific inflation or being triggered by product improvements—managers cannot simply tack on the product cost increase to sales price. They should carefully take into account variable expenses that are dependent on (driven by) sales revenue.

Suppose that the company's unit product cost goes up $.54 (from $6.50 to $7.04). The manager cannot simply raise the sales price $.54. In the example, the company's sales-revenue-driven variable operating expenses are 10 percent of sales revenue. The manager should determine the sales price increase as follows:

$$\$.54 \text{ product cost increase} \div .90$$
$$= \$.60 \text{ sales price increase}$$

Dividing by .9 recognizes that only 90 percent of a sales dollar is left over after deducting sales-revenue-driven variable expenses. Only 90 cents on the dollar is available to provide for the increase in the unit product cost. If the company raises its sales price exactly $.60, then its contribution margin would remain exactly the same, which can be seen as follows:

	Before	Change	After
Sales price	$10.00	$0.60	$10.60
Product cost	6.50	0.54	7.04
Gross margin	$ 3.50	$0.06	$ 3.56
Volume-driven expenses	0.61		0.61
Revenue-driven expenses	1.00	$0.06	1.06
Contribution margin	$ 1.89		$ 1.89

Thus, the company's total contribution margin would be the same at the $10.60 sales price, assuming sales volume remains the same.

VARIABLE COST INCREASES AND SALES VOLUME

As just mentioned, one basic type of product cost increase is when the product itself is improved. These quality improvements may be part of the marketing strategy to give customers a better product at the same sales price, to stimulate demand. In addition to product cost, variable operating expenses could be increased to improve the quality of the service to customers.

For example, faster delivery methods such as overnight Federal Express could be used, even though this would cost more than the traditional delivery methods. This would increase the sales-*volume*-driven expense. The company could increase sales commissions to improve the personal time and effort the sales staff spends with each customer, which would increase the sales-*revenue*-driven expense.

In the our example, suppose management is considering a new strategy for product and service quality improvement that would increase product cost and the two variable operating expenses by 4 percent. Tentatively, management has decided not to increase the sales price because demand should increase for the improved product and service. It goes without saying that the improvement in demand depends on customers being made aware and convinced of the improvements. Before a final decision is made, management would like to know how much sales volume would have to increase just to keep profit the same.

Figure 12.1 presents this keep-even, or standstill, income statement based on 4 percent increases in the product cost and the two variable operating costs. Product cost increases $.26 per unit, sales-volume-driven variable operating expenses increase $.03 (rounded) per unit, and sales-revenue-driven variable operating expenses increase from 10.0 percent of sales revenue to 10.4 percent. Fixed expenses are held constant. Figure 12.1 shows that sales volume would have to increase to 727,086 units, which can be computed directly as follows:

$1,134,760 contribution margin target ÷ $1.56 unit contribution margin = 727,086 sales volume needed

So sales volume would have to increase 20.8 percent: 727,086 units required to be sold ÷ 601,904 present sales volume = 20.8% increase. This is a rather substantial increase. Why would sales volume have to increase almost 21 percent when variable costs increase only 4 percent? As before, the key point is the drop in the contribution margin due to the cost increases from $1.89 to $1.56 per unit, which is a 17 percent decrease. It takes a lot of sales volume increase to make up for the drop in the unit contribution margin.

Actual income statement (from Figure 8.1)			Pro forma standstill income statement for 4% higher variable costs		+20.8%
Sales volume =	601,904 units		727,086 units		
	Per unit	Totals	Per unit	Totals	
Sales revenue	$10.00	$6,019,040	$10.00	$7,270,860	
Less: cost-of-goods-sold expense	6.50	3,912,376	6.76	4,915,101	
Gross margin	$ 3.50	$2,106,664	$ 3.24	$2,355,759	
Less: variable operating expenses					
Sales-volume-driven	0.61	370,000	0.64	464,829	
Sales-revenue-driven	1.00	601,904	1.04	756,169	
Contribution margin	$ 1.89	$1,134,760	$ 1.56	$1,134,760	
Less: fixed costs					
Operating expenses		551,384		551,384	
Depreciation expense		112,792		112,792	
Operating earnings		$ 470,584		$ 470,584	
Less: interest expense		76,650		76,650	
Earnings before income tax		$ 393,934		$ 393,934	
Less: income tax expense		133,938		133,937	
Net income		$ 259,996	Same	$ 259,996	

Sales volume would have to increase 20.8% in this example just to keep net income the same. Why? Notice the $.33 drop in the contribution margin per unit, which is more than 17%. This has to be overcome by a 20.8% increase in sales volume, assuming that the sales price remains constant, as it does in this example. Increasing sales volume by almost 21% would be quite a task, to say the least!

FIGURE 12.1 *Higher sales volume needed to cover 4 percent higher variable costs.*

Also, there is more bad news. More capital would be needed at the higher sales volume level; total net operating assets would be higher due mainly to increases in accounts receivable and inventory. The impact on cash flow at the higher sales volume level should be analyzed. Figure 12.2 presents the impact on operating cash flow from profit (before depreciation) that would be caused by the higher sales volume level.

As you can see, cash flow would decrease $269,964, mainly because of the large increases in accounts receivable and inventory. Cash would be drawn down by almost $270,000, which is more than the company's cash balance (from Figure 4.2). Additional capital would have to be raised from debt and/or equity sources, even though profit would remain the same. ROE would suffer if the owners (stockholders) supplied some of the additional capital.

BETTER PRODUCT AND SERVICE LEADING TO HIGHER SALES PRICE

Instead of determining how many more units would have to be sold because of the higher variable costs, the alternative strategy would be to raise the sales price. Figure 12.3 presents the income statement for the exact higher sales price that would keep profit the same as before, given the 4 percent higher product cost and other variable expenses. In other words, all the variable cost increases are loaded into the sales price and none in the sales volume increase.

Following this strategy, the sales price would have to be increased to $10.36 (rounded).* In this case, the company has improved the product and the service to its customers. There is no increase in profit. In Figure 12.3, notice that sales revenue, cost of goods sold, and variable expenses all would increase. So the total net operating assets of the business would increase, which in turn would require more total capital. If the owners (stockholders) supplied part of the additional capital, ROE would decrease because a larger owners' equity number would be divided into the same net income number.

This "upgrade" scenario would be customer driven—if the company failed to improve its product and/or service, then it might lose sales because the customers want the improvements and are willing to pay. This may seem to be a strange state of affairs, but you see examples everyday where the customer wants a

* This required sales price is computed as follows: ($6.76 product cost + $.64 volume-driven cost per unit + $1.89 contribution margin per unit) ÷ (1.000 − .104) = $10.362262 sales price. In words: the sales price, net of the sales-revenue-driven cost per unit as a percent of sales price, must cover the product cost and the sales-volume-driven expense per unit, and provide the same contribution margin per unit as before.

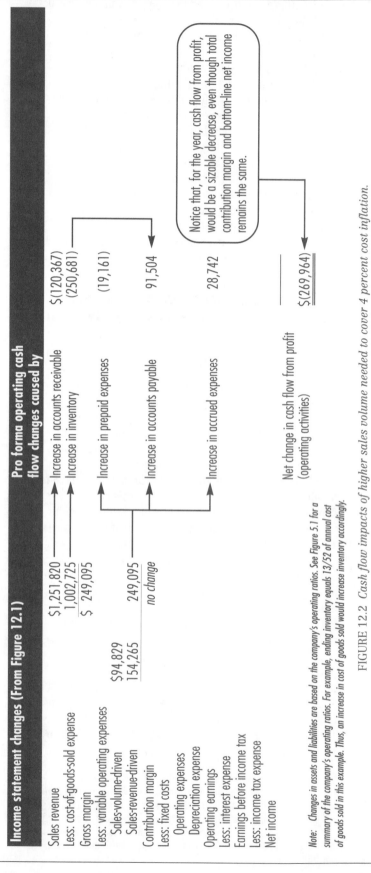

Income statement changes (From Figure 12.1)

Sales revenue		$1,251,820
Less: cost-of-goods-sold expense		1,002,725
Gross margin		$ 249,095
Less: variable operating expenses		
Sales-volume-driven	$94,829	
Sales-revenue-driven	154,265	249,095
Contribution margin		no change
Less: fixed costs		
Operating expenses		
Depreciation expense		
Operating earnings		
Less: interest expense		
Earnings before income tax		
Less: income tax expense		
Net income		

Pro forma operating cash flow changes caused by

Increase in accounts receivable	$(120,367)
Increase in inventory	(250,681)
Increase in prepaid expenses	(19,161)
Increase in accounts payable	91,504
Increase in accrued expenses	28,742
Net change in cash flow from profit (operating activities)	$(269,964)

Notice that, for the year, cash flow from profit, would be a sizable decrease, even though total contribution margin and bottom-line net income remains the same.

Note: Changes in assets and liabilities are based on the company's operating ratios. See Figure 5.1 for a summary of the company's operating ratios. For example, ending inventory equals 13/52 of annual cost of goods sold in this example. Thus, an increase in cost of goods sold would increase inventory accordingly.

FIGURE 12.2 *Cash flow impacts of higher sales volume needed to cover 4 percent cost inflation.*

Actual income statement (from Figure 8.1)		Pro forma standstill income statement for 4% higher variable costs	
Sales volume = 601,904 units	→ Same →	601,904 units	
Per unit	**Totals**	**Per unit**	**Totals**
Sales revenue $10.00	$6,019,040	$10.36	$6,237,087
Less: cost-of-goods-sold expense 6.50	3,912,376	6.76	4,068,871
Gross margin $ 3.50	$2,106,664	$ 3.60	$2,168,216
Less: variable operating expenses			
Sales-volume-driven 0.61	370,000	0.64	384,800
Sales-revenue-driven 1.00	601,904	1.08	648,657
Contribution margin $ 1.89	$1,134,760	$ 1.89	$1,134,759
Less: fixed costs			
Operating expenses	551,384		551,384
Depreciation expense	112,792		112,792
Operating earnings	$ 470,584		$ 470,583
Less: interest expense	76,650		76,650
Earnings before income tax	$ 393,934		$ 393,933
Less: income tax expense	133,938		133,937
Net income	$ 259,996	→ Same →	$ 259,996

Sales price would not have to increase by 4.0% because the sales price is a higher base amount. The objective is to keep net income the same amount. So the sales price would have to increase only $.36 per unit (rounded), which is a little less than 4.0%.

FIGURE 12.3 *Higher sales price needed to cover 4 percent higher variable costs.*

better product and/or service and is willing to pay more for the improvements.

DECREASES IN PRODUCT COST AND VARIABLE EXPENSES CAUSING SALES VOLUME DECREASES

Suppose a business were able to lower its unit product costs and its variable expenses per unit. On the one hand, such savings may be true efficiency or productivity gains. Purchase costs may be reduced by sharper bargaining. (If the business is a manufacturer, productivity gains reduce unit product costs.) Or wasteful expenses could be eliminated.

The key question is whether the product itself remains the same, as well as the product's real and perceived quality, and whether the quality of service to customers remains the same. Maybe not. Product cost decreases may represent quality decreases or disimprovements, or possibly reduced sizes such as smaller candy bars or fewer ounces in breakfast cereal boxes. Reducing variable operating expenses may adversely affect the quality of service to customers—for instance, spreading fewer personnel over the same number of customers.

If the company can lower its costs and still deliver the same product and the same quality of service, then sales volume should not be affected, everything else remaining the same, of course. Customers should see no differences in the products or service. In this case, the cost savings would improve the unit contribution margin and profit would increase accordingly.

Improvements in the unit contribution margin are very powerful; these increases have the same type of multiplier effect as operating leverage. For example, suppose that, because of true efficiency gains, the business lowers its product costs or its volume-driven or sales-revenue-driven expenses, such that it improves its contribution margin, say, $.10 per unit. Now this may not seem like much, but remember that the company sells 601,904 units over the year, so the improvement in its unit contribution margin would add $60,190 to the total contribution margin profit line, that is, profit before fixed expenses, interest, and income tax. Even with the government taking out its 34 percent, this would improve bottom-line profit $39,726, which would be a gain of over 15 percent in net income!

Total quality management (TQM) is getting a lot of press today, indicated by the fact that it has been reduced to an acronym. Clearly managers have always known that product quality and quality of service to customers are absolutely critical factors, though perhaps they lost sight of this in pursuit of short-term profits. Today, however, managers obviously have been made acutely aware of how quality conscious customers are. (I find it surprising that today's gurus are preaching this gospel as if it were just discovered.)

Cost savings may cause degradation in the quality of the product or service to customers. It would be no surprise, therefore, if sales volume would decrease. The unit contribution margin would improve, but the drop in sales volume may offset the gain in the profit margin. Or sales prices may have to be dropped to maintain the same sales volume, in which case, the unit contribution margin would not improve.

SUBTLE AND NOT-SO-SUBTLE CHANGES IN FIXED OPERATING EXPENSES

Why do fixed operating expenses increase? The increase may be due to general inflationary trends. For instance, utility bills and insurance premiums seem to drift relentlessly upward; they hardly ever go down. In contrast, fixed operating expenses may be deliberately increased to expand capacity. The business could rent a larger space or hire more employees on fixed salaries.

And there's a third reason: Fixed expenses may be increased to improve the sales value of the present location. The business could invest in better furnishings and equipment (which would increase its annual depreciation expense). Fixed expenses could *decrease* for the opposite reasons, of course. But we'll focus on increases in fixed expenses.

Suppose in the company example that total fixed operating expenses were to increase due to general inflationary trends. There were no changes in the capacity of the business, nor in the retail space or appearance (attractiveness) of the space. As far as customers can tell, there have been no changes that would benefit them. The company could attempt to increase its sales price—the additional fixed expenses could be spread over its present sales volume.

However, this assumes that sales volume would remain the same at the higher sales price. Sales volume might decrease at the higher sales price, unless customers accept the increase as a general inflationary-driven increase. Sales volume might be sensitive to even small sales price increases. Many customers keep a sharp eye on prices, as you know. The business should probably allow for some decrease in sales volume when sales prices are raised.

END POINT

This and the previous chapter examine certain basic trade-offs; both chapters rest on the premise that seldom does one profit factor change without changing or being changed by one or more other profit factors. It was mentioned before, but bears repeating here, that managers must keep their attention riveted on *unit contribution profit margin.* Profit performance is very sensitive to changes in this key operating profit number, which several different situations in this and the preceding chapter demonstrate.

The preceding chapter examines the interplay between sales price and volume changes. Sales prices are the most external part of the business, as mentioned before. In contrast, product cost and variable expenses are more internal to the business. Customers may not be aware of these expense decreases, unless such cost savings show through in lower product quality or worse service. Frequently cost "savings" are not cost savings at all, in the sense that customer demand is adversely affected.

Cost increases can be due to inflation, general or specific, or can be caused by product improvements in size or quality, or the quality of service surrounding the product. To prevent profit deterioration, cost increases have to be recovered through higher sales volume or through higher sales prices. This chapter examines the critical differences between these two alternatives.

Depending on higher sales volume to offset cost increases may not be very realistic; sales volume would have to increase too much. This type of analysis does give managers a useful point of reference, however. Cost increases generally have to be recovered through higher sales prices. This chapter demonstrates the analysis tools for determining the higher sales prices.

Survival Analysis:
Turning Loss into Profit

A successful formula for making profit can take a wrong turn anytime. Every step on the pathway to profit is slippery; each step requires constant attention. Managers have to keep a close watch on all profit factors and continuously look for opportunities to improve profit. Nothing can be taken for granted. A popular term these days is *environmental scan,* which is a good term here also. Managers should make profit radar scans to see if there are any blips on the screen that signal trouble.

WHEN THINGS GO WRONG

This chapter looks at the profile of a business suffering a loss instead of making a profit. The lessons of the previous chapters are applied to analyze the reasons for the loss and to identify which factors must be improved to turn the situation around. Basically the question is: What's wrong? Managers must know how to answer this question.

Often, the answer is found in the *frustrating fringe* surrounding the basic pathway to profit. This broad term refers to several different negative pressures on profit performance that managers have to deal with day in and day out, which might be called the sinkholes and pitfalls on the pathway to profit. Chapter 16 presents a survey of these profit robbers.

PROFILE OF A LOSER

Suppose you're the manager in charge of a product line, territory, division, or some other major organizational unit of a large corporation. You are responsible for the operating profit performance (earnings before interest and income tax) of your unit. You do not have direct responsibility for the operating assets and liabilities of your organizational unit, nor authority over financing the net operating assets of your unit. These financial functions are centralized at a higher level in the organization.

Since your responsibility is limited to operating profit performance, your unit is called a *profit center* in management accounting. A manager may have both profit responsibility as well as broader responsibility and authority for the unit's operating assets and operating liabilities. In this arrangement, the manager would be charged a cost of capital or expected to meet established cost-of-capital objectives based on the net operating assets used by the unit. This type of organizational unit is called an *investment center* and uses the tools for evaluating business investment performance explained in Chapter 6.

We shall focus mainly on operating profit (earnings before interest and income tax) in the following discussion, although cost-of-capital and return on equity aspects are also considered along the way. Profit performance should not be completely divorced from capital performance.

Your most recent annual profit report is presented in Figure 13.1, titled the "bad news profit report" to emphasize the loss for the year. This report is shown in a fairly condensed format to limit attention to essential profit factors. For example, only one variable operating expense is included that is sales volume driven. The company example in previous chapters includes both sales-volume- and sales-revenue-driven variable operating expenses, but this distinction takes a backseat in the following analysis.

Since we focus on operating profit, the profit report does not include interest expense or income tax expense. Only the total is given for all fixed operating expenses; depreciation is included in the total but is not separated out in this example.* New to the example is the inclusion of annual capacity and the breakeven volume, in addition to actual sales volume for the year just ended.

You have taken a lot of heat lately from your boss for the $145,000 operating loss. Your job is to turn things around, and fairly fast. Your bonus next year, and perhaps keeping your job, depend on moving your unit into the black.

 **FIRST: SOME QUESTIONS ABOUT FIXED EXPENSES**

One thing you might do first is to take a close look at your $870,000 fixed operating expenses. Your fixed

* It should be mentioned that this report does not contain enough detail to serve as a management control report or for management decision making in the normal, noncrisis situations discussed in previous chapters. Chapter 16 explains that much more detail is needed for management control.

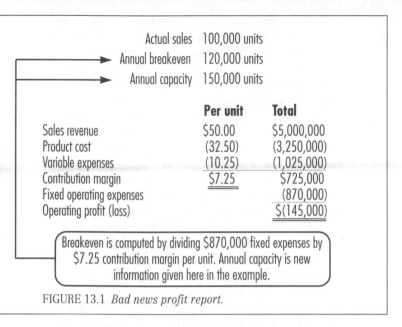

	Per unit	**Total**
Actual sales		100,000 units
Annual breakeven		120,000 units
Annual capacity		150,000 units

	Per unit	**Total**
Sales revenue	$50.00	$5,000,000
Product cost	(32.50)	(3,250,000)
Variable expenses	(10.25)	(1,025,000)
Contribution margin	$7.25	$725,000
Fixed operating expenses		(870,000)
Operating profit (loss)		$(145,000)

Breakeven is computed by dividing $870,000 fixed expenses by $7.25 contribution margin per unit. Annual capacity is new information given here in the example.

FIGURE 13.1 *Bad news profit report.*

expenses may include, in part, an *allocated* amount from a larger pool of fixed expenses from the higher organizational unit that your profit center reports to, or they may include a share of fixed expenses from corporate headquarters. Any basis of allocation is open to question; virtually every allocation method is somewhat arbitrary and can be challenged on one or more grounds.

For instance, consider the legal expenses of the corporation. Should these be allocated to each profit responsibility center throughout the organization? On what basis: relative sales revenue, frequency of litigation of each unit, or according to some other formula? Likewise, what about the costs of centralized data processing and accounting expenses of the business? Many fixed expenses are allocated on some arbitrary basis, which is open to question.

It's not unusual for many costs to be allocated across different organizational units; every manager should be aware of the methods, bases, or formulas that are used to allocate costs. The worst mistake is to assume that there is some natural or objective basis for cost allocation. The great majority of cost allocation schemes are arbitrary and, therefore, subject to manipulation. Chapter 15 discusses cost allocation in more detail.

Questions about the proper method of allocation should be settled *before* the start of the year. Raising such questions after the fact—after the profit performance results are reported for the period—is too late. In any case, if you argue for less (a smaller allocation of fixed expenses to your unit), then you are also arguing that other units should get more of the organization's fixed expenses, which will initiate a counter argument from those units, of course. Also, it may appear that you're making excuses rather than fixing the problem.

Another question to consider is this: Is a significant amount of depreciation expense included in the fixed expenses total? Accountants treat depreciation as a fixed expense, based on generally accepted methods that allocate original cost over the estimated useful economic lives of the assets. For instance, under current income tax laws, buildings are depreciated over 39 years and cars and light trucks over 5 years. Just because accountants adopt such methods doesn't mean that depreciation is, in fact, a fixed expense.

Contrast depreciation with, for example, annual property taxes on buildings and land (real estate). Property tax is an actual cash outlay each year. Whether or not the business made full use of the building and land during the year, the entire amount of tax should be charged to the year as fixed expense. There can be no argument about this. On the other hand, depreciation raises entirely different issues.

Suppose your loss is due primarily to sales volume that is well below your normal volume of operations. You can argue that less depreciation expense should be charged to the year and more should be shifted to future years. The reasoning is that the assets were not used as much—the machines were not operated as many hours, the trucks were not driven as many miles, and so on. On the other hand, depreciation may be truly caused by the passage of time. For instance, depreciation of computers is based on their expected technological life. Using the computers less probably doesn't delay the date of replacing the computers.

DANGER! Generally speaking, arguing for less depreciation is not going to get you very far. Most businesses are not willing to make such a radical change in their depreciation policies, that is, to slow down recorded depreciation when sales volume takes a dip. Also, this would look suspicious—the business would appear to be selecting different expense methods to manipulate reported profit.

WHAT'S THE PROBLEM?

Your first thought might be that sales volume is the main problem since it is less than breakeven (see Figure 13.1). To review briefly, the breakeven volume is determined as follows:

$870,000 fixed expenses ÷ $7.25 contribution margin per unit
= 120,000 units breakeven volume

Actual sales volume is only 100,000 units; just to reach the breakeven point, sales volume would have to increase 20,000 units. This would add $145,000 more contribution margin:

20,000 additional units × $7.25 contribution margin per unit
= $145,000 increase in contribution margin

Total contribution margin would just equal total fixed operating expenses at the 120,000 units sales volume. By the way, notice that breakeven is 80 percent of capacity: 120,000 units/150,000 units = 80%, which by almost any standard is far too high. Of course, breakeven is not your ultimate goal.

Suppose you were able to increase sales volume beyond the breakeven point all the way up to sales capacity of 150,000 units, an increase of 50,000 units from the actual sales level of 100,000 units. A 50 percent increase in sales volume may not be very realistic, to say the least. At any rate, your annual profit report would look as shown in Figure 13.2.

As you can see, even if sales volume were increased to full capacity, operating profit would be only $217,500, which equals only 2.9 percent of sales revenue. For the large majority of businesses—the only exceptions being those with very high inventory turnover ratios—an operating profit (i.e., earnings before interest and income tax) equal to only 2.9 percent on sales revenue is seriously inadequate. The operating earnings goal for your profit center probably would be in the range of 10.0 to 15.0 percent on sales revenue.

Thus, increasing sales volume is not the entire answer. You have two other basic options: (1) reduce fixed expenses and (2) improve your unit contribution margin.

There may be some flab in your fixed expenses. It goes without saying that you should cut the fat. The more serious question is whether to downsize, which means to reduce fixed operating expenses and decrease capacity. For instance, assume you could slash fixed expenses by one-third ($290,000) but this would reduce capacity by one-third, down to 100,000 units. If

	Actual sales	150,000 units
	Annual breakeven	120,000 units
	Annual capacity	150,000 units

	Per unit	Total
Sales revenue	$50.00	$7,500,000
Product cost	(32.50)	(4,875,000)
Variable expenses	(10.25)	(1,537,500)
Contribution margin	$7.25	$1,087,500
Fixed operating expenses		(870,000)
Operating profit		$217,500

Notice that, even at full capacity, operating profit is only 2.9% of sales revenue, which in almost all industries is far too low to earn an adequate ROE.

FIGURE 13.2 *Full-capacity profit report.*

no other factors changed, your profit performance would be as shown in Figure 13.3.

Operating profit would be $145,000, which is better than a loss. But profit would still be only 2.9 percent of sales revenue, which is much too low, as previously explained. Keep in mind that making profit requires a substantial amount of net operating assets. The capital invested in the net operating assets is supplied by debt and equity sources and carries a cost, which is discussed extensively in Chapter 6.

Suppose, to illustrate, that the $5,000,000 sales revenue level requires $2,000,000 net operating assets—one-half from debt at 8.0 percent annual interest, and one-half from equity on which the annual ROE target is 15.0 percent. The interest expense is $80,000 ($1,000,000 debt × 8.0%), leaving only $65,000 earnings before tax. Net income after income tax is not enough to meet the company's ROE goal, which would be the $1,000,000 owners' equity capital times 15.0 percent ROE, or $150,000 net income.

By cutting fixed operating expenses you have removed any room for growth, since sales volume would be at capacity. In summary, it's fairly clear that the main problem is that your unit contribution margin is too low.

 IMPROVING UNIT CONTRIBUTION MARGIN

Now for the tough question: How would you improve unit contribution margin? Is sales price too low? Or are product cost and variable expenses too high? Do all three need improving? Answering these questions strikes at the essence of the manager's function. Man-

	Actual sales	100,000 units
	Annual breakeven	80,000 units
	Annual capacity	100,000 units

	Per unit	**Total**
Sales revenue	$50.00	$5,000,000
Product cost	(32.50)	(3,250,000)
Variable expenses	(10.25)	(1,025,000)
Contribution margin	$7.25	$725,000
Fixed operating expenses		$(580,000)
Operating profit		$145,000

> Notice that, even if fixed expenses are reduced by one-third, operating profit is only 2.9% of sales revenue, which in almost all industries is far too low to earn an adequate ROE.

FIGURE 13.3 *One-third less fixed costs profit report.*

agers are paid for knowing what to do and what has to be changed, as well as how to make the changes. Analysis techniques don't provide the final answers to these questions. But the analysis methods certainly help the manager to size up and quantify the impact of changes in the factors that determine unit contribution margin.

One useful approach is to set a reasonably achievable profit goal—say $500,000—and load all the needed improvement on each factor to see how much change would be needed in each. To move from $145,000 loss to $500,000 profit is a $645,000 swing. If sales volume stays the same at 100,000 units, then achieving this improvement would require that the unit contribution margin be increased $6.45 per unit, compared with the present $7.25 per unit. The manager could load the $6.45 improvement amount on each profit factor. Doing this gives the following improvement percents that would be needed:

$$\$6.45 \div \$50.00 \text{ sales price} = 13\% \text{ increase}$$
$$\$6.45 \div \$32.50 \text{ product cost} = 20\% \text{ decrease}$$
$$\$6.45 \div \$10.25 \text{ variable expenses} = 63\% \text{ decrease}$$

Making changes of these magnitudes would, at best, be very tough.

Raising sales prices 13 percent would surely depress demand. Lowering product cost 20 percent is not realistic in most situations, and lowering variable expenses 63 percent may be just plain impossible. A combination of improvements would be needed, instead of loading all the improvement on just one factor. Also, sales volume probably would have to be increased.

Suppose you develop the following plan. Sales prices will be increased 5 percent and sales volume will be increased 10 percent, based on better marketing and advertising strategies. Product cost will be reduced 4 percent by sharper purchasing, and variable expenses will be cut 8 percent by exercising tighter control over these expenses. Last, you think you can eliminate about 10 percent fat from fixed expenses (without reducing sales capacity). If you could actually achieve all these goals, your profit report would look as shown in Figure 13.4.

You would make your profit goal and then some, but only if *all* the improvements were actually achieved. Profit would be 9.1 percent of sales revenue ($522,700 ÷ $5,775,000 = 9.1%). You may still face pressure to increase the return on sales. You may still have to go back to the drawing board to figure out additional improvements.

END POINT

It might not appear so, but this is a review chapter that returns to many of the analysis tools discussed in previous chapters and applies them to the case of business

	Per unit	Total
Actual sales	110,000 units	
Annual breakeven	65,965 units	
Annual capacity	150,000 units	
Sales revenue	$52.50	$5,775,000
Product cost	(31.20)	(3,432,000)
Variable expenses	(9.43)	(1,037,300)
Contribution margin	$11.87	$1,305,700
Fixed operating expenses		(783,000)
Operating profit		$522,700

FIGURE 13.4 *Improvement plan profit report.*

survival, of turning loss into profit. Managers use the tools under a great deal of pressure in these situations. There is no room for mistakes of analysis. The central importance of the contribution profit margin per unit come to the forefront again.

Not much was said about cash flow in this chapter, in order to focus on how to turn around performance from loss to profit. But it should be said in closing that a loss drains the company's cash balance or sucks up cash flow from depreciation capital recovery, in which case the money is not available for replacing or expanding fixed assets, or the company uses cash from the sale of fixed assets and other asset liquidations, or it is financed from additional borrowing or additional capital invested by owners. None of these ways of paying for a loss are sustainable for any period of time. A business may be able to get through one, two, or even three years of loss, but sooner or later it will hit the wall. Chapter 11 bankruptcy proceedings may be the result.

14

Service Businesses

Ask business consultants and I'd bet most of them would say that the first thing new clients tell them is: "Our business is different." Which is true, of course; every business is unique. On the other hand, all businesses draw on a common core of concepts, principles, and techniques. Take people. Every individual is different and unique. Yet basic principles of behavior and motivation apply to all of us. Take products. Breakfast cereals are different from computers, which are different from autos, and so on. Yet basic principles of marketing apply to all products.

DIFFERENT, YET THE SAME

Applying the basics is the really hard part, which managers are paid to do and do well. The manager must adapt the basic concepts and general principles to the specific circumstances of her or his particular business. Likewise, the examples used in previous chapters have to be adapted and modified to fit the characteristics and problems of each particular business.

This chapter applies the profit analysis tools and techniques discussed in previous chapters to *service* businesses. These business entities do not sell a product, or if a product is sold, it is quite incidental to the service. There are very interesting differences in profit and cash flow behavior between product and service businesses.

SERVICE BUSINESS EXAMPLE

Service businesses range from dry cleaners to film processors, from hotels to hospitals, from airlines to freight haulers, from CPAs to barbers, from rental firms to photocopying stores, and from movie theaters to amusement parks. The service sector is the largest general category in the economy—although extremely diverse.

Nevertheless, we can develop a general example to serve as a relevant framework for a large swath of service businesses. This benchmark example can be modified to fit the particular characteristics of any service business.

By now you should be fairly familiar with the product company example that has been used since the first chapter. Instead of introducing a new example, the product business example is converted to a service company example—to point out the basic differences between the two types of business. Figure 14.1 presents (one last time) the financial statements of the product company, but with certain accounts crossed out. These are the accounts you don't find in the financial statements of a service company.

 A service company does not sell a product, so the inventory account and the other inventory-dependent accounts are also crossed out. Accounts payable for inventory purchases in the balance sheet is crossed out. In the income statement, the cost-of-goods-sold expense account and the gross margin profit line are crossed out. And in the cash flow statement, the change in the inventory account is crossed out, and accounts payable would be affected also.

Figure 14.2 presents the company example for a service business that is used through the rest of the chapter. A service company does not have to carry an inventory, so it needs less capital. Accordingly, the debt and equity capital sources are decreased in the service company example. The notes in Figure 14.2 comment on the changes from the product company example. Bottom-line profit (net income) is a little higher due to the lower interest expense (a smaller amount of debt capital is used in the service company example). But the most important change involves the removal of the cost-of-goods-sold expense from the income statement.

Notice in Figure 14.2 that the cost-of-goods-sold expense and the gross profit (margin) lines are deleted, because the service company does not sell a product. In this example, the amount of the cost-of-goods-sold expense is transferred to the company's fixed operating expenses. All of the cost-of-goods-sold expense amount is moved down to the fixed operating expense account, which is the largest expense in the income statement.

Even though, by definition, a service business sells a service and not a product, an incidental product is often sold with the service. For example, a copying business (such as Kinko's) sells paper to its customers. Of course, the main thing sold is the copying service, not the paper. Likewise, airlines sell transportation, but also provide food and beverages in flight. Hotels are not really in the business of selling towels and ashtrays, but they know that many guests take these with them on the way out. True, many personal and professional service firms, such as architect and CPA firms, sell no product at all.

Some expenses of a service business vary with total sales *revenue*. Credit card discounts and sales commissions come to mind. Service businesses also have some expenses that vary with sales *volume*—for example, the number of passengers flown by an airline and the number of hotel guests would directly affect certain variable expenses of the business.

 Most service businesses are saddled with large fixed expenses. Service takes people; most service businesses have a large number of employees on fixed salaries or are paid fixed hourly rates based on a forty-hour work week. Also, many service businesses, such as movie theaters and airlines, have large capital investments in buildings and/or equipment, or they lease these assets at fixed rents. Thus, the example includes a fairly large amount of fixed expenses.

The company's two variable operating expenses are relatively small compared with its sales revenue, which is quite different from a product business. Notice that the contribution margin is a very large percentage of sales revenue.

$5,047,136 contribution margin ÷ $6,019,040 sales revenue
= 83.9% contribution margin percent

Assume the company's annual sales volume is 601,904 units of service, whatever these units might be—billable hours for a law firm, number of tickets for a movie theater, passenger seat miles for an airline, or so on. Thus, the company sells its service for $10.00 per unit and earns a contribution profit margin of $8.39 per unit.

TEN PERCENT CHANGES

What would be the profit impact from a 10 percent increase in sales price compared with a 10 percent increase in sales volume for the service business example? Figure 14.3 shows the answers to these questions. Notice that the sales volume factor has been added in this exhibit. For a long distance trucking company, for instance, it is ton-miles hauled. Most service businesses use a common denominator for sales volume activity.

Figure 14.3 demonstrates that a 10 percent sales volume change would increase contribution margin nearly as much as a 10 percent sales price change. (The sales-*volume*-driven expense would not increase with the higher sales price.) This comparison is in sharp contrast with product-based businesses, in which sales price changes cause much larger profit swings than sales volume changes.

For the service company, a sales price increase added on to its relatively high contribution profit mar-

INCOME STATEMENT FOR YEAR

> A service business does not sell products, so it has no cost-of-goods-sold expense and no gross profit line.

Sales revenue	$6,019,040
~~Cost of goods sold expense~~	~~(3,912,376)~~
~~Gross Margin~~	~~$2,106,664~~
Variable operating expenses:	
Sales-volume-driven	(370,000)
Sales-revenue-driven	(601,904)
Contribution margin	$1,134,760
Fixed expenses:	
Operating expenses	(551,384)
Depreciation expense	(112,792)

BALANCE SHEET AT END OF YEAR

> A service business does not have inventory or accounts payable from inventory purchases.

Operating assets

Cash	$256,663
Accounts receivable	578,754
~~Inventory~~	~~978,094~~
Prepaid expenses	$117,176
Property, plant, and equipment at original cost	1,986,450
Accumulated depreciation	(452,140)-
Total operating assets	$3,464,997

Operating liabilities

Accounts payable:	
~~Inventory~~	~~$300,952~~
Operating expenses	87,882
Total accounts payable	$388,834

CASH FLOW STATEMENT FOR YEAR

Operating activities

Net income	$259,996
Changes in operating cycle	
Assets and liabilities:	
Accounts receivable Increase	(96,404)
~~Inventory increase~~	~~(150,481)~~
Prepaid expenses increase	(24,341)
Accounts payable increase	58,318
Accrued expenses increase	40,283
Income tax payable increase	1,720
Operating cash flow	$89,091
Depreciation	112,792
Cash flow from profit	$201,883

FIGURE 14.1 Cross-outs for service business.

Operating earnings	$470,584
Interest expense	(76,650)
Earnings before income tax	$393,934
Income tax expense	(133,938)
Net income	$259,996

Accrued expenses:	
Operations	$175,764
Interest	12,775
Total accrued expenses	$188,539
Income tax payable	13,394
Total operating liabilities	$590,767
Net operating assets	$2,874,230

Sources of capital

Short-term notes payable	$425,000
Long-term notes payable	550,000
Total interest-bearing debt	$975,000
Capital stock	$725,000
Retained earnings	1,174,230
Total stockholders' equity	$1,899,230
Total debt and owners' equity	$2,874,230

Investing activities

Purchases of property, plant, and equipment	$(389,400)

Financing activities

Net increase in short-term debt	$50,000
Long-term borrowings	75,000
Capital stock issue	100,000
Cash dividends to stockholders	(93,750)
Increase (decrease) in cash during year	$(56,267)

FIGURE 14.1 (Continued)

INCOME STATEMENT FOR YEAR

Sales revenue	$6,019,040
Variable operating expenses:	
Sales-volume-driven	(370,000)
Sales-revenue-driven	(601,904)
Contribution margin	$5,047,136
Fixed expenses:	
Operating expenses	(4,463,760)
Depreciation expense	(112,792)
Operating earnings	$470,584
Interest expense	(32,000)
Earnings before income tax	$438,584

BALANCE SHEET AT END OF YEAR

Operating assets

Cash	$256,663
Accounts receivable	578,754
Prepaid expenses	418,128
Property, plant, and equipment at original cost	1,986,450
Accumulated depreciation	(452,140)
Total operating assets	$2,787,855

Operating liabilities

Accounts payable:	
Operating expenses	$313,596
Accrued expenses:	
Operations	627,192
Interest	5,333
Total accrued expenses	$632,525
Income tax payable	14,912

Changes (compared with Figure 14.1 for the product company example):

- There are no inventory and no accounts payable for inventory purchases. An incidental product may be sold with the service; the unused stock of these items is usually included in prepaid expenses, which is true in this example.

- In place of cost-of-goods-sold expense, service businesses typically have large fixed operating expenses. So all of the cost-of-goods-sold expense from the other example is moved to fixed operating expenses.

- Debt and equity capital is reduced because less capital is needed to finance the smaller amount of net operating assets.

FIGURE 14.2 *Example of service business income statement and balance sheet.*

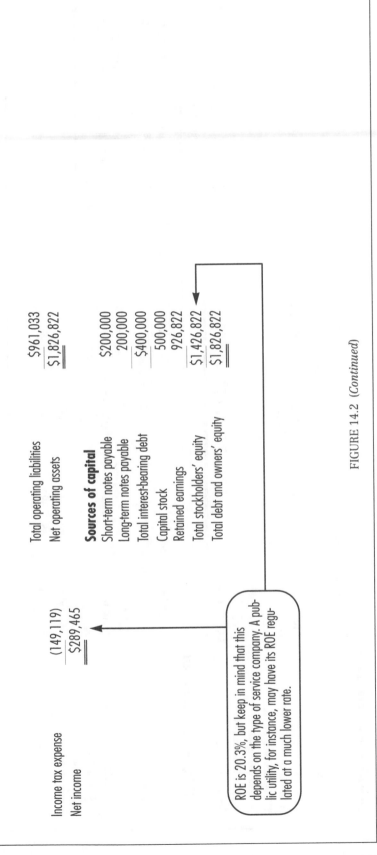

Income tax expense	(149,119)
Net income	$289,465

Total operating liabilities	$961,033
Net operating assets	$1,826,822
Sources of capital	
Short-term notes payable	$200,000
Long-term notes payable	200,000
Total interest-bearing debt	$400,000
Capital stock	500,000
Retained earnings	926,822
Total stockholders' equity	$1,426,822
Total debt and owners' equity	$1,826,822

ROE is 20.3%, but keep in mind that this depends on the type of service company. A public utility, for instance, may have its ROE regulated at a much lower rate.

FIGURE 14.2 (Continued)

10% higher sales price case

| | Baseline example | | Changes | |
| | 601,904 units | | | |
	Totals	**Per unit**	**Totals**	**Per unit**
Sales volume			*No change*	
Sales revenue	$6,019,040	$10.00	$601,904	$1.00
Variable operating expenses:				
Sales-volume-driven	370,000	0.61		
Sales-revenue-driven	601,904	1.00	60,190	0.10
Contribution margin	$5,047,136	$8.39	$541,714	$0.90

10% higher sales volume case

| | Baseline example | | Changes | |
| | 601,904 units | | +60,190 units | |
	Totals	**Per unit**	**Totals**	**Per unit**
Sales volume				
Sales revenue	$6,019,040	$10.00	$601,904	
Variable operating expenses:				
Sales-volume-driven	370,000	0.61	37,000	
Sales-revenue-driven	601,904	1.00	60,190	
Contribution margin	$5,047,136	$ 8.39	$504,714	

There is not much difference in the contribution margin increase between the two types of changes—the only difference is that the sales-volume-driven expenses increase in the sales volume increase case and don't in the sales price situation. The sales volume increase might require that fixed expenses be increased if the company were already operating at or close to its capacity.

FIGURE 14.3 *Comparison of 10 percent sales price increase versus 10 percent sales volume increase for service business.*

gin per unit does not carry as much impact as a sales price increase does for a product company, in which the contribution margin per unit is a much smaller base on which to add a sales price increase. In short, both a sales price and a sales volume change push up sales revenue 10 percent and both push up the sales-revenue-driven expenses 10 percent; the only difference is that one also pushes up sales-volume-driven expense and the other doesn't.

The other key issue for profit analysis concerns the large base of fixed operating expenses. Figure 14.3 assumes that the fixed costs remain constant for either alternative, although, as noted in the figure, if the company were already operating at or close to its capacity, then the fixed costs may have to be increased in the sales volume increase situation.

Fixed costs provide capacity, which refers to the total number of hours the employee workforce could turn out over the year for a personal service firm or the number of passenger miles that an airline could fly, etc. The main concern is whether capacity is being fully used or not. Some slack or unused capacity is normal, but when sales volume falls too far below capacity and management sees no way to rebuild the sales volume, the only option is to downsize the workforce.

CASH FLOW CHANGES

We should take a quick look here at the cash flow impacts of a 10 percent change—say the 10 percent sales price change. Figure 14.4 presents the impact on operating cash flow from profit (before depreciation) for the sales price increase. The change in net income equals the $541,714 increase in contribution margin (see Figure 14.3) less the 34 percent income tax of $184,183—so net income increases $357,531.

Accounts receivable would increase a fair amount and prepaid expenses not so much. These two negative changes on cash flow would be partially offset by increases in the two operating liabilities and the increase in income tax payable. Overall, the cash flow from profit increase is not too much less than the profit increase. Of course, we have not examined whether or not the company could pass along a 10 percent price increase without adversely affecting its demand. So, we next turn to the trade-off between sales price and sales volume.

TRADE-OFF DECISIONS: BE CAREFUL

Suppose the service company is considering a 10 percent sales price *decrease*. The business predicts that sales volume would increase at least 10 percent, perhaps more. We have already analyzed this

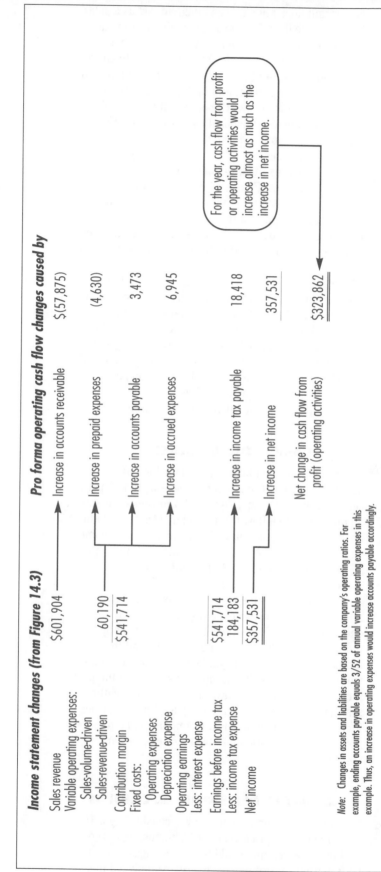

Income statement changes (from Figure 14.3)

Sales revenue	$601,904
Variable operating expenses:	
Sales-volume-driven	
Sales-revenue-driven	60,190
Contribution margin	$541,714
Fixed costs:	
Operating expenses	
Depreciation expense	
Operating earnings	
Less: interest expense	
Earnings before income tax	$541,714
Less: income tax expense	184,183
Net income	$357,531

Pro forma operating cash flow changes caused by

Increase in accounts receivable	$(57,875)
Increase in prepaid expenses	(4,630)
Increase in accounts payable	3,473
Increase in accrued expenses	6,945
Increase in income tax payable	18,418
Increase in net income	357,531
Net change in cash flow from profit (operating activities)	$323,862

> For the year, cash flow from profit or operating activities would increase almost as much as the increase in net income.

Note: Changes in assets and liabilities are based on the company's operating ratios. For example, ending accounts payable equals 3/52 of annual variable operating expenses in this example. Thus, an increase in operating expenses would increase accounts payable accordingly.

FIGURE 14.4 *Cash flow impacts of 10 percent higher sales price for service business.*

trade-off situation for a product business (see Chapter 11). The result there was a very large *decrease* in profit. Is the same true for a service business? Figure 14.5 shows that the results for the service are not nearly as bad as the steep decline in the product company case. The service company still would make a profit, but it would be using more of its capacity (workforce) to make less money—not a good trade-off.

Contribution margin would decrease $91,171, which is only a 1.8 percent drop. But the impact on the bottom line would be a decrease of $60,173 after tax, which would be a 20.8 percent drop. This is much less compared with the huge decreases that occur in the product company examples. The main reason for the much smaller percentage of profit decrease is that the contribution margin per unit would not take such a big hit as compared with the product company cases. The unit contribution margin here drops $.90, or 10.7 percent. This is bad; the increase in sales volume does not quite make up for this decline in the unit contribution margin.

It bears repeating here that whenever sales volume increases, management should take a close look at the company's fixed expenses to make certain that they would not have to be increased to provide for the higher sales volume.

What about the opposite 10 percent trade-off? Suppose the sales price were increased 10 percent, causing only a 10 percent decrease in sales volume. For product businesses, this trade-off increases profit by a large percentage. But not for service companies. The gain in profit can be determined by looking at Figure 14.5 again. Sales revenue would *decrease* $60,190, the same as shown in Figure 14.5. (Selling 90 units at $110 gives the same result as selling 110 units at $90; either way, your total sales revenue is $9,900 or 1 percent less than selling 100 units at $100 per unit.)

So the sales-revenue-driven expenses would decrease $6,019 because they equal 10.0 percent of sales revenue in this company example. And the sales-volume-driven expenses would decrease by 10.0 percent, or $37,000. But these two expense decreases are not enough to offset the sales revenue decrease. The company would give up some contribution margin, and its bottom-line profit would suffer.

Boosting sales price 10 percent and taking 10 percent less sales volume is not a smart move, unless the company could reduce its fixed expenses substantially at the lower sales volume. As mentioned before, downsizing an established business is very difficult, and giving up market share goes against the grain of most managers.

END POINT

In many ways, the financial statements of service businesses are not all that different from those of product

Actual income statement (see Figure 14.2)

Sales volume = 601,904 units

	Per unit	Totals
Sales revenue	$10.00	$6,019,040
Variable operating expenses:		
Sales-volume-driven	0.61	370,000
Sales-revenue-driven	1.00	601,904
Contribution margin	$8.39	$5,047,136
Fixed costs:		
Operating expenses		4,463,760
Depreciation expense		112,792
Operating earnings		$ 470,584
Less: interest expense		32,000
Earnings before income tax		$ 438,584
Less: income tax expense		149,119
Net income		$ 289,465

Pro forma changes caused by 10% lower sales price and 10% higher volume

+60,190 units

Per unit	Totals
$(1.00)	$(60,190)
	37,000
(0.10)	(6,019)
$(0.90)	$(91,171)
	$(91,171)
	(30,998)
	$(60,173)

−1.8%

−20.8%

The company would suffer only a slight decrease in its total contribution margin, but the dollar amount of the decrease is a large percentage of operating earnings, so bottom-line net income decreases over 20%.

FIGURE 14.5 Profit impact of 10 percent lower sales price yielding 10 percent higher sales volume for service business.

companies—although there are some differences, of course. There is no cost-of-goods-sold expense in the income statement and no inventory or accounts payable for inventory purchases in the balance sheet for service businesses. Some service businesses, such as transportation companies and gas and electricity utilities, are very capital intensive. Other service companies, including professional service firms such as CPAs and lawyers, need relatively few long-term operating assets.

The same tools of analysis are useful for both types of business. This chapter demonstrates how to use the profit analysis and cash flow tools for service businesses. The tools for evaluating business investment performance, as well as the other tools discussed in the book, also are used by service businesses.

15

Sales Mix and Cost Allocation

This chapter explores two different issues confronting managers, which on the surface may seem unrelated but are, in fact, traveling companions. Tools for analyzing *sales mix* are explained first. Sales mix refers to the relative proportions or the comparative weights of different products in the total sales of the business. You probably have observed that most businesses sell a broad range and diversity of products. The central marketing strategy of business is to determine the optimal sales mix that maximizes profit. Over time, however, the sales mix of a business is almost certain to change, and managers should understand the profit impact of these changes.

Any discussion of sales mix is incomplete without discussing fixed cost allocation. Typically, two or more products share a common base of fixed expenses. For instance, consider the sales of a department store in one building. There are many building occupancy expenses, including rent (or depreciation), utilities, property taxes, fire and hazard insurance, and so on. All products sold in the store benefit from the fixed expenses. Or consider a sales territory managed by a sales manager whose salary and other office costs cover all the products sold in the territory. Should such fixed expenses be allocated among the different products?

Allocation may appear to be logical. The more basic question is whether or not allocation really helps management decision making and control. Allocation is a controversial issue, especially where product lines (or other product groupings) are organized as separate profit centers, for which the managers have profit responsibility and whose compensation may depend (in part at least) on the profit performance of the organizational unit.

The topics of sales mix and cost allocation fit together naturally. If a company sold only one product, there would be no cost allocation problems between products—although there may be common costs extending over two or more separate sales regions (territories). The main concern in the following discussion is the allocation of fixed expenses among products.

SALES MIX ANALYSIS

Suppose you're the general manager of a major division, one of the several autonomous profit centers in the organization. Your division sells one product line, consisting of four products sold under the company's label plus one product sold as a generic (no label) product to a supermarket chain. Your profit report for the most recent year is presented in Figure 15.1.

The format of the profit report is different from that of the income statement presented earlier in the book; it starts with unit sales prices, then deducts unit product costs and unit variable expenses to determine unit contribution profit margins. Recall that contribution margin is profit before fixed operating expenses (and before interest and income tax). A profit report such as that shown in Figure 15.1 that displays this vital information is the basic tool of analysis for managers. In the report, notice that fixed expenses are not allocated among the five products; allocation methods are discussed later.

All five products are earning a contribution margin, though these unit profit margins vary in dollar amount and by percent of sales price across the five products. The premier product has the highest percent of profit margin (35 percent), as well as the highest dollar amount of profit margin per unit ($33.25). You might notice that the generic model has a higher percentage of contribution profit margin and generates more total contribution margin than the economy model.

Production costs are cut to the bone on the generic product, and no advertising or sales promotion of any type is done on the product—the variable expenses are mainly delivery costs. Product cost is highest for the premier product because the best raw materials are used and additional labor time is required to make its quality top of the line. Also, variable advertising and sales promotion costs are very heavy for this product; variable expenses are 22 percent of sales price for this product: $21.15 variable expenses ÷ $95.00 sales price = 22%.

The economy model accounts for 18 percent of sales volume but only 11 percent of total contribution margin. The premier model accounts for only 9 percent of sales volume but yields 21 percent of total contribution margin. Which brings up the very important issue of what is the best, or optimal, sales mix. The comparative information, product by product, presented in Figure 15.1 is very important for marketing decision

Products

	Generic	Economy	Standard	Deluxe	Premier	Product line totals — Units	Product line totals — Dollars
Sales price	$28.25	$42.50	$60.00	$75.00	$95.00		$5,261,000
Product cost	(20.05)	(26.65)	(32.00)	(36.00)	(40.60)		(2,886,500)
Variable expenses	(1.13)	(6.80)	(11.80)	(16.50)	(21.15)		(922,390)
Unit contribution profit margin	$7.07	$9.05	$16.20	$22.50	$33.25		
% of sales price	25%	21%	27%	30%	35%		
Sales volume in units	28,000	18,000	35,000	10,000	9,000	100,000	
% of total sales volume	28%	18%	35%	10%	9%	100%	
Total contribution margin	$197,960	$162,900	$567,000	$225,000	$299,250		$1,452,110
% of total contribution margin	14%	11%	39%	15%	21%	100%	
Fixed expenses	?	?	?	?	?		(766,000)
Operating profit	?	?	?	?	?		$686,110

The question is whether or not to allocate the total fixed expenses among the five products, to determine the operating profit attributable to each product line.

FIGURE 15.1 Product line profit report.

167

analysis. Shifts in sales mix and trade-offs among the products are important to understand.

The marketing strategy of many businesses is to encourage their customers to trade up, or move up to the higher-priced items in their product lines. As a rule, higher-priced products have higher unit contribution profit margins. This general rule applies mainly for mature products, which are those products in the middle age or old phases of their life cycles.

Newer products in the infant and adolescent stages of their life cycles often have a competitive advantage. During the early phases of their life cycles, new products may enjoy high contribution profit margins until competition catches up and forces sales price and/or sales volume down. In fact, the CEO of Eastman Kodak made this very point a few years ago in an article in the *New York Times*.

Compare two of the company's products, the standard versus the deluxe. You make $6.30 higher unit contribution profit margin on the deluxe product: $22.50 deluxe – $16.20 standard = $6.30. Giving up one unit of standard in trade-off for one unit of deluxe would increase total contribution margin, without any change in total fixed expenses. Marketing strategies should be based on contribution profit margin information such as that presented in the product line profit report (Figure 15.1).

The position of the economy model is interesting because its contribution profit margin is by far the lowest of the company-label models and not that much more than the generic model. The economy model may be in the nature of a loss leader or, more accurately, a minimum profit leader—a product you don't make much margin on but one necessary to get the attention of customers, and which serves as a springboard or stepping-stone for customers to trade up to higher-priced products.

However, the opposite may happen. In tough times, many customers may *trade down* from higher-priced models and buy products that yield lower profit margins. Large numbers of customers may trade down to the standard or the economy models. Dealing with this downshifting is a challenging marketing problem. Perhaps the sales prices on the lower-end products could be raised to increase their contribution profit margins per unit; perhaps not.

Should you be making and selling the generic product? On the one hand, this product brings in 28 percent of your total sales volume and 14 percent of total contribution margin. On the other hand, these units may be taking sales away from your other four products—though this is hard to know for sure. This question has to be answered by market research.

If the generic product were not available in super-markets, would these customers buy one of your other models? If all these customers would buy the economy model, you would be better off; you'd be giving up sales on which you make a unit contribution profit margin of $7.07 for replacement sales on which you would earn $9.05, or almost $2.00 more per unit. If customers shifted up to the standard or higher models, you would be ahead that much more, though it would seem that customers who buy generic products are not the likely type to trade up.

Many different marketing questions can be raised. Indeed, the job of the manager is to consider the whole range of marketing strategies, including the positioning of each product, setting sales prices, the most effective means of advertising, and so on. Deciding sales strategy requires information on contribution profit margins and sales mix such as presented in Figure 15.1. The exhibit is a good tool of analysis for making marketing decisions regarding the optimal sales mix.

 FIXED EXPENSES: ALLOCATE OR NOT?

When selling two or more products, inevitably there are fixed operating expenses that cannot be directly matched or coupled with the sales of each product. The unavoidable question is whether or not to allocate the total fixed operating expenses among the products. Refer to Figure 15.1 again; notice that fixed expenses are not allocated. Should these fixed expenses be distributed among the five different products in some manner?

Fixed expenses generally fall into two broad categories: (1) sales and marketing expenses and (2) general and administrative expenses. Most fixed operating expenses are *indirect;* the expenses cannot be directly associated with particular products. The example here assumes there are no direct fixed expenses for any of the products. On the other hand, there could be some direct fixed expenses.

For example, an advertising campaign may feature only one product. Suppose you bought a one-time insertion in the *Wall Street Journal* for the premier product. The cost of this one-time ad should be deducted from the total contribution margin of the premier product as a direct fixed expense. Typically, however, most fixed expenses are indirect; they cannot be directly matched to any one product.

Indirect fixed expenses *can* be allocated to products, although the purposes and methods of allocation are open to much debate and difference of opinion. For instance, allocation could be done on the basis of sales volume, which means that each unit sold would be assigned an equal amount of the total fixed expense; on the basis of sales revenue, which means that each dollar of sales revenue would be assigned an equal amount of total fixed expense; or according to some more complex formula.

Figure 15.2 shows two alternative income statements for the product line example: one in which total fixed expenses are allocated on the basis of sales volume and the second on the basis of sales revenue of each product. Total operating profit for the entire product line is the same for both, but the operating profit reported for each product differs between the two allocation methods.

Both sales volume and sales revenue for allocating fixed costs have obvious shortcomings and both methods are rather arbitrary. Either method rests on a dubious premise: either that each and every unit has the same fixed cost or each and every sales revenue dollar has the same fixed cost. Recent attention has been focused on the theory of cost drivers to allocate fixed expenses, which goes under the rubric of *activity-based costing* (ABC). This approach should really be called activity-based cost allocation, because it's a method to allocate indirect costs to products.

The ABC tool of analysis challenges the premise that fixed expenses are truly and completely indirect. Total fixed expenses are subdivided into separate cost pools; a separate cost pool is determined for each basic *activity* or support service. Instead of lumping all fixed costs into one conglomerate pool of "general" support, each basic type of support activity is identified with its own separate cost pool. Each product is then analyzed to determine and measure the usage the product makes of each activity for which separate fixed expense pools are established.

In this example, all products except the generic model are advertised, and all advertising is done through the advertising department of the corporation. The advertising department is defined as one separate fixed cost pool and its activity is measured according to some common denominator of activity, such as number of ad pages run in the print media (newspapers and magazines). Each product is allocated its share of the total advertising department's cost pool based on how many ad pages were run for each product. Advertising is the cost driver, the activity that causes the cost. The number of ad pages is the measure of this activity that is used to allocate the cost among the products advertised.

Alternatively, different types of advertising (print versus electronic media, for example) could be identified and each product line could be charged with its share of the advertising department's cost based on two separate cost driver measures: one for the number of print media pages and a second for the number of minutes on television or radio.

Method A—fixed expenses allocated on basis of sales volume

	Generic	Economy	Standard	Deluxe	Premier	Totals
Sales revenue	$791,000	$765,000	$2,100,000	$750,000	$855,000	$5,261,000
Cost-of-goods-sold expense	(561,400)	(479,700)	(1,120,000)	(360,000)	(365,400)	(2,886,500)
Gross margin	$229,600	$285,300	$980,000	$390,000	$489,600	$2,374,500
Variable expenses	(31,640)	(122,400)	(413,000)	(165,000)	(190,350)	(922,390)
Contribution margin	$197,960	$162,900	$567,000	$225,000	$299,250	$1,452,110
Fixed expenses—allocated	(214,480)	(137,880)	(268,100)	(76,600)	(68,940)	(766,000)
Operating profit (loss)	$(16,520)	$25,020	$298,900	$148,400	$230,310	$686,110

Method B—fixed expenses allocated on basis of sales revenue

	Generic	Economy	Standard	Deluxe	Premier	Totals
Sales revenue	$791,000	$765,000	$2,100,000	$750,000	$855,000	$5,261,000
Cost-of-goods-sold expense	(561,400)	(479,700)	(1,120,000)	(360,000)	(365,400)	(2,886,500)
Gross margin	$229,600	$285,300	$980,000	$390,000	$489,600	$2,374,500
Variable expenses	(31,640)	(122,400)	(413,000)	(165,000)	(190,350)	(922,390)
Contribution margin	$197,960	$162,900	$567,000	$225,000	$299,250	$1,452,110
Fixed expenses—allocated	(115,169)	(111,384)	(305,759)	(109,200)	(124,488)	(766,000)
Operating profit	$82,791	$51,516	$261,241	$115,800	$174,762	$686,110
Difference (B − A)	+$99,311	+$26,496	$(37,659)	$(32,600)	$(55,548)	$0

No change.

Additional operating profit due to alternative method of allocating fixed expenses.

Operating profit taken away from the products due to alternative method of allocating fixed expenses.

FIGURE 15.2 Two methods of allocating fixed expenses.

Some fixed expenses are quite indirect and far removed from particular products, such as the accounting department, legal department, the annual CPA audit fee, cost of security guards, and general liability insurance. The cost driver concept would get stretched to its limit for certain fixed expenses. Also, the number of separate activities, each with its own expense pool, can get out of hand. Three to five, perhaps even seven to ten, separate cost drivers for fixed cost allocation may be understandable and feasible, but there is a limit.

The more fundamental management question is whether any allocation scheme is worth the effort. What's the purpose? Does allocation help decision making? The basic management purpose should not be to find the "true" operating profit for each product or other sales revenue source. The fundamental question is whether management is making optimal use of the resources and potential provided by the company's fixed operating expenses.

The bottom line is finding which sales mix maximizes total contribution margin. Allocation of indirect fixed expenses in and of itself doesn't help to do this. Indirect fixed expenses may have to be allocated for legal or contract purposes; if so, the method(s) for such allocation should be spelled out in advance rather than waiting until after the fact to select the allocation rationale.

Sometimes a business may allocate fixed expenses to minimize the *apparent* operating profit on a product. I was hired to be an expert witness for the plaintiff in a patent infringement lawsuit against a well-known corporation. The defendant had already lost in the first stage; it had been found guilty of patent infringement. For three years the defendant corporation had manufactured and sold a product, the patent of which the plaintiff owned, without compensating the plaintiff. The second stage was to assess the amount of damages to be awarded to the plaintiff.

The plaintiff was suing for recovery of the profit made by the defendant corporation on sales of the product. The defendant allocated every indirect fixed cost it could think of to the product—including part of the CEO's annual salary—to minimize the profit that was allegedly earned from sales of the product. The jury threw out this heavy-handed allocation and awarded $16 million to the plaintiff.

FIXED MANUFACTURING OVERHEAD COST ALLOCATION

There is one area in which fixed costs must be allocated among different products; nonallocation is not an option. Fixed *manufacturing* overhead (indirect production) costs must be allocated in some manner among the different products manufactured during the period. Manufacturing accounting procedures and problems are discussed in Chapter 17. A very brief summary is presented here, focusing mainly on the cost allocation aspect.

The manufacturer keeps detailed records to accumulate direct materials costs and direct labor costs, from the beginning to the end of the production process, for each and every product. This requires an enormous amount of detailed and meticulous bookkeeping for the direct costs of each product or each batch (lot) of products. For example, the assembly of automobiles is estimated to require 10,000 to 15,000 different parts; a brewery takes over 1,000 separate steps to make a barrel of beer. Direct costs of raw materials and labor are not a significant accounting problem, though they do put heavy demands on the company's accounting system. Manufacturing overhead costs are another matter entirely.

By their very nature, overhead costs are *nondirect* costs. These costs cannot be directly connected with any particular batch of products, workstation, or production department. Consider the annual salary of the production vice president or the annual real estate property tax on the company's production land and building. Overhead costs, therefore, have to be *allocated* or *apportioned* in some manner to determine the full and complete manufacturing cost per unit.

Traditionally, manufacturers used a *common denominator* of production activity for the purpose of allocating manufacturing overhead costs to different products. Direct labor hours were a common denominator because all products required direct labor. Thus, each product was charged for manufacturing overhead costs based on the burden rate per direct labor hour. At a recent meeting in Chicago, a partner with Arthur Andersen, the international accounting and consulting firm, cited studies and said from his own experience that, because of automation, direct labor is often only 15 percent or less of total manufacturing cost in many industries.

Many other studies make the same observation. The Arthur Andersen partner observed that direct materials often are 50 percent or more of total product cost. Perhaps some measure of materials, such as weight or size, would be a better common denominator for manufacturing fixed overhead cost allocation. Alternatively, two or more burden rates may be developed for allocating manufacturing overhead costs—each for a separate type or pool of overhead costs.

Activity-based costing (cost allocation) methods are getting a lot of attention today as a better way to allocate fixed manufacturing overhead costs. The basic support activities necessary to manufacture products are carefully identified, and separate fixed manufacturing overhead cost pools are determined for each activity.

As previously discussed for other fixed expenses, the key step is to identify the major categories of support activity for carrying on the production process. The costs for each of these basic activities are accumulated in a separate pool. Burden rates are computed for each of these cost pools based on the most relevant measure of activity of the cost pool. In this way, the total cost of the activity is allocated to products on the basis of how much of the total activity each product uses.

For example, the manufacture of many products starts with engineering design and development of product specifications. The company would measure how much of the engineering department's time and effort is required for each product and allocate the cost of the department on this basis.

Traditional cost accounting methods threw in the engineering department's cost with many other service department costs, including such diverse departments as purchasing, plant security, and plant maintenance. A very broad-based common denominator (such as direct labor hours) was used to allocate the total pool of fixed overhead costs among the company's several products. ABC methods certainly appear to be more accurate compared with traditional gross-level methods based on direct labor hours. Traditional cost accounting followed the more simplistic approach of using one burden rate to make a swath across all products.

It is now believed by many management accounting theorists that the traditional overhead cost allocation process has led to misleading unit product costs.* It's a little too early, in my opinion, to say with any certainty whether traditional cost accounting allocation methods have been all that misleading or not. There was a fairly enthusiastic initial reception to this book, but time will tell. Everyone wants to believe that there is a better method of allocation—one that is more "realistic" and more "relevant."

In any case, no matter which basis and method is used to allocate manufacturing overhead costs, the manager should be aware that all allocation methods are arbitrary—it's just a matter of degree. Some products are favored and others penalized, no matter which allocation method is used. Managers should take manufacturing overhead burden rates with a grain of salt. One product can be made to look less profitable (or even unprofitable) or more profitable merely by changing the method of allocating fixed manufacturing overhead costs.

* See, for example, Johnson and Kaplan, *Relevance Lost: The Rise and Fall Of Management Accounting* (Boston: Harvard Business School Press, 1987).

END POINT

Sales mix analysis is very important in profit management. Different products have different contribution profit margins. The manager should carefully consider whether the present mix of products being sold can be improved by strategic trade-offs among the products, especially by moving customers from lower-margin to higher-margin products. Also, the manager should know the profit impact of customers moving down the product line.

Multiple products bring with them an unavoidable side effect: fixed expenses that cannot be directly associated or matched with individual products. These fixed expenses benefit a broad range or line of products, but the costs are indirect to any one of the products. The question facing management is whether or not to allocate the common fixed expenses among the products to determine a measure of operating profit from each product.

It's questionable whether allocation would help to make better decisions or develop a better marketing strategy. The key to this sort of analysis is to focus on contribution profit margins before fixed expenses. But allocation may be done for other purposes. Allocation methods are arbitrary and usually have to be taken with skepticism, although the newer method called activity-based costing (ABC) overcomes some of the limits of traditional allocation methods.

Manufacturers have no choice regarding their fixed manufacturing overhead costs: These costs must be allocated to the products produced during the period according to some systematic method to determine the full product cost per unit, which is needed for inventory cost valuation and to measure the cost-of-goods-sold expense. Chapter 17 discusses manufacturing accounting.

PART 3

Management Control

16

Management Control and Budgeting

Decision making lays down a plan of action for accomplishing the company's objectives. Achieving the objectives requires *management control*. In the broadest sense, management control refers to everything managers do in moving the business toward its objectives. Decisions start things in motion, and then control brings things to a successful conclusion. Good decisions with bad control can turn out just as disastrously as making bad decisions in the first place. Good tools for decision-making analysis must be complemented with good tools of control.

THRUST OF MANAGEMENT CONTROL: FOLLOW-THROUGH ON DECISIONS

Management control is both preventive and positive in nature. Managers have to prevent, or at least minimize, wrong things from happening. Murphy's Law is all too true; if something can go wrong it will. And managers have to make sure right things are happening and happening on time. Managers shouldn't be only reactive to problems; they must also be proactive and push things along in the right direction. Management control is not just the absence of problems but the presence of actions to achieve the goals and objectives of the business.

One of the best definitions of management control I've heard is by a former student. I asked the class for a good but concise definition. He defined management control in two words: "watching everything." This pithy definition captures the essence of it, I think. There's no generally accepted conceptual model or official definition of management control. All management theorists include control in their conceptual scheme, but there's little consensus on exact definitions of control.

Most definitions of management control emphasize the need for feedback information on actual performance that is compared against goals, objectives, targets, budgets, and plans to detect any deviations and variances, so that managers can take corrective action to bring performance back on course.

Management control is an information-dependent process, that's for sure. Clearly, managers need actual performance information reported to them on a timely basis. In short, feedback information is the main tool of management control. Managers need this information quickly, and, in this respect, time is a tool of control also. Information received too late can result in costly delays before problems are corrected.

MANAGEMENT CONTROL INFORMATION

Figure 16.1 modifies Figure 1.1, which presents an overview of the accounting system. The external financial reporting and tax functions of accounting are not shown in Figure 16.1, in order to take a closer look at the internal flow of information to managers.

Generally, management control information consists of three types: (1) periodic comprehensive financial statements (including supporting schedules) that are designed for control purposes, (2) periodic control reports more limited in scope than complete financial statements, and (3) specific focus or key item information.

Management control information can be good news or bad news (see Figure 16.1). Good news is when actual performance is going according to plan. Management's job is to keep things moving in this direction. Management control information usually reveals bad news as well—problems that have come up and unsatisfactory performance areas that need attention. Not all problems come to the manager's attention through the accounting system, of course.

Managers draw on a very broad range of information sources for their overall control purposes. For example, managers monitor customer satisfaction, employee absenteeism and morale, production schedules, and quality control inspection results. Managers listen to customers' complaints, shop the competition, and may even decide that some industrial intelligence and espionage is necessary to get information about the competition. But the accounting system is one of the most important sources for control information.

Managers are primarily concerned with problems that directly impact on the financial performance of the business, such as sales quotas not being met, sales prices being discounted lower than predicted, product costs higher than expected, expenses running over budget, and cash flow running slower than planned. Or

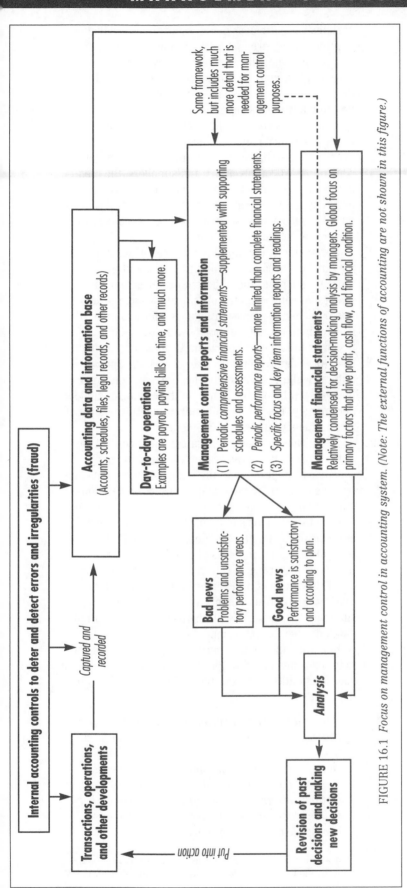

FIGURE 16.1 *Focus on management control in accounting system.* (*Note: The external functions of accounting are not shown in this figure.*)

Internal accounting controls to deter and detect errors and irregularities (fraud)

Accounting data and information base
(Accounts, schedules, files, legal records, and other records)

Day-to-day operations
Examples are payroll, paying bills on time, and much more.

Management control reports and information
(1) Periodic *comprehensive financial statements*—supplemented with supporting schedules and assessments.
(2) Periodic *performance reports*—more limited than complete financial statements.
(3) *Specific focus* and *key item* information reports and readings.

Management financial statements
Relatively condensed for decision-making analysis by managers. Global focus on primary factors that drive profit, cash flow, and financial condition.

Same framework, but includes much more detail that is needed for management control purposes.

Bad news
Problems and unsatisfactory performance areas.

Good news
Performance is satisfactory and according to plan.

Analysis

Revision of past decisions and making new decisions

Put into action

Transactions, operations, and other developments

Captured and recorded

perhaps sales are over quota, sales prices are higher than predicted, product costs are lower than expected, and so on. Even when things are moving along very close to plan, managers need control reports to inform them of this. In short, managers need control information to know what's going on.

Control reports should be designed to fit the specific areas of authority and responsibility of individual managers. The purchasing (procurement) manager gets control reports on inventory and suppliers, the credit manager gets control reports on accounts receivable and customers, the sales manager gets control reports on sales and salespersons, and so on. These periodic control reports are detail rich.

For example, the monthly sales report for a territory may include breakdowns on hundreds, and perhaps more than a thousand, different products and customers. Moving up in the organization—to a product line manager or a division manager, for example—the span of management authority and responsibility becomes broader and broader. At the top management level (president/chief executive officer), the span of authority and responsibility encompasses the whole business. At the higher rungs on the organizational ladder, managers need control information in the form of comprehensive financial statements.

Financial statements for management control have much more detail and are supplemented by many schedules compared with the financial statements illustrated earlier in the book that are used for decision-making purposes. For example, management control financial statements should include detailed schedules of receivables that are past due, inventory that has been in stock too long, lists of products that have unusually high rates of return by customers, which expenses are most over budget, and so on. Decision-making financial statements are more like executive summaries, compared with the enormous amount of detail needed for management control.

In addition to regular periodic reports, a manager may select one or a few specific factors or key items for special attention. An example of this approach is the following:*

> *During a recent cost-cutting drive, James Orr, chairman and chief executive of Anima Corp., an insurer in Portland, Maine, asked for a daily count on the number of company employees. He was told he couldn't get it. Some data were kept by divisions and so were hard to gather together in one place. Some were in a payroll data base accessible only to programmers.*

* William M. Bulkeley, "Special Systems Make Computing Less Traumatic for Top Executives," *The Wall Street Journal* (June 20, 1988), p. 17.

> *Mr. Orr persisted, however, and now the
> answer is at his fingertips whenever he wants it:
> A specially designed executive information sys-
> tem links personnel data to a personal computer
> in Mr. Orr's office. "Management knows I'm
> watching the count very closely," he says.
> "Believe me, they don't add staff carelessly."*

It's a good idea to identify the few relative critical success factors and keep a close and constant watch on
them. Knowing what these factors are is one secret of
good management. Product quality is almost always
one such key success factor.

By their very nature, management control reports
are confidential and are not discussed outside the company. Also, management control reports are quite sensitive because they disclose "mistakes" of decisions and
how decisions went wrong. Often, unexpected and
unpredictable developments upset the applecart of
good decisions. Of course, some degree of inherent
uncertainty surrounds all business decisions. Nevertheless, management control reports do have a strong element of passing judgment on the manager's savvy and
ability to make good predictions.

THE FOUNDATION: INTERNAL ACCOUNTING CONTROLS

You might have noticed one other addition at the top in
Figure 16.1, which was not mentioned until now. Good
management control information depends on good
internal accounting controls. The reliability of the
accounting system that supplies the essential information for management control rests in large measure on
the internal controls built into the system and how well
these controls are working. Specific forms are used and
procedures are enforced to eliminate or at least minimize errors in capturing, processing, storing, and
retrieving the large amount of detailed data and information needed to run a business. Forms and procedures are not too popular, but without them an
organization couldn't function.

Internal accounting controls are also designed to
protect against *theft* and *fraud* by employees, suppliers,
customers, and managers themselves. Unfortunately,
my father-in-law was right. He told me many years ago
that, based on his experience, "there's a little bit of larceny in everyone's heart." He could have added that
there's a lot of larceny in the hearts of a few.

It's an unpleasant fact of business life that some customers will shoplift, some vendors will overcharge or
short-count on deliveries, some employees will embez-
zle or steal assets, and some managers will commit
fraud against the business or take personal advantage
of their position of authority in the business. The finan-

cial press reports instances of fraud and corruption with alarming frequency.

The ideal internal accounting control is one that deters and detects, and is cost effective. Some controls may be simply too costly to justify, such as a body search of every employee on exit from work—though diamond and gold mines take these precautions, I hear, and a recent article in the *New York Times* on General Electric indicated that some of its employees must go through a search on exit. Having an audit by an independent CPA firm is one tool of control. Based on their audit, the CPA firm expresses an opinion on the external financial report of the business.* However, the CPA audit goes only so far in detecting errors and irregularities (fraud).

Managers should understand the limits of audits by CPAs in this regard. Auditors are responsible for discovering material errors and fraud (called "irregularities" in the official pronouncement). However, it simply is not cost effective to have the outside auditors do a thorough and exhaustive examination that would catch all errors and irregularities. It would take too long and cost too much. The first line of defense is the internal accounting controls of the business.

Recently, the national organization of CPAs, the American Institute of Certified Public Accountants (AICPA), released an important guide dealing with internal accounting controls.† It's an excellent summary and reflects the long experience of CPAs in auditing a wide range of businesses. The AICPA's guidelines are an excellent checklist for the types of internal accounting controls that a business should establish and enforce with due diligence.

THE CASH FLOW STATEMENT: A TOOL FOR FRAUD DETECTION

The cash flow statement is a good tool for the detection of possible fraud, a tool that evidently is overlooked by most managers. Most fraud schemes and scams go after money. Willie Sutton said when asked why he robbed banks, "Because that's where the money is." To get to the money and to conceal the fraud as long as possible, an asset or a liability—most often accounts receivable, inventory, and sometimes accounts payable (other assets and liabilities may be involved also)—has to be manipulated and misstated by the perpetrator.

* See Chapter 18 in my book, *How to Read a Financial Report*, 4th ed. (New York: John Wiley & Sons, 1994), which explains audits of external financial reports by independent CPAs.
† "Consideration of the Internal Control Structure in a Financial Statement Audit," Statement on Auditing Standards No. 55, (April 1988), issued by the Auditing Standards Board, American Institute of Certified Public Accountants, Inc.; New York.

For example, suppose an employee or midlevel manager steals inventory and sells the products for cash, which goes into his or her pocket. A good management control reporting system keeps a very close watch on inventory levels and cost-of-goods-sold expense ratios. If a material amount of inventory is stolen, the inventory shrinkage number and/or profit margin figures should sound alarms. The sophisticated thief realizes this and will cover up the missing inventory. Indeed, this is exactly what was done in many fraud cases.

The company's internal controls were not effective in preventing the cover-up; the accounting system reported inventory that, in fact, was not there. Thus, inventory showed a larger increase (or a smaller decrease) than it should have. Recall that an increase in inventory has a negative impact on cash flow from profit (see Chapter 4). You might think that managers would be alert to any inventory increases. But in the majority of fraud cases, managers did not pursue the reasons for the inventory increase. If they had, they might have discovered the inventory theft.

In similar fashion, fraud may involve taking money out of collections on accounts receivable, which is covered up by overstating the accounts receivable account. Other fraud schemes may use accounts payable to conceal the fraud. Managers should keep in mind that the reported profit performance of the business is overstated as the result of undiscovered fraud. This is terribly embarrassing when it is discovered and financial statements from prior periods have to be revised and restated. But fraud can be disastrous. Furthermore, it may lead to firing the executive who failed to discover the theft or fraud; one responsibility of managers is to prevent fraud by subordinates and to devise ways and means of making certain that no fraud is going on.

In brief, managers should keep alert to increases in accounts receivable and inventory, as well as accounts payable, that are reported in the cash flow statement. Not only do these increases cause negative cash flow effects, such increases could signal a suspicious change that is not consistent with changes in sales activity and other facts and information known to the manager.

GUIDELINES FOR MANAGEMENT CONTROL REPORTING

Need for Comparative Reports

More than anything else, management control is directed towards achieving profit goals and meeting the other financial objectives of the business. Goals and objectives are not established in a vacuum. Prior period performance is one framework for comparison. Ideally, however, the business should adopt goals and objectives for improvement that are put into a framework of clear-cut benchmarks and standards that actual performance is compared against. Budgeting, which is discussed later in this chapter, is one way of doing this.

In practice, many companies simply compare actual performance this period against last period. This is certainly better than no comparison at all, and it does focus attention on trends, especially if several past periods are used for comparison and not just the most recent period. But this approach may sidetrack one of management's main responsibilities, which is to forecast changes in the business environment.

Changes from last period may have been predictable and should have been built into the plan; the changes between this period and last period don't really present any new information relative to what should have been predicted. The manager should get in a forward planning mode, such as explained in Chapter 7, for planning the capital needs of growth. The danger of using last period for comparison with this period is that the manager gets into the rear-view style of management—looking behind but not ahead.

 Frequency of Control Reports

A tough question to answer is how often to prepare control reports. Managers cannot wait until the end of the year for control reports, although a year-end review is usually a good idea and serves as the platform for developing next year's plan. Daily or weekly control reports are not practical for most businesses, although some companies, such as airlines and banks, monitor sales volume and other vital operating statistics on a day-to-day basis,

Monthly or quarterly management control reports are the most common. Each business develops its own practical solution to the frequency question; there's no one general answer that fits all companies. The main objective is to strike a balance between preparing control reports too frequently and too late. With computers and other electronic means of communication today, it is tempting to bombard managers with too much control information too often. Sorting out the truly relevant from the less relevant and truly irrelevant information is at the very core of the manager's job.

 Profit Control Reports

The internal management income statement illustrated in previous chapters for decision making should be the starting point for designing internal management profit control reports. First and foremost, contribution margin and the other profit margins below this line should be the main focus of attention and should be clear and easy to follow. Contribution and profit margins should be reported for each major product or product line (backed up with detailed schedules for virtually every individual product) in internal management profit performance reports. This is very confidential data which is not divulged in external income statements, nor, for that matter, very widely within the organization.

Variable expenses should be divided between those that depend on sales volume versus those that depend on sales revenue and broken down into a large number of specific accounts. Sales volumes for each product and product line should be reported. Fixed expenses should be broken down into major components: salaries, advertising, occupancy costs, and so on. Sales capacity should be reported. Any significant change in capacity due to changes in fixed expenses should be reported.

Internal management control reports should analyze *changes in profit*. In particular, the impact of sales volume changes should be separated from changes in sales price, product cost, and variable expenses, as explained in earlier chapters. If trade-off decisions were made—for example, cutting sales price to increase sales volume—there should be follow-up analysis in the management control profit reports that tracks how the decision actually worked out. Did sales volume increase as much as expected?

As explained below, there is a frustrating fringe of negative factors that constantly threaten profit margins and bloat fixed expenses. Each of these negative factors should be singled out for special attention in management profit control reports. Inventory shrinkage, for example, should be reported on a separate line, as should sales returns, unusually high bad debts, and any extraordinary losses or gains recorded in the period.

If there is a general fault with internal profit reports for management control purposes, it is, in my opinion, the failure of the accounting staff to explain and analyze why profit increased or decreased relative to last period or relative to the budget for the period. Such profit change analysis would be very useful to include in the profit reports. But managers generally are left on their own to do this. Managers should find the tools discussed in previous chapters very helpful in this analysis.

 Financial Condition and Cash Flow Control Reports

In management control balance sheets and cash flow statements, the most important point is to keep close tabs on changes in each major asset and liability. In particular, the manager should keep a close watch on changes in each operating asset and each operating liability—to spot any change in the operating ratios of the business. These changes have immediate impact on the cash flow of the business, as explained in previous chapters. Such changes need quick management response.

Sales revenue and expenses drive the operating assets and liabilities of the business. Changes in each operating asset and liability need to be compared with changes in the sales revenue or expense that determines the asset or liability. If sales revenue increased 10 percent, did accounts receivable go up 10 percent? Significant deviations must be investigated. Controlling cash flow from profit means controlling changes in the company's operating assets and liabilities.

Investment Performance Measures in Control Reports

Management control financial statements should include business capital investment performance measures, which are discussed in Chapter 6. Return on (net operating) assets (ROA), return on equity (ROE), and any significant changes in financial leverage should be reported. If the business falls below its ROE goal, there should be a very clear explanation that pinpoints which factors are to blame.

BRIEF OVERVIEW OF BUDGETING

Chapter 7, which explains the tools used in planning for the capital needs of growth, presents a little taste of budgeting. Sales growth means more capital will be needed to invest in the net operating assets of the business. The company's managers must analyze how much more capital will be needed and decide on the strategy for securing the additional capital from debt and equity sources. Planning for capital needs is just one purpose of budgeting. There are many other purposes. The technical aspects and procedures of budgeting are not discussed here; fundamentals are the focus.

Management decisions taken all together should constitute an integrated and coordinated strategy and overarching plan of action for achieving profit and financial objectives. Decisions are like the blueprint for a building; control should be carried out in the context of the decision blueprint. Clearly, decisions should be the reference and framework for management control. *Budgeting* is one tool to integrate management decision making and management control, akin to constructing a building according to its blueprint.

Decisions are made explicit in a budget, which is the concrete plan of action for achieving the profit and financial objectives of the business according to a timetable. Actual results are evaluated against budget period by period, line by line, and item by item. Variances have to be explained; they serve as the catalyst for taking corrective action where needed or for revising the plan as needed.

No budgeting doesn't mean that there is no management control. Budgeting is helpful but not absolutely essential for management control. Many businesses do little or no budgeting, yet they make a good profit and remain solvent and financially healthy. They depend on the management control reports discussed previously in this chapter to track their actual profit performance, financial position, and cash flow. But they have no formal or explicit budget against which to compare actual results. More than likely, they use last year as the reference for comparison.

The larger the organization, the more likely you'll find a formal and comprehensive financial budgeting process in place. The company's strategic plan is put in the form of a detailed, comprehensive, and integrated budget. The budget is the primary means of communication and authorization down the line in the organization. The budget provides the key benchmarks for evaluating performance of managers at all levels. Actual is compared against budget, and significant variances are highlighted, and investigated and reported up the line. Managers are rewarded for meeting or exceeding the budget, and they are held accountable for unfavorable variances.

There are persuasive reasons for and advantages to budgeting. On the other side of the coin, budgeting is costly and may lead to a lot of game playing and dysfunctional behavior. Some reasons for budgeting are not applicable to smaller businesses. Smaller businesses do not need budgets for communication and coordination purposes that are much more important in larger organizations in which top management is distant from day-to-day operations.

Profit budgeting depends heavily on the ability of managers to forecast changes in the key factors that drive profit—in detail and with fairly good accuracy. Nothing is so counterproductive and more discouraging than an unrealistic profit budget built on flimsy sales projections. If no one believes the sales budget numbers, the budget process becomes a lot of wasted motion or, worse, an exercise in hypocrisy.

The profit budget should be accepted as realistically achievable by those managers responsible for meeting the objectives and goals of the profit plan and to serve as the benchmarks against which actual performance will be compared. If budget goals are too unrealistic, managers may engage in all sorts of manipulations and artificial schemes to meet their budget profit targets. There are enormous pressures in a business organization to make budget, even if managers think the budget is not fair and realistic.

Then there are always unexpected developments—events that simply cannot be foreseen at the time of making up the profit budget. The budget should be adjusted for such developments, but budget revision is not easy. Once adopted, budgets tend to become carved in stone. Higher levels of management quite naturally are suspicious that requests for budget adjustments may be attempts to evade budget goals or may be excuses for substandard performance. Budgeting works best in a stable and predictable environment.

The master budget is made up of the separate profit and other budgets for each organizational unit—such as sales territories, departments, product lines, branches, divisions, and subsidiaries. Each subunit's budget is like a building stone in a large pyramid that leads up to the master budget at the top. Starting at the bottom end, sales and expense budgets dovetail into larger-scale profit budgets, which in turn are integrated with cash flow and financial condition (balance sheet) budgets.

As mentioned before in this chapter, management control deals with a thousand and one details. Control deals with detail, detail, and more detail. Day to day and month to month, the manager has to pay attention to an avalanche of details. Keeping all the details in perspective is a challenge. Control reports comparing actual with budget should not let the details take over, causing managers to lose sight of the overall progress toward the profit goal.

The whole point of budgeting, but one which is easy to lose sight of, is to achieve profit and other financial objectives. Budgeting is not an end in itself. Detailed expense and cost reporting is required, so that the manager can keep close watch on the total effect on the key expense and cost factors that were forecast in the profit budget. Often, managers ask for reams of detailed expense and cost reports, but they do not necessarily read all the detail.

A complete budget plan requires a budgeted financial condition report (balance sheet) and a cash flow budget, as well as the profit budget (income statement) for the coming period. As explained in previous chapters, the financial condition of the business is driven mainly by the profit-making operations of the business. Capital expenditures for replacements and expansions of long-term operating assets of the business must be included in the cash flow budget and the budgeted year-end financial condition.

A total financial plan—the profit budget integrated with the financial condition and cash flow budgets—is a very convincing package when applying for a loan or renewing an existing line of credit. It shows that the company's total financial plan has been thought out. Managers may prefer to leave many details to their accounting and budgeting staffs, but they have to supply all the essential forecasts and assumptions on which the financial budget plan is based.

As the bard says, "The best-laid schemes . . . ," which leads to the next section, which surveys the reasons why the profit goal set out in the budget is difficult to reach. Profit can slip away in many ways.

THE FRUSTRATING FRINGE OF PROFIT ROBBERS

The pathway to profit is surrounded by a frustrating fringe of negative pressures that cut into profit margins, hurt sales volume, and drive up fixed expenses. This umbrella term refers to the several different negative pressures on profit performance that managers have to deal with day in and day out. These might be called the sinkholes and pitfalls, or detours, on the road to profit.

KEY CONCEPT

Sales Price Negatives

When eating in a restaurant, you don't argue about the menu prices, and you don't bargain over the posted prices at the gas pump or in the supermarket. In contrast, sales price negotiation is the way of life in many industries. Many businesses advertise or publish *list prices*. Examples are sticker prices on new cars, manufacturers' suggested retail prices on consumer products, and standard price sheets for industrial products.

List prices are not the final prices, just the point of departure. In some cases, such as new car sales, neither the seller nor the buyer takes the list price as the real price—the list price simply sets the stage for bargaining. In other cases, the buyer agrees to pay list price but demands other types of price concessions and reductions or other special accommodations.

Prompt payment discounts usually are offered when making sales on credit to other businesses. For example, a 2 percent discount may be given for payments received within 10 days after the sales invoice date. These are called *sales discounts*. As a buyer, you should view them as penalties for delayed payment. Also, *quantity discounts* for large orders and *special customer discounts* for government agencies and educational institutions are common.

Rebates and *coupons* are offered by many consumer product companies; these lower the final net sales price, of course. Sales prices also may be reduced by giving *allowances* or *adjustments* after the point of sale because some customers complain about the quality of the product or when minor product flaws are discovered after taking delivery. Instead of the customer returning the product, the company reduces the original sales price.

Managers must decide how these sales price negatives are reported to them in their internal management income statement. One alternative is to report sales revenue net of all such reductions. I don't recommend this method. The better approach is to report sales revenue at established list prices. All sales price negatives should be accumulated in sales *contra* accounts that are deducted from gross sales revenue.

Figure 16.2 presents the top part of an internal income statement that includes about every type of sales revenue negative that a business might have.* Seven different reductions from list sales prices are illustrated in this exhibit. A business may not have all the sales contra accounts shown here, but three or four are not unusual. The amounts of each contra account may not be as large as shown (hopefully not).

In external income statements, only net sales revenue ($8,303,000 in this example) is reported, as a general rule. For internal management reporting, however, gross (list price) sales revenue before all sales price reductions should be reported. Sales price reductions should be accumulated in contra (deduction) accounts, which are illustrated in Figure 16.2, so that managers can monitor each one relative to established sales policies, for comparison with previous periods and for comparison of actual performance against goals (or budget) for the period. Managers should find this information useful for other decisions. For instance, sales prices may be increased, not by increasing list prices but by reducing rebates or other sales revenue negatives.

 Product Cost and Variable
CONCEPT **Expense Negatives**

Inventory *shrinkage* is a serious problem for many businesses, especially retailers. Shrinkage is a euphemism for inventory losses caused by shoplifting by customers, employee theft, and short-counts from

Gross sales revenue, at list prices		$10,000,000
Less:		
Sales discounts	$(150,000)	
Special discounts	(200,000)	
Sales returns	(175,000)	
Quantity discounts	(275,000)	
Rebates	(650,000)	
Coupons	(165,000)	
Price allowances	(82,000)	(1,697,000)
Net sales revenue		$ 8,303,000

Remainder of income statement

FIGURE 16.2 *Income statement illustrating sales revenue negatives.*

* Other examples could be given, such as a lawsuit that a business has lost that requires substantial refunds to customers or simple mistakes in billing customers that have to be corrected.

suppliers. The term also includes inventory losses due to product damage and deterioration, as well as inventory write-downs to recognize product obsolescence. Many businesses suffer inventory obsolescence, which means they end up with some products that cannot be sold or have to be sold below cost. When this becomes apparent, inventory should be decreased by write-down entries.* (The inventory asset account is decreased and an expense account is increased.) Inventory shrinkage of 1.5 to 2.0 percent of retail sales is not unusual.

Inventory loss due to theft is a particularly frustrating expense. The business has to buy (or manufacture) these products, then hold them in inventory, which requires carrying costs, only to have them stolen by "customers" or employees. On the other hand, inventory shrinkage due to damage from handling and storing products, and product deterioration over time, and product obsolescence is a normal and inescapable economic risk of doing business.

Internal management control reports definitely should separate inventory shrinkage expense from cost-of-goods-sold expense. Inventory shrinkage is hardly ever reported as a separate expense in external financial reports; it is combined with cost of goods sold or some other expense. Managers need to keep a close watch on inventory shrinkage and cannot do so if it is buried in the larger cost-of-goods-sold expense.

Another reason for separating out inventory shrinkage is that this expense does not behave the same way as cost-of-goods-sold expense. Cost-of-goods-sold expense varies with sales volume.† Inventory shrinkage may include both a fixed amount that is more or less the same regardless of sales volume and the remainder, which may vary with sales volume.

Strong internal controls and effective preventive measures help minimize inventory shrinkage, but at a cost. Even elaborate and expensive controls cannot eliminate *all* inventory shrinkage. Almost every business tolerates some amount of inventory shrinkage. For instance, most businesses look the other way when it comes to minor employee theft; they don't encourage it, of course, but they don't do anything about it either. Preventing all shrinkage would be too costly or might offend customers and hurt sales volume.

---

* Managers may be reluctant to authorize write-downs because it means an additional expense has to be deducted from sales revenue. Inevitably, the question of blame comes up: Who's responsible for the inventory loss?

† The inventory accounting method used by the business may produce a cost-of-goods-sold expense amount that does not vary in strict proportion with changes in sales volume. Both the last-in, first-out (LIFO) method and the first-in, first-out (FIFO) method can cause this problem. In Chapter 21 of my *How to Read a Financial Report*, 4th ed. (New York: John Wiley & Sons, 1994), I argue that the sales pricing strategy of the business should determine the accounting method.

Would you shop in a retail store that carried out body searches on all customers leaving the store? I doubt it. Many retailers hesitate even to require customers to check bags before entering their stores. On the other hand, closed-circuit TV monitors are common in many stores. Retailers are constantly trying to find controls that do not offend their customers. For example, many product packages are designed to make it difficult to shoplift the product, such as compact music discs, which are put in oversized packages that are difficult to conceal.

Recently, business has worked to adopt industrywide standard specifications for an electronic strip that could be placed on or in most retail products. If not deactivated at the point of sale, the strip sets off an alarm when the shoplifter passes through an inconspicuous detection device when attempting to leave the store.

DANGER! Product *recalls* can be very costly. Also, abnormally high *warranty* and *repair* costs add significant amounts to product cost or variable expenses of making sales. A business may fail to take advantage of *prompt payment discounts* or buy in small quantities and forgo *volume* (large-quantity) *discounts*. Several other product cost and variable operating expense negatives could be discussed. Only one is mentioned: excessive purchase costs due to a company's purchasing agents accepting bribes, kickbacks, under-the-table payments, or other favors from vendors. A purchasing agent I know made me aware of how serious a problem this is. He didn't exactly say that all purchasing agents are corrupt, but he certainly said that the temptation is there and many succumb.

In internal management control reports, the negative factors just discussed should be set out in separate expense accounts, if they are relatively material, or listed separately in a supplementary schedule. Managers may have to specifically instruct their accountants to isolate these expenses. In external income statements, these costs are grouped in a larger expense account (such as cost of goods sold or general and administrative expenses).

KEY CONCEPT ## Sales Volume Negatives

Sales *returns* can be a problem, although this varies quite a bit from industry to industry. Many retailers accept sales returns without hesitation as part of their overall marketing strategy. Customers may be refunded their money or they may exchange for different products. On the other hand, some products, such as new cars, are seldom returned (even when recalled).

Sales returns definitely should be accumulated in a separate sales *contra* account that is deducted from gross sales revenue (see Figure 16.2 again). The total of sales returns is very important control information. On the other hand, in most external income statements, only net sales revenue (gross sales revenue less sales returns and all other sales revenue negatives) is reported.

Lost sales due to temporary *stock-outs* (zero inventory situations) are important for managers to know about. Such nonsales are not recorded in the accounting system. No sales transaction takes place, so there is nothing to record in the sales revenue account. However, missed sale opportunities should be accumulated in the accounting system and reported to managers, even though no sales actually took place. Managers need a measure of how much additional profit margin could have been earned on these lost sales.

Many times, customers are willing to *back order* the products, or sales are made for future delivery if customers do not need immediate delivery, which are called sales backlogs. Information about back orders and sales backlogs should be reported to managers, but not as sales revenue, of course. If a customer refuses to back order or will not wait for future delivery, the sale may be lost. As a practical matter, it is difficult to keep track of lost sales. The manager may have to rely on other sources of information, such as complaints from customers and the company's sales force.

 Excess Capacity: A Ticking Downsizing Time Bomb?

The accounting problem of the excess production capacity of manufacturers is discussed in Chapter 17, which explains manufacturing accounting procedures and problems. The key question concerns the cost of idle capacity—production capacity that was "paid for" and available but not used to manufacture products during the year. Unless idle capacity is extraordinarily large, the cost of unused production capacity is included in unit product costs. In short, the cost of the units actually manufactured includes some cost for manufacturing capacity that did not produce any products.

This section is directed to excess *sales* capacity and excess *administrative* or *management capacity*. The business may have too much office space, too many employees, too many managers, too much retail space, too many delivery vehicles, and so on. Production capacity is usually a known number. In contrast, most businesses do not attempt to estimate in any formal quantitative manner either their sales capacity or their administrative capacity.

Some ratios are helpful tools, even if there is no measure of sales capacity as such. For example, many retailers keep an eye on *sales revenue per employee* and *sales revenue per square foot* of retail space. Most retailers have rough rules of thumb, such as $300 or $400 of sales per square foot of retail space, or

$150,000 of sales per employee. These amounts vary widely from industry to industry.

Trade associations collect such data from their members and publish industry averages. Retailers can compare their performances against local and regional competition, as well as national averages. Hotels and motels carefully watch their *occupancy rates,* which is another example of a useful ratio to measure actual sales against capacity.

Reducing any fixed expense is not easy, as you know. Employees have to be fired (or temporarily laid off), major assets have to be sold, contracts may have to be broken, and so on. Downsizing decisions are difficult to make. For one thing, they are an admission of the inability of the business to generate enough sales volume to justify their fixed expenses. Nonetheless, part of the manager's job is to make these painful decisions.

The tendency is to put off the decision, to delay the tough choices that have to be made. In a recent article in the *Wall Street Journal,* the former CEO of Westinghouse observed that one of the biggest failings of American chief executives is procrastinating—that executives are reluctant to face up to making these decisions at the earliest possible time.

END POINT

Management control is very difficult in practice. Good control reports are very important; they supply essential feedback information that managers need to know in following through on their decisions. But in the final analysis, it comes down to good management.

Managers are paid to solve problems, but many problems do not lend themselves to easy or obvious solutions. Good management starts with good decisions. Control procedures are certainly required. However, the best control in the world can't reverse a bad decision. The main thrust of the book is to explain the tools for analyzing profit, financial condition, and cash flow for making good decisions.

Budgeting certainly is, in part, a tool of management control. But budgeting is done for more than just control purposes; it's a broader management tool that encompasses strategic planning, communication with and by managers, motivation of managers, the basis for incentive compensation plans, delegation of authority, and more.

This chapter includes a short summary on budgeting, which, I must admit, does not do this broad topic justice. However, this book is concerned primarily with management analysis tools for decision making. These tools of analysis are used in the budgeting process. Budgeting is a tool of management control, but its nature and purposes are much broader.

This chapter concludes with a brief look at the frus-trating fringe of profit robbers—the culprits that drive down sales revenue and drive up expenses. There are many. One main theme is that managers must keep a close watch on each of these significant negative fac-tors. Sales revenue contra accounts and separate expense accounts for these robbers should be included in internal management control reports.

CHAPTER 17

Manufacturing Accounting

If you're in the manufacturing business, this chapter is an absolute must. The chapter presents a concise explanation of the accounting methods used by virtually all manufacturers to determine and measure *product cost*. Nothing happens until the business knows its product costs. To set sales prices, to control costs, to plan for the future, the business must know the costs of manufacturing its products.

SO, YOU'RE NOT A MANUFACTURER

But suppose you're not in the business of manufacturing the products you sell. You may have your enthusiasm under control for this chapter. I would point out, however, that all managers use product cost information and that all products begin their life by being manufactured. Even if your company does not manufacture products, understanding how manufacturing costs are accumulated and allocated to products and how certain accounting problems are dealt with by manufacturers is very important.

 **PRODUCT MAKERS VERSUS**
PRODUCT RESELLERS

Manufacturers are producers: They make the products they sell. Retailers (as well as wholesalers and distributors) do not make the products they sell; they are channels of distribution. Product cost is *purchase* cost for retailers; it comes on a purchase invoice. Product cost is much different for manufacturers; it's the composite of diverse costs of production. It has to be computed.

The manufacturing process may be simple and short, or complex and long. It may be either labor intensive or capital (asset) intensive. Products, such as breakfast cereal, may roll nonstop off the end of a continuous mass-production assembly line. These are called *process cost* systems. Or production may be discontinuous and done on a one-batch-at-a-time basis; these are called *job order* systems. For instance, printing and binding 10,000 copies of a book is an example of a job order system.

The example in this chapter is for an established manufacturing business—one that has been operating several years. Its managers have already assembled and organized machines, equipment, tools, and employees into a smooth-running production process that is dependable and efficient—a monumental task, to say the least. Plant location is critical; so is plant layout, employee training, materials procurement, complying with an ever-broadening range of governmental regulations, employee safety laws, environmental protection laws, and so on. These points are mentioned in passing, before moving on to product cost determination.

 **BASIC MANUFACTURING COSTS CONCEPT AND COMPANY EXAMPLE**

Some manufacturers determine their product costs monthly; others quarterly. There is no one standard period. It could be done weekly or even daily. The year is a natural time period for management planning and financial reporting. Thus, the year is the time period for this example.

For convenience of discussion, the company in this example manufactures one product in its one production plant. Figure 17.1 presents the company's profit report for the year down through its operating profit line (earnings before interest and income tax expenses) and includes the supporting manufacturing cost report, which has not been presented before.

The company recorded $8,220,000 total manufacturing costs and produced 12,000 units during the year. Of this amount, $7,535,000 is charged to cost-of-goods-sold expense for the 11,000 units sold during the year, and $685,000 is allocated to the 1,000 units inventory increase.* Thus, $685,000 of the manufacturing costs for the year will not be expensed until next year or sometime further into the future when the inventory is sold.†

---

* During the production process, which can take several weeks or months, manufacturing costs are first accumulated in an inventory account called *work-in-process*. When production is completed, the cost of the completed units is transferred to the *finished goods* inventory account.

† We do not explore here the differences between the FIFO and LIFO methods for assigning unit product costs to cost-of-goods-sold expense and to inventory. This choice of costing methods is available to manufacturers as well as retailers and wholesalers. Unit product costs usually vary from period to period. Thus, the cost-of-goods-sold expense and the amount allocated to the increase in inventory varies between the two methods. The FIFO and LIFO methods are explained in Chapter 21 of my book, *How to Read a Financial Report,* 4th ed. (New York: John Wiley & Sons, 1994).

Manufacturing costs consist of four basic cost components or natural groupings. *Raw materials* are purchased parts and materials that become part of the finished product. *Direct labor* refers to those employees who work on the production line. Direct labor costs include fringe benefits which typically add 30 to 40 percent to basic wages. For instance, employer Social Security and Medicare tax rates presently are 7.65 percent of base wages; also, there are unemployment taxes, employee retirement and pension plan contributions, health and medical insurance, workers' compensation insurance, and paid vacations and sick leaves.

Manufacturing *overhead* refers to all other production costs. Some of these costs vary with total output, such as electricity that powers machinery and equipment. These *variable* overhead costs are separated from *fixed* overhead costs. Over the short run, many manufacturing overhead costs are fixed in amount and do not depend on the level of production activity. Examples are property taxes, fire insurance on the production plant, and plant security guards who are paid a fixed salary.

In this example, the company's annual production *capacity* is 12,000 units. Its $2,100,000 total fixed overhead costs provide the physical facilities and human resources to produce 12,000 units under normal practical conditions of operation. Actual production output for the year in the example equals the company's production capacity. In practice, actual output usually falls somewhat below capacity; we look at this issue later.

COMPUTATION OF UNIT PRODUCT COST

Unit product cost is determined by dividing the total manufacturing costs for the period by total production output for the period:

$$\$8{,}220{,}000 \text{ total manufacturing costs} \div 12{,}000 \text{ units total output} = \$685 \text{ unit product cost}$$

Notice immediately three things about unit product cost. First, it's a *calculated* amount. It doesn't exist until it's computed. Clearly, both the numerator and the denominator of the computation must be correct, or else the unit product cost would be wrong. Second, unit product cost is an *average*. Total cost over a period of time is divided by total output over that same period, one year in this example. Costs and quantities may vary daily, weekly, monthly—but the definition and computation of unit product cost is the average over a certain period of time.*

---

* In a job order costing system, the total cost of the job (i.e., one batch or one group of products manufactured as a separate lot) is divided by the total number of units in the job to determine unit product cost.

Operating profit report for year

Sales volume = 11,000 units

	Per unit	Total
Sales revenue	$1,400	$15,400,000
Cost-of-goods-sold expense	(685)	(7,535,000)
Gross profit (or gross margin)	$715	$7,865,000
Variable operating expenses	(305)	(3,355,000)
Contribution margin	$410	$4,510,000
Fixed operating expenses		$(2,300,000)
Operating profit (before interest and income tax)		$2,210,000

Manufacturing cost report for year

Annual production capacity = 12,000 units
Actual output = 12,000 units

Basic cost components

	Per unit	Total
Raw materials	$215	$2,580,000
Direct labor	260	3,120,000
Variable overhead	35	420,000
Fixed overhead	175	2,100,000
Total manufacturing costs	$685	$8,220,000
To: 11,000 units sold	$685	$7,535,000
To: 1,000 units inventory increase	685	685,000
Total manufacturing costs		$8,220,000

Cost-of-goods-sold expense equals the sales volume times the unit product cost.

Both sales-volume- and sales-revenue-driven expenses are shown here in one total amount.

These expenses are nonmanufacturing costs, i.e., not part of the production process. They are called *period costs* because they are charged off to the period in which they are recorded and do not become part of product cost.

These four basic types of manufacturing costs are called *product costs*. They become attached to the product and thus are not charged off to expense until the product is sold.

The cost of the 1,000 units manufactured but not sold is added to the inventory asset account. It is assumed that this is a reasonable increase relative to annual sales and the beginning inventory level.

FIGURE 17.1 *Operating profit and manufacturing cost report.*

Third, only *manufacturing* costs are included, not the nonmanufacturing expenses of operating the business, such as marketing (sales promotion, advertising, etc.), delivery costs, administration and general management costs, legal costs, and interest expense. A Chinese wall should be built between manufacturing costs and all other, nonmanufacturing, costs. The proper classification and separation between costs is critical.

Sales and marketing costs, such as advertising, are not included in product cost; these are viewed as costs of making sales, not of making products. Research and development (R&D) costs are not classified as product cost, even though these costs may lead to new products, new methods of manufacture, new compounds of materials, or other technological improvements.

Raw materials and direct labor costs are clearly manufacturing costs. Taken together, they are called *prime costs.* Direct materials and direct labor are matched with or traced to particular products being manufactured. Variable overhead, on the other hand, presents problems of matching with particular products. And fixed overhead is a real headache. The term *overhead* means *indirectly* from the products being manufactured.

Consider, for example, the print order for the production of 10,000 copies of a book. The paper and ink cost (raw materials) can be identified to each production run. Likewise, the employees setting up and operating the presses (direct labor) can be identified and matched to the job. However, variable overhead costs cannot be directly identified with particular press runs; instead, these costs must be *allocated.* For instance, the cost of electricity to power the presses can be allocated on the basis of the machine hours of each print run.

Much more troublesome are *fixed* manufacturing overhead costs, which include a wide variety of costs such as property taxes on the production plant, depreciation of the production equipment, fixed salaries of plant nurses and doctors, and the fixed salary of the vice president of production. Fixed manufacturing overhead costs have to be allocated according to some basis for sharing these costs among the different products manufactured by the company. The company in this example makes only one product. So fixed overhead as well as variable overhead costs are all assigned to this one product. (Cost allocation issues and methods are discussed in Chapter 15.)

 ## DELIBERATE MISCLASSIFICATION OF MANUFACTURING COSTS

To minimize taxable income, some manufacturers have been known to intentionally misclassify some of their costs. Certain costs were recorded as marketing or as general and administration expenses that should have been booked as manufacturing costs. These misclassified costs were not included in the calculation of unit product cost. The purpose was to maximize costs that are charged off immediately to expense. By minimizing current taxable income, the business could delay payment of income taxes.

The 1986 Tax Reform Act took a special interest in the problem of manufacturing overhead cost classification. The experience of the Internal Revenue Service was that many manufacturers were misclassifying some of their costs. The income tax law now spells out in some detail which costs must be classified as manufacturing overhead costs and therefore capitalized. To *capitalize* means to put the cost into an inventory asset account by including the cost in the calculation of unit product cost. Remember that the cost of inventory remains an asset and is not charged to expense until the products are sold.

The following costs should definitely be classified as manufacturing costs: production employee benefits costs; rework, scrap, and spoilage costs; quality control costs; and routine repairs and maintenance on production machinery and equipment. Of course, depreciation of production machinery and equipment and property taxes on the production plant should be classified as manufacturing overhead costs.

To illustrate the effects of misclassifying manufacturing costs, suppose that $480,000 of the company's manufacturing fixed overhead costs had been recorded in fixed operating expenses instead of in fixed manufacturing overhead costs. Otherwise, everything else remains the same as shown before in the company example. Figure 17.2 shows the effects of this misclassification error. Pay particular attention to the operating profit line, which is taxable income before the interest expense deduction.

In Figure 17.2, fixed operating expenses are inflated $480,000 (from $2,300,000 to $2,780,000). This amount is shifted from fixed manufacturing overhead costs, which decrease from $2,100,000 to $1,620,000. Thus $480,000 manufacturing fixed overhead escapes being charged to the 12,000 units produced, which decreases unit product cost $40, from $685 to $645.

Remember that 1,000 of the 12,000 units manufactured during the year go into ending inventory, not out the door to customers. Each of the 1,000 units carries $40 less fixed overhead cost, for a total of $40,000 less cost in ending inventory. Operating profit, that is, taxable income before interest, is $40,000 less as the result of the misclassification error, so income tax for the year would be less. In one sense, we have cooked the books to record $40,000 less operating profit simply by reclassifying some costs away from manufacturing.*

Target sales prices may be determined by marking up unit product cost a certain percentage. Thus, managers should be very clear regarding whether all manufacturing overhead costs are included in the calculation of unit product cost. If not, the markup percent should be adjusted since it would be based on an understated unit product cost. The better course of action would seem to be to properly classify all manufacturing overhead costs in the first place.

KEY CONCEPT — **IDLE PRODUCTION CAPACITY**

Most manufacturers have fairly large fixed manufacturing overhead costs: depreciation of plant and equipment, salaries of a wide range of employees (from the vice president of production to janitors), fire insurance costs, property taxes, and literally hundreds of other costs. Fixed manufacturing overhead costs provide *production capacity*. Managers should measure or at least make their best estimate of the production capacity provided by their fixed manufacturing overhead costs. Capacity is the maximum potential production output for a period of time provided by the manufacturing facilities that are in place and ready for use.

Suppose the company's annual production capacity were 15,000 units instead of the 12,000 units assumed in the previous example. The business has correctly classified costs between manufacturing and other operating costs. All other profit and production factors are the same as before. The company manufactured only 12,000 units during the year. The 3,000-unit gap between actual output and production capacity is called *idle* capacity. In short, the company operated at 80 percent of its capacity: 12,000 units actual output ÷ 15,000 units capacity = 80%.

It should be pointed out that 20 percent idle capacity is not unusual. An Associated Press report recently stated:

> *The nation's industrial operating rate was unchanged in January at 82.2 percent of capacity. . . . Manufacturers of durable goods . . . operated at 79.9 percent of capacity . . . while manufacturers of nondurable goods operated at 86.1 percent of capacity. Normally, when operating rates get about 85 percent, economists begin to worry about bottlenecks and rising prices. [(Boulder) Daily Camera, February 19, 1988, p. 6B]*

* Although it would be rather unusual, a manufacturer could start and end the period with no inventory. In this case, profit would be the same no matter how costs were classified, although for internal management reports the proper classification of costs is important.

Operating profit report for year

		Sales volume =	11,000 units
		Per unit	**Total**
Sales revenue		$1,400	$15,400,000
Cost-of-goods-sold expense		(645)	(7,095,000)
Gross profit (or gross margin)		$755	$8,305,000
Variable operating expenses		(305)	(3,355,000)
Contribution margin		$450	$4,950,000
Fixed operating expenses			$(2,780,000)
Operating profit (before interest and income tax)			$2,170,000

Manufacturing cost report for year

		Annual production capacity =	12,000
		Annual production output =	12,000
		Per unit	**Total**
Raw materials		$215	$2,580,000
Direct labor		260	3,120,000
Variable overhead		35	420,000
Fixed overhead		135	1,620,000
Total manufacturing costs		$645	$7,740,000
To: 11,000 units sold		$645	$7,095,000
To: 1,000 units inventory increase		$645	$645,000
Total manufacturing costs			$7,740,000

Cost-of-goods-sold expense equals the sales volume times the unit product cost, which is now only $645 per unit.

Includes $480,000 of manufacturing cost, which is incorrect.

This is taxable income before interest deduction. It is $40,000 too low because of the misclassification of manufacturing costs.

This total does not include $480,000 of manufacturing overhead costs that have been misclassified as shown above.

The cost of the 1,000 units manufactured but not sold is added to the inventory asset account, but here is based on the lower unit product cost of $645.

FIGURE 17.2 *Misclassification of manufacturing costs.*

Producing below capacity in any one year does not necessarily mean that management should downsize its production facilities. Production capacity has a long-run planning horizon. Most manufacturers have some capacity in reserve, to provide for growth and for unexpected surges in demands for its products. Our concern focuses on how to determine unit product cost given the 20 percent idle capacity.

In most situations, 20 percent idle capacity would be considered within the range of normal production output levels. So the company would compute unit product cost the same way as shown earlier. The 12,000 units actual output is divided into the $2,100,000 total fixed manufacturing overhead costs to get the fixed overhead cost *burden rate,* which is $175. This is the burden rate included in unit product cost in Figure 17.1.

The theory is that the actual number of units produced should absorb all fixed manufacturing overhead costs for the year, even though a fraction of the total fixed manufacturing costs was "wasted" because the company did not produce up to its full capacity. In this way, the cost of idle capacity is buried in the unit product cost, which would have been lower if the company had produced at its full capacity and thus spread its fixed manufacturing costs over 15,000 units.

The main alternative is to divide total fixed manufacturing overhead costs by capacity. This would give a fixed overhead cost burden rate of $140: $2,100,000 total fixed manufacturing overhead costs ÷ 15,000 units annual capacity = $140 burden rate. In terms of total dollars, the company had 20 percent idle capacity during the year, so 20 percent of its $2,100,000 total fixed overhead costs, or $420,000, would be charged to an idle capacity expense for the year. This amount would bypass the unit product cost computation and go directly to expense for the year.*

Managers may not like treating idle capacity cost as a separate expense, which draws attention to it. In the manufacturing cost report, the manager could easily see that the business produced at only 80 percent of its capacity, so he or she should be aware that the unit product cost is higher than if it were based on capacity.

If, on the other hand, actual output were substantially less than production capacity, the fixed overhead burden rate should not be based on actual output. The idle capacity cost definitely should be reported as a separate expense in the internal management profit

---

* Cost of-goods-sold-expense would be $7,150,000 (11,000 units sold × $650 unit product cost = $7,150,000); idle capacity expense would be $420,000, and the total of these two would be $7,570,000, which is $35,000 more than the $7,535,000 cost-of-goods-sold expense shown in Figure 17.1. In short, operating profit would be $35,000 less and ending inventory would be $35,000 less.

report. (External financial reports seldom report the cost of idle capacity as a separate expense.)

The generally accepted accounting rule is that the fixed manufacturing overhead burden rate included in the calculation of unit product cost should be based on a *normal* output level—not necessarily equal to 100 percent of production capacity but typically in the 75 to 90 percent range of capacity. However, it must be admitted that there are no hard and fast guidelines on this. In short, some amount of normal idle capacity cost is loaded into the unit product cost because the fixed overhead burden rate is based on an output level less than full capacity.

MANUFACTURING INEFFICIENCIES

The ideal manufacturing scenario is one of maximum production efficiency—no wasted materials, no wasted labor, no excessive reworking of products that don't pass inspection the first time through, no unnecessary power usage, and so on. The goal is optimum efficiency and maximum productivity for all variable costs of manufacturing. Today the word is *TQM,* or total quality management, as the means to achieve these efficiencies and to maximize quality.

Management control reports should clearly highlight productivity ratios for each factor of the production process—each raw material item, each labor step, and each variable cost factor. One key productivity ratio, for instance, is the direct labor hours per unit. Ten to fifteen years ago it took ten hours to make a ton of steel, but today it takes only about four hours; a recent article in the *New York Times* commented that the relatively few workers seen on the production floor of the modern steel plant is remarkable.

The computation of unit product cost is based on the essential premise that the manufacturing process is reasonably efficient, which means that productivity ratios for every cost factor are fairly close to what they should be. Managers should watch productivity ratios in their production control reports, and they should take quick action to deal with the problems. Occasionally, however, things get way out of control and this causes an accounting problem regarding how to deal with gross inefficiencies.

To explain, suppose the company in the example had wasted raw materials during the year. Assume the $2,580,000 total cost of raw materials in the original scenario (see Figure 17.1) had included $660,000 of raw materials wastage. These materials were scrapped and not used in the final products. This may have been caused by inexperienced or untrained employees, or perhaps inferior quality materials not up to its product quality control standards were used as a cost-cutting measure.

This problem should have been stopped before it amounted to so much; quicker action should have been taken. In any case, assume the problem persisted and the result was that raw materials costing $660,000 had to be thrown away and were not used in the production process. The preferred approach is to take out the $660,000 from the computation of unit product cost, which would lower the unit product cost by $55: $660,000 wasted raw materials cost ÷ 12,000 units output = $55. The $660,000 excess raw materials cost would be deducted as a one-time extraordinary expense or loss in the profit report.

The wasted raw materials costs could be included in unit product cost, but this could result in a seriously misleading cost figure. Nevertheless, exposing excess raw materials cost in a management profit report is a touchy issue. Would you want the blame for this laid at your doorstep? It might be better to bury the cost in unit product cost and let it flow against profit in this way, rather than as a naked item for other top-level managers to see in a report.

Many manufacturing businesses use a *standard cost system.* Perhaps the term *system* here is too broad. What is meant is that certain procedures are adopted by the business to establish performance benchmarks, and then actual costs are compared against these standards to help managers carry out their control functions.

Quantity and price standards for raw materials, direct labor, and variable overhead costs are established as yardsticks of performance, and any *variances* (deviations) from the standards are reported. Despite the clear advantages of standard cost systems, many manufacturers do not use any formal standard cost system. It takes a fair amount of time and cost to develop and to update standards.

If the standards are not correct and up to date, they can cause more harm than good. Nevertheless, actual costs should be compared against benchmarks of performance. If nothing else, current costs should be compared against past performance. Many trade associations collect and publish industry cost averages, which are helpful benchmarks of comparison.

KEY CONCEPT — EXCESSIVE PRODUCTION

Please refer one more time to Figure 17.1. Notice that the $685 unit product costs includes $175 of fixed manufacturing overhead costs. If the units are sold, the fixed overhead cost ends up in the cost-of-goods-sold expense; if the units were not sold, then $175 fixed overhead cost per unit is included in ending inventory. Inventory increased 1,000 units in this example, so ending inventory carries $175,000 of fixed overhead costs that will not be charged off to expense until the products are sold in a future period. The inclusion of fixed manufacturing overhead costs in inventory is called *full-cost absorption*. Sounds very reasonable, doesn't it?

Growing businesses need enough production capacity for the sales made during the year and to increase inventory in anticipation of higher sales next year. However, sometimes a manufacturer makes too many products. Production output is much more than sales volume for the period and there is a large increase in inventory—much more than what would be needed for next year.

Suppose, for example, that the company had sold only 6,000 units during the year, even though it manufactured 12,000 units. Figure 17.3 presents the profit and manufacturing cost report for this "disaster" scenario. Notice that the company's inventory would have increased 6,000 units—as many units as it sold during the year!

The inventory buildup could be in anticipation of a long strike looming in the near future, which would shut down production for several months. Or perhaps the company predicts serious shortages of raw material parts during the next several months. There could be such legitimate reasons for a large inventory buildup, but assume not.

Instead, assume the company fell way short of its sales goals for the year and failed to adjust its production output. And assume the sales forecast for next year is not all that encouraging. The large inventory overhang at year-end presents all sorts of problems. Where to store it? Will sales price have to be reduced to move the inventory? And what about the fixed manufacturing overhead cost included in inventory? This last question presents a very troublesome accounting problem.

If only 6,000 units had been produced instead of the 12,000 actual production, the company would have had 50 percent idle capacity—an issue discussed earlier in the chapter. By producing 12,000 units, the company seems to be making full use of its production capacity. But is it, really? Producing *excessive* inventory is a false and illusory use of production capacity.

A good case can be made that no fixed manufacturing overhead costs should be included in *excessive* quantities of inventory; the amount of fixed overhead cost that usually would be allocated to the inventory should be charged off as expense to the period. Unless the company were able to slash its fixed overhead costs, which is very difficult to do in the short run, it will have these fixed overhead costs again next year. It should bite the bullet this year, it is argued.

Assume the company will have to downsize its inventory next year, which means it will have to slash production output next year. Unless it can make substantial cuts in its fixed manufacturing overhead costs, it will have substantial idle capacity next year.

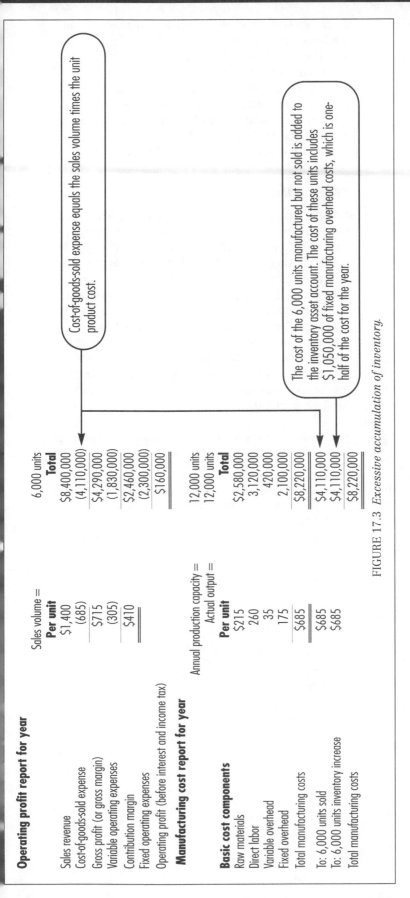

Operating profit report for year

Sales volume = 6,000 units

	Per unit	Total
Sales revenue	$1,400	$8,400,000
Cost-of-goods-sold expense	(685)	(4,110,000)
Gross profit (or gross margin)	$715	$4,290,000
Variable operating expenses	(305)	(1,830,000)
Contribution margin	$410	$2,460,000
Fixed operating expenses		(2,300,000)
Operating profit (before interest and income tax)		$160,000

Manufacturing cost report for year

Annual production capacity = 12,000 units
Actual output = 12,000 units

Basic cost components	Per unit	Total
Raw materials	$215	$2,580,000
Direct labor	260	3,120,000
Variable overhead	35	420,000
Fixed overhead	175	2,100,000
Total manufacturing costs	$685	$8,220,000
To: 6,000 units sold	$685	$4,110,000
To: 6,000 units inventory increase	$685	$4,110,000
Total manufacturing costs		$8,220,000

Cost-of-goods-sold expense equals the sales volume times the unit product cost.

The cost of the 6,000 units manufactured but not sold is added to the inventory asset account. The cost of these units includes $1,050,000 of fixed manufacturing overhead costs, which is one-half of the cost for the year.

FIGURE 17.3 *Excessive accumulation of inventory.*

The question is whether the excess quantity of ending inventory should be valued at only *variable* manufacturing costs and exclude fixed manufacturing overhead costs. As a practical matter, it is very difficult to draw a line between excessive and normal inventory levels. Unless ending inventory is extremely large, the full-cost absorption method is used for ending inventory. The fixed overhead burden rate is included in the unit product cost for all units in ending inventory.*

END POINT

Manufacturers must determine their unit product costs; they have to develop relatively complex accounting systems to keep track of all the different costs that go into manufacturing their products. Direct costs of raw materials and labor and variable overhead costs are relatively straightforward. Fixed manufacturing overhead costs are another story. This chapter examines the problems of excess (idle) production capacity, excess manufacturing costs due to inefficiencies, and excess production output. Managers have to stay on top of these situations if they occur and know how their unit product costs are affected by the accounting procedures for dealing with the problems.

* One theory is that *no* fixed manufacturing overhead costs should be included in ending inventory, whether normal or abnormal quantities are held in stock. Only variable manufacturing costs would be included in unit product cost. This is called *direct costing,* though more properly it should be called *variable* costing. It is not acceptable for external financial reporting or for income tax purposes.

Capital Investment

Determining Future Returns for Capital Investment

Chapter 6 discusses the business entity as an investment enterprise and user of capital. From the capital investment viewpoint, a business is an investment venture that requires a portfolio of operating assets and liabilities. The business must raise the capital needed for investment in its net operating assets. Capital has a cost; interest is paid on debt capital, and enough net income has to be earned to achieve a satisfactory ROE on equity capital.

MACRO VERSUS MICRO BUSINESS INVESTMENT ANALYSIS

In contrast to the company-as-a-whole or big-picture approach (which is introduced in Chapter 6), business managers also have to make decisions on specific individual investments. For example, a business could invest in highly automated equipment that requires less labor; alternatively, it could choose more labor-intensive methods that use older and cheaper equipment. The automated equipment choice would require more initial capital to be invested up front but would yield substantial cost savings in the future. Another investment example is the lease-versus-purchase decision. Instead of purchasing them, a business can lease equipment and machinery, trucks and other vehicles, as well as several other operating assets.

At the macro (company as a whole) level, capital investment analysis focuses on how much total operating profit has to be earned to cover total interest expense, total income tax, and total net income, which depend on the debt and equity capital structure of the business. The basic premise is that the company will continue in business indefinitely and continue reinvesting capital to keep the business going. Accountants call this the *going-concern* assumption.

So, at the company-as-a-whole level, the basic premise is one of continuity of investment, but at the micro level of analysis, the investment under review has a finite life and a planned termination point. As capital is recovered from an individual investment, it leaves the investment and returns to the general pool of capital available to the business. Capital recovered each period is *not* reinvested in the specific investment; each investment is a self-liquidating project. The pattern of capital recovery over the life of the investment is important information to managers that should be sorted out in the analysis.

KEY CONCEPT   CAPITAL INVESTMENT EXAMPLE

Suppose the company is considering buying new, state-of-the-art point-of-sale (POS) electronic cash registers that read bar-coded information on most of the products the business sells. The main purpose is to automate the marking of sales prices on products. The company would avoid the labor cost of marking initial sales prices and sales price changes on its products, which takes many hours each time products are stocked and when prices are changed. Also, the new registers would provide better control over the prices rung up at the point of sale. In the past, the company's cashiers sometimes punched in wrong prices using the old cash registers, either by error or intentionally as a "favor" to their friends.

The investment in the new cash registers would generate future labor cost savings. The company's future annual cash outlays for wages and fringe benefits would decrease if the new cash registers were used. Avoiding a cash outlay is as good as a cash inflow. Both increase the cash balance of the business. The cost of the new cash registers—net of the trade-in allowances on the old cash registers and including the cost of installing the new cash registers—would be $250,000 and would be paid immediately.

The company adopts a five-year planning horizon for this capital investment. In other words, the business limits the recognition of cost savings to five years, even though there may be benefits beyond this time frame. Labor time savings and wage rates are difficult to project beyond a five-year period and many other things can change. At the end of five years, the cash registers are forecast to have no residual value, which is probably very conservative.

The future annual labor cost savings have been estimated based on how many work hours would be saved. These estimates could turn out to be wrong, of course. But there isn't much choice; some forecast has to be made. The labor cost savings are estimated to be $80,000 per year for five years. (The annual cost savings could vary year to year.) For convenience of analysis, assume that the cost savings occur at each year-end, though the savings would occur throughout the year.

The total *future cash returns* from the capital investment would be $400,000 ($80,000 annual labor cost savings × 5 years = $400,000)—an amount that is $150,000 more than the $250,000 cost, or initial capital investment. In other words, the company's operating earnings (profit before interest and income tax) would increase $150,000 over the five years after deducting the cost of the investment. Is this enough to pay interest and income tax and still yield enough net income to meet the company's ROE objective?

This question leads to the capitalization structure of the business, which is summarized as follows:

Capitalization structure and cost-of-capital assumptions

- 1-to-2 debt-to-equity mix
- 8.4% annual interest rate on debt
- 34% income tax rate
- 15.0% annual ROE objective

These assumptions conform closely with the company example that has been used throughout the book. At the end of its most recent year, the (interest-bearing) debt of the company was $975,000 and its total owners' equity was $1,899,230 (see Figure 4.2), which is close to the 1-to-2 debt-to-equity ratio adopted here. The interest rate, income tax rate, and ROE target rate are the same as used previously in the company example.

There may be other incentives to invest in the new cash registers. The company may anticipate that there will be increasing difficulties in hiring qualified employees. The new cash registers would be easier to train new employees on. The new cash registers would enable the company to collect key marketing data on a real-time basis, which it cannot do at present. These may be very important reasons for buying the new cash registers. However, attention here focuses on the financial aspects of the decision.

ANALYSIS OF THE INVESTMENT

The basic approach of the following analysis is to compute the takeouts from each year's cash return. The four basic demands on the annual cash returns are the following:

1. *Interest* on debt capital used during the year
2. *Income tax* on the taxable income for the year
3. *ROE* on equity capital used during the year
4. *Capital recovery,* which is the residual amount after deducting the three preceding items

Figure 18.1 presents this four-way apportionment from each year's cash return. To explain this approach, we will walk down the four steps for year one in some detail. The same steps are repeated in each successive year.

The cash return from labor cost savings is $80,000, all of which is put at the end of the year. The company's cash balance at year-end is $80,000 better off as the result of using the new cash registers. There are four claims on the cash return. First, interest is taken out equal to $7,000—$83,333 debt at start of year × 8.4% interest rate = $7,000. Second, income tax is deducted. The company's taxable income is higher because of the labor cost savings; the incremental income tax increase has to be taken into account.

Income tax each year depends on which depreciation method is used for tax purposes. As you can see in Figure 18.1, the straight-line method is assumed, which is $50,000 per year for five years with a zero salvage value. (The accelerated depreciation method may be used instead.) Notice that the interest expense for the year is deducted to determine taxable income (see the income tax computation for each year in Figure 18.1).

Third, the amount of net income, or earnings on equity capital used during the year, is deducted based on the established ROE objective of 15.0 percent per year. ROE is $25,000 for the first year—$166,667 equity capital at start of year × 15.0% ROE = $25,000. What we are doing is inserting the minimum 15.0 percent ROE rate, which is the company's ROE goal. We don't know whether or not the forecast cash returns from the investment are enough to actually achieve this goal. What we are doing is using the ROE benchmark rate to see whether the predicted cash returns are enough to earn at least a 15.0 percent annual ROE.

The fourth and final claim on each year's cash return is for *recovery of capital*. Capital recovery is the residual amount remaining after deducting interest, income tax, and the ROE amount for the year. For year one, capital recovery is $40,180 (see Figure 18.1). This amount of cash returns to the central bank of the company. It is *not* reinvested in additional cash registers— the company has all the cash registers it needs.

The cash registers example is a self-liquidating capital investment in depreciable operating assets. *Self-liquidating* means that the investment has a finite life (five years in this example) and that capital recovered is not rolled over or reinvested in new cash registers. At the end of the investment's life, there is no more capital invested in this particular investment. In year one, the company liquidates $40,180 of its investment; this much of the initial capital that was invested in the assets is recovered and is no longer tied up in *this* particular project.

Therefore, the amount of capital invested during the second year is reduced by $40,180—$250,000 initial capital – $40,180 capital recovery in first year =

	Year one	Year two	Year three	Year four	Year five	Totals
Cash returns (at year-end)						
Labor cost savings	$80,000	$80,000	$80,000	$80,000	$80,000	
Distribution of cash returns						
Interest (@ 8.4% annual interest rate)	$7,000	$5,875	$4,617	$3,209	$1,635	
Income tax (see schedule below)	7,820	8,203	8,630	9,109	9,644	
ROE (@ 15.0% annual ROE rate)	25,000	20,982	16,488	11,461	5,839	
Recovery of capital	40,180	44,941	50,265	56,220	62,881	
Total (equal to cash return above)	$80,000	$80,000	$80,000	$80,000	$80,000	$254,488
Capital balances at start of year						
Debt (⅓ of total capital)	$83,333	$69,940	$54,960	$38,205	$19,465	
Equity (⅔ of total capital)	166,667	139,880	109,920	76,410	38,929	
Total capital invested in assets	$250,000	$209,820	$164,879	$114,614	$58,394	
Income tax computation						
Operating profit increase	$80,000	$80,000	$80,000	$80,000	$80,000	
Depreciation deduction (straight-line)	(50,000)	(50,000)	(50,000)	(50,000)	(50,000)	
Interest expense (see above)	(7,000)	(5,875)	(4,617)	(3,209)	(1,635)	
Taxable income	$23,000	$24,125	$25,383	$26,791	$28,365	
Income tax @ 34% (entered above)	$7,820	$8,203	$8,630	$9,109	$9,644	

FIGURE 18.1 *Analysis of capital investment.*

Taking out 15.0% annual ROE results in total capital recovery over the five years that is a little more than the $250,000 initial capital invested. Therefore, the actual ROE is somewhat higher than 15.0%. The investment is attractive because its ROE is more than the minimum target ROE established by the company, based on its capitalization structure.

Every year, the total capital invested is divided between debt and equity based on the company's debt-to-equity ratio of 1 to 2.

$209,820 capital balance at start of year two. Capital investment analysis does not follow where the $40,180 capital recovery goes. This capital leaves this project (the cash registers investment). The company may put this money into another investment, increase its cash balance, reduce debt, or pay a higher cash dividend. We don't know.

Each successive year, the investment sizes down. Notice that the annual amounts of interest and net income for ROE decrease year to year, because the total capital invested decreases year to year. In contrast, income tax increases year to year because interest decreases; as you recall, interest is deductible for determining taxable income.

Now, to get to the crux of the analysis: How do we know whether or not the future cash returns are enough to yield a 15.0 percent or higher ROE? The answer is found in the total capital recovery over the life of the investment. If, after taking out the interest, income tax, and ROE from the annual cash returns, the total capital recovery equals or is more than the initial capital invested in the project, then the cash returns are enough.

This is the key test: will total capital recovery over the life of the investment equal or be more than the initial amount of capital invested?

Capital recovery from investment

Year one	$40,180
Year two	44,941
Year three	50,265
Year four	56,220
Year five	62,881
Total capital recovery	$254,488
Initial capital invested	(250,000)
Excess capital recovery	$4,488

As you can see, the total capital recovered is $4,488 more than the initial capital invested. This excess of $4,488 is not really capital recovery; it constitutes additional earnings over and above the annual earnings on equity already included in the list, based on the 15.0 percent ROE rate. In other words, the actual ROE rate is higher than the 15.0 percent used in Figure 18.1. The cash registers investment is attractive from the cost-of-capital point of view because the company would earn a rate higher than its 15.0 percent ROE hurdle rate.

What is the precise ROE rate for this investment? This rate can be solved for; we can change the ROE rate so that the total capital recovery is exactly $250,000. Is this really the most important question, however? The forecast of labor cost savings may turn out to be too high. Perhaps the more relevant question to ask is: How much could the annual labor cost savings drop and still earn a 15.0 percent ROE on the investment? Managers probably should ask for the minimum annual labor cost savings that would justify the capital investment.

DETERMINING FUTURE RETURNS TO EARN TARGET ROE

The tool of analysis shown in Figure 18.1 for the cash registers capital investment example is organized and entered in a computer spreadsheet (EXCEL®). One reason for using a spreadsheet program is to do all the calculations quickly and surely. The spreadsheet also provides the template for examining relevant alternatives or what-if changes in the example. Any of the several factors in the analysis can be changed to test impacts of different data and assumptions. We now change the future cash returns to find the amount of annual labor cost savings that would yield exactly a 15.0 percent annual ROE. All other factors are held the same—only the annual labor cost savings amount is changed.

Finding the answer requires a trial-and-error process that is repeated until the exact amount of future cash returns is found that makes total capital recovery $250,000. This may seem to be complex and time consuming, but just the reverse is true. Only a few trials or passes are required to zero in on the exact answer. From Figure 18.1 we already know that $80,000 is too high, so a first guess might be $79,000. This would still be too high. After a few tries we find the exact amount.

Figure 18.2 presents the analysis schedule for this amount. As you can see, the total capital recovery is exactly $250,000. The annual ROE rate is 15.0 percent, the minimum established by the company, given its capitalization structure. The manager must now make the decision whether or not the company would realistically be able to achieve the annual $78,927 cost savings. This is the hard part, of course. But at least the manager knows that if the annual labor cost savings are this much or more, then making the investment will turn out to be a good decision.

As said before, any of the factors in the analysis can be changed to see how sensitive the outcome of the analysis would change. This is a major reason for using spreadsheets. For example, consider the depreciation method. Different depreciation methods are allowed for income tax purposes. In the example, the straight-line method is used. Alternatively, the business might choose an accelerated method. Any acceptable depreciation schedule can be easily programmed into the spreadsheet.

One important point to take note of in Figure 18.2 is that the depreciation tax deduction schedule is *not* the capital recovery schedule. For instance, the first-year depreciation tax deduction is $50,000 (using the

	Year one	Year two	Year three	Year four	Year five	Totals
Cash returns (at year-end)						
Labor cost savings	$78,927	$78,927	$78,927	$78,927	$78,927	$394,633
Distribution of cash returns						
Interest (@ 8.4% annual interest rate)	$7,000	$5,895	$4,659	$3,276	$1,730	$22,559
Income tax (see schedule below)	7,455	7,831	8,251	8,721	9,247	41,505
ROE (@ 15.0% annual ROE rate)	25,000	21,053	16,638	11,700	6,177	80,568
Recovery of capital	39,471	44,148	49,379	55,229	61,773	250,000
Total (equal to cash return above)	$78,927	$78,927	$78,927	$78,927	$78,927	$394,633
Capital balances at start of year						
Debt (⅓ of total capital)	$83,333	$70,176	$55,460	$39,001	$20,591	
Equity (⅔ of total capital)	166,667	140,352	110,920	78,001	41,182	
Total capital invested in assets	$250,000	$210,529	$166,380	$117,002	$61,773	
Income tax computation						
Operating profit increase	$78,927	$78,927	$78,927	$78,927	$78,927	$394,633
Depreciation deduction (straight-line)	(50,000)	(50,000)	(50,000)	(50,000)	(50,000)	(250,000)
Interest expense (see above)	(7,000)	(5,895)	(4,659)	(3,276)	(1,730)	(22,559)
Taxable income	$21,927	$23,032	$24,268	$25,650	$27,197	
Income tax @ 34% (entered above)	$7,455	$7,831	$8,251	$8,721	$9,247	$41,505

Notice that these two are equal, so annual ROE is exactly 15.0%.

FIGURE 18.2 Future returns that yield target ROE.

straight-line method), but the first-year capital recovery is $39,471. Total depreciation and total capital recovery amounts are both $250,000 for the five years combined. But they differ year to year.

This is a nuisance in capital investment analysis, especially in using the discounted cash flow methods for capital investment analysis (explained in the next chapter). To repeat an earlier point, using the spreadsheet tool is a practical and relatively painless way of dealing with the differences between tax depreciation and capital recovery amounts year to year.

KEY CONCEPT
LEASE VERSUS BUY

Business managers are faced with the lease-versus-buy choice. Almost any long-term operating asset (building, trucks, equipment, machinery, etc.) can be leased either directly from the manufacturer or indirectly through a third-party leasing specialist. The cash registers discussed earlier in the chapter probably could have been leased instead of purchased. Managers generally are interested in leasing, especially if the business is short of cash. Perhaps the lessor has a lower cost of capital than the lessee, in which case the business would be better off leasing rather than investing its own capital in the assets.

Suppose the company could have leased the cash registers instead of buying them; assume the lessor had offered an annual rent of $78,927 for five years, which is precisely the minimum annual labor cost savings necessary to earn 15.0 percent ROE (see Figure 18.2). Generally, the lessee bears all costs of possession and use of the assets that it would have if it had bought them outright. For example, the company would pay the fire and theft insurance on the assets whether they were owned or leased. By leasing the cash registers, the company would reduce its annual labor costs by $78,927 but would pay annual lease rent of the same amount. From the financial point of view, leasing versus buying is a standoff.

Leases involve certain other considerations beyond just the financial aspects. For example, the company prefers not to assume the economic risks of owning the cash registers. In a fast-changing technological environment, the business may be unwilling to assume the risks of buying cash registers today that may be obsolete in two or three years. So the company may shop around for a two- or three-year lease.

To illustrate the lease-versus-buy analysis, consider the following new example. Suppose the company has just installed new production machinery and equipment in its plant to expand its annual output capacity. These assets have just been installed and are ready for use. The contract price for the machinery and equipment and their installation is $575,000.

The contractor that built and installed the machinery and equipment has offered to lease everything to the company for five years at quarterly rents of $53,371.50, or $213,486 annually. At the end of the lease, the company would have the option to purchase the assets for $35,000. The company estimates that the assets will have a fair value considerably more than this after five years. If the company buys the assets, it would depreciate them over five years for income tax purposes. Is the lease attractive, given the capitalization structure and cost of capital of the company?

The spreadsheet analysis tool used for the cash registers capital investment example earlier in the chapter is equally useful for the lease-versus-buy decision. The basic idea is that by investing $575,000 today the company could avoid the lease payments—the lease payments are equivalent to the labor cost savings factor in the cash registers example.

Figure 18.3 presents the analysis of the lease. The lease rents are put on an annual basis at the end of each year. (This is for convenience of presentation and does not make any significant difference to the answer.) Also, notice that the $35,000 purchase option price at the end of the lease would be avoided by purchasing the assets and, therefore, is shown as a future return on the investment.

The analysis in Figure 18.3 shows that the lease rents would yield a 24.0 percent ROE, which is much higher than the company's 15.0 percent ROE benchmark. Thus, leasing is not a good decision because the company could earn 24.0 percent ROE by purchasing the assets today for $575,000. Putting it another way, the lessor (the contractor who made and installed the machinery and equipment) would earn a 24.0 percent ROE if it had the same capitalization structure as the company. Of course, the lessor may have a different debt-to-equity mix, and its interest rate and ROE goal may be different, as well as its income tax situation.

In theory, the company should rank all its capital investment opportunities and select the one with the highest ROE first, and so on. Looking at only this one particular choice between lease and purchase, the company should favor the purchase. Perhaps the company has other investment opportunities for its available capital that promise an even higher ROE than 24.0 percent. If this is true, the company should look at these alternatives, although this would raise the question of why the company is satisfied with a 15.0 percent ROE on its main line of business.

END POINT

Business managers make many capital investment decisions. The analysis hinges on the cost-of-capital requirements of the business, which are determined by the

	Year one	Year two	Year three	Year four	Year five	Totals
Cash returns (at year-end)						
Lease rents	$213,486	$213,486	$213,486	$213,486	$213,486	$1,067,432
Purchase option					35,000	35,000
					$248,486	$1,102,432
Distribution of cash returns						
Interest (@ 8.4% annual interest rate)	$16,100	$13,933	$11,380	$8,371	$4,826	$54,611
Income tax (see schedule below)	28,011	28,748	29,616	30,639	43,745	160,759
ROE (@ 24.0% annual ROE rate)*	92,000	79,620	65,030	47,837	27,575	312,062
Recovery of capital	77,375	91,185	107,460	126,639	172,342	575,000
Total (equal to cash returns above)	$213,486	$213,486	$213,486	$213,486	$248,486	$1,102,432
Capital balances at start of year						
Debt (% of total capital)	$191,667	$165,875	$135,480	$99,660	$57,447	
Equity (% of total capital)	383,333	331,750	270,960	199,320	114,894	
Total capital invested in assets	$575,000	$497,625	$406,440	$298,980	$172,341	
Income tax computation						
Operating profit increase	$213,486	$213,486	$213,486	$213,486	$248,486	$1,102,432
Depreciation deduction (straight-line)	(115,000)	(115,000)	(115,000)	(115,000)	(115,000)	(575,000)
Interest expense (see above)	(16,100)	(13,933)	(11,380)	(8,371)	(4,826)	(54,611)
Taxable income	$82,386	$84,553	$87,106	$90,115	$128,661	$160,759
Income tax @ 34% (entered above)	$28,011	$28,748	$29,616	$30,639	$43,745	

These two amounts are key in the analysis; they must be equal. The other totals are useful check figures.

*The lessor would earn 24.0% annual ROE, which is considerably more than the company's 15.0% ROE. This ROE rate has to be solved for by trial and error, although this goes very fast on a computer spreadsheet program.

FIGURE 18.3 *Lease-versus-buy analysis.*

company's mix of debt and equity capital, the cost of each, and the income tax situation of the business. The cost of equity capital is not a contractual rate like interest. The ROE (return on equity) goal and objective of the business must be determined by top management.

Given the benchmark ROE goal of the business, the manager should put the projected future returns from the investment to this cost-of-capital test. Alternatively, starting with the entry cost of the investment, the manager should determine how much the future returns would have to be to at least satisfy the ROE goal of the business. Then the manager has to judge whether these future returns can be actually achieved.

The chapter offers a practical and straightforward tool of analysis to help managers apply the cost-of-capital imperatives of the business to capital investment decisions. A computer spreadsheet program is the best way of using this tool of analysis. The versatility of computer spreadsheet programs makes them a very powerful tool of analysis. Analysis is important, to be sure. More fundamental is the ability of managers to find good capital investment opportunities and blend them into the overall strategy of the business.

CHAPTER 19

Discounting Future Returns from Capital Investment

T he pivotal idea and central premise behind the analytical tools discussed in both this and the previous chapter is the *time value of money*. Capital has a time-cost; the cost of using capital over a period of time must be taken into account in evaluating a capital investment and comparing it with alternative uses of the capital.

SPREADSHEET VERSUS MATHEMATICAL ANALYSIS OF CAPITAL INVESTMENTS

The analysis method explained in the previous chapter uses a spreadsheet program. Even if the manager is not a spreadsheet user, the logic and layout of the printout is very important to understand. The versatility of a spreadsheet program makes it a very useful tool. Different scenarios can be examined quickly and efficiently, which is an enormous advantage. In most practical business capital investment situations, several critical assumptions and forecasts have to be made, and the manager should test the sensitivity to each critical input factor.

Furthermore, the spreadsheet tool makes it easy to present all relevant information—both in the management decision-making analysis phase and also for management control after a decision is made. The year-by-year format shown in Figure 18.2 for the cash registers investment, which is a very typical example, provides essential benchmark information for monitoring and controlling the actual results of the investment as it plays out year by year. Spreadsheets are certainly a very useful tool for analysis, calculations, and presentation of information.

Another reason for using the spreadsheet approach in the previous chapter is to avoid mathematically based procedures for analyzing capital investments. In the previous chapter, not one mathematical equation was presented. In my experience, managers are put off by the mathematical approach, which is usually loaded with rather arcane equations and unfamiliar symbols.

Before spreadsheets came along, certain mathematical tools and techniques of analysis were developed that have become the touchstones of capital investment analysis. The names of these mathematical tools have become household words and are used freely in the business and financial world. Managers, business and financial professionals, and investors should know what the terms mean and how they are used. This chapter presents a quick tour of the basic mathematical tools for capital investment analysis, which rest on one basic equation.

THE BASIC EQUATION OF MATHEMATICAL TECHNIQUES

Chapter 6 explains that return on investment (ROI) is the basic tool for analysis for capital investments. As explained earlier, ROI must be defined and put into the context of which particular type of investment is being examined. ROI has to be matched with the type of investor. The main concern of this book is the business entity as the investor.

The particular ROI rate used in the mathematical techniques is the *after-tax weighted-average cost of capital* of the business. This rate is either used directly and explicitly in the analysis or it serves as the benchmark for evaluating the capital investment. It is often called the *hurdle rate* because it is the minimum acceptable rate of earnings on capital investments by the business—the company should do at least this well and, hopefully, better.

For the same example used in the previous chapter, the company's after-tax weighted-average cost of capital is determined as follows:

After-tax weighted-average cost-of-capital rate computation				
Source of capital	Weight	Cost of capital rates		
Debt:	⅓ ×	(8.4%)(1 − 34%)	=	1.848%
Equity:	⅔ ×	15.0%	=	10.000%
				11.848%

- The contractual interest rate paid to lenders is 8.4 percent and the income tax rate is 34 percent. So the after-tax cost of interest is: $(8.4\%)(.66) = 5.544\%$.

- The ROE goal of the company is 15.0 percent per year, which, by definition, is the after-tax rate.

In the example, the company's ratio of debt-to-equity capital is 1 to 2, or one dollar of debt for every two dollars of equity. In the computation, therefore, debt capital is given one-third weight and equity capital is given two-thirds weight.

Because interest is deductible to determine taxable income, the interest rate is multiplied by 1 minus the tax rate to put it on an after-tax basis. The purpose is to put interest on the same basis as the ROE rate in the computation. ROE is an after-tax rate. Net income (which is after tax) is divided by owners' equity to determine ROE. In short, both cost-of-capital rates are after tax.

There is no standard acronym for the after-tax weighted-average cost-of-capital rate, such as ATWA-COC (which would be quite a mouthful). It is frequently represented by r in equations, which we use in the following discussion. The shorter term, *cost of capital,* will be used interchangeably with the much longer term, *after-tax weighted-average cost of capital.*

The basic capital investment equation is

$$PV = FV \div (1 + r)^n$$

- PV means the *present value* of the capital investment.

- FV means *future value* and refers to one specific future after-tax cash return from the capital investment.

- r is either (a) *the after-tax weighted average cost-of-capital* rate, or (b) the discount rate that is solved for in the analysis.

- n means the *number of periods* until the FV (future cash return) is received.

The n and r in the equation must be for the same time interval; in other words, r is the rate for one period of time. If we know any three of the four variables in the equation, we can solve for the unknown fourth variable. The r factor in the equation may be the unknown variable that is solved for—a very important technique explained later in the chapter.

DISCOUNTED CASH FLOW (DCF)
One Period, One Future Return

We start with a hypothetical example that has only one future cash return. Suppose one year from now the company receives an after-tax cash return of $111,848 from an investment. Inserting the variables into the equation we get

$$PV = \$111,848 \div (1 + .11848)^1$$

Solving for PV gives $100,000, which you can eyeball from the equation: $111,848 ÷ 1.11848 = $100,000.

The present value (PV) is the maximum amount the company should invest today, given its cost of capital. The $111,848 future cash return to be received one year from today is "worth" $100,000 today. In other words, if the entry cost is $100,000, the company would earn exactly its after-tax weighted-average cost-of-capital rate on the investment.*

Computing the present value is called *discounting* the future cash flow. Hence, the term *discounted cash flow* (DCF), which is the generic name for this tool of analysis. The required amount to cover the company's cost of capital is discounted from the future cash return from the investment. This leaves the capital recovery from the investment. In other words, present value is the amount of capital recovered from the investment after deducting the amount of earnings required to cover the company's cost of capital.

If the entry cost today of the investment is $100,000 but the future cash return is not known, the entry cost can be substituted for PV in the equation and the equation is solved for FV

$$\$100,000 = FV \div (1 + .11848)^1$$

or

$$\$100,000 \times (1 + .11848)^1 = FV$$

The future after-tax cash return one year from today would have to be at least $111,848 to satisfy the company's cost of capital.

KEY CONCEPT   Two Periods, Two Future Returns

Assume the company has identified a capital investment opportunity that would require a $100,000 entry cost today and promises two future returns: Each cash return is $59,052, the first to be received one year from today and the second two years from today. The company's after-tax weighted-average cost of capital is 11.848 percent per year, as previously computed. Two present values can be computed and the two results added to get the total present value of the investment, as follows:

$$PV_1 = \$59,052 \div (1 + .11848)^1$$
$$PV_2 = \$59,052 \div (1 + .11848)^2$$
$$PV_1 + PV_2 = \text{Total PV of investment}$$

These calculations are burdensome. The theory is the same, but the arithmetic becomes irksome.

---

* The before-tax future cash return would have to be $117,952. Interest would be: $33,333 debt × 8.4% = $2,800. There is no taxable income from this $2,800 because interest is deductible. The company would have to earn $15,152 before-tax on equity capital which, at the 34 percent tax rate, would give after-tax net income of $10,000: $10,000 net income ÷ $66,666 equity capital = 15.0% ROE.

A financial calculator can be used to compute the two PV amounts: $PV_1 = \$52,796$ and $PV_2 = \$47,204$.* The total PV equals $100,000, the same as the entry cost of the investment. The present values of this and the previous example are the same, so the investments are equally satisfactory—although this investment would be a two-year commitment compared with only one year in the previous case.

The PV approach has one serious disadvantage. The unfolding of the investment over the two years is not clear from the calculation. Rather than opening up the investment for closer inspection, the PV computation closes it down and telescopes the information into only one number, which does not reveal the other information about the investment over its life. It's better to take a full look at the investment, such as is presented in Figure 19.1.

This presentation shows that the cash return at the end of year one is split between $11,848 to cost of capital and $47,204 to capital recovery. The capital recovery aspect of every investment is extremely important. The capital recovery portion of the cash return at the end of year one reduces the amount of capital invested during year two. Only $52,796 is invested during the second year: $100,000 – $47,204 = $52,796. It is vital to understand the decreasing balance and self-liquidating nature of capital investments. The pattern of capital recovery period by period is very important to the analysis.

By the way, Figure 19.1 offers proof that this investment would yield exactly an 11.848 percent rate of earnings on the investment. Why? Notice that the total capital recovered, after taking out 11.848 percent cost of capital each year, is $100,000, which equals the entry cost. Thus the 11.848 percent discount rate must be correct; the company would earn its cost of capital and recover the entry cost of the investment.

KEY CONCEPT Two Periods, One Future Return

Suppose at the end of the first year there is no cash return; instead, only one cash return is received at the end of year two in the amount of $125,100. The present value equation in this case is as follows:

$$PV = \$125,100 \div (1 + .11848)^2$$

The main difference here is that there are two periods of waiting to get to the cash return from the investment. The future cash return is divided by (1 + cost-of-capital rate) raised to the second power, which equals

---

* The mathematical formula for the computation is not shown here. Virtually no one explicitly uses the formula to compute present value. Such computations are done with a financial calculator or with the financial functions in a spreadsheet program.

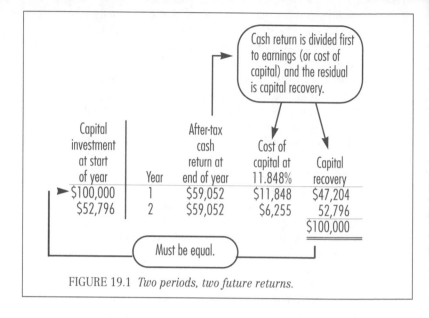

Cash return is divided first to earnings (or cost of capital) and the residual is capital recovery.

Capital investment at start of year	Year	After-tax cash return at end of year	Cost of capital at 11.848%	Capital recovery
$100,000	1	$59,052	$11,848	$47,204
$52,796	2	$59,052	$6,255	52,796
				$100,000

Must be equal.

FIGURE 19.1 *Two periods, two future returns.*

1.25100. So the PV equals exactly $100,000, the entry cost of the investment.

The PV calculation obscures important information that is revealed in Figure 19.2. This example demonstrates the *compounding* of earnings. The company had $100,000 invested during year one and, at 11.848 percent, the business earned $11,848 for the year. But no cash return is received at the end of the first year.

The amount earned but not received is compounded or added into the capital investment balance at the start of year two. For year two, the 11.848 percent is based on the higher investment balance, which you can see in Figure 19.2. The capital recovery column shows a negative number for year one. This means that the earnings for the year would not be available for withdrawal from the investment and, therefore, would have to be reinvested through the second year. It's as if the company received the $11,848 earnings at the end of year one, but immediately had to turn around and put the money back into the investment to keep it going.

Compound interest is commonly used to describe the reinvestment of earnings, although the term *interest* is too restrictive. The term actually refers to earnings in general and not just interest income. Compound interest (earnings) can be compared with retained earnings in the balance sheet—net income earned but not paid out as dividends and reinvested in the business.

In this investment, the company would make 11.848 percent ROI each year, but none of the earnings would be available in cash until the end of year two. Total earnings over the two years would be slightly higher

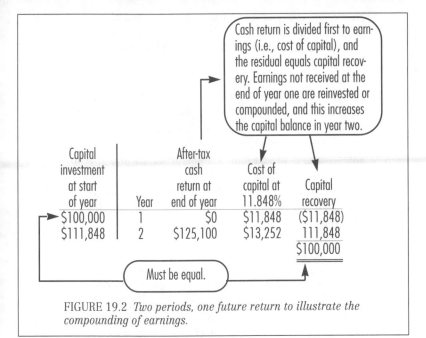

Cash return is divided first to earnings (i.e., cost of capital), and the residual equals capital recovery. Earnings not received at the end of year one are reinvested or compounded, and this increases the capital balance in year two.

Capital investment at start of year	Year	After-tax cash return at end of year	Cost of capital at 11.848%	Capital recovery
$100,000	1	$0	$11,848	($11,848)
$111,848	2	$125,100	$13,252	111,848
				$100,000

Must be equal.

FIGURE 19.2 *Two periods, one future return to illustrate the compounding of earnings.*

because more capital is invested during the second year compared with the earlier example.

Net Present Value (NPV) and Internal Rate of Return (IRR)

Another scenario for a two-period, two-future-cash-returns example is now introduced to highlight another tool for capital investment analysis. The entry cost today is $100,000 for the investment. The future after-tax cash returns would be $62,689 at the end of year one and year two; these are higher future values compared with the earlier example. Using the company's 11.848 percent after-tax weighted-average cost of capital as the discount rate, the PV of the investment is computed as follows:

$$PV_1 = \$62,689 \div (1 + .11848)^1$$
$$PV_2 = \$62,689 \div (1 + .11848)^2$$
$$PV_1 + PV_2 = \$106,160$$

As you can see, the PV is $6,160 more than the entry cost. The *net present value* (NPV) is the "excess" recovered from the investment, over and above the initial capital invested. So, in this example, NPV is $6,160. It represents additional earnings over and above the earnings based on the 11.848 percent cost-of-capital rate. The NPV has informational value, but it is not an ideal measure to compare with other investment opportunities.

Instead, the *internal rate of return* (IRR) can be determined for the investment. The IRR is that precise discount rate that makes PV exactly equal to the $100,000 entry cost. The IRR is a very useful measure of the investment's performance. Given the $100,000

entry cost today and two future cash returns of
$62,689, the IRR can be solved for; it is 16.5 percent,
which is higher than the company's 11.848 percent
cost-of-capital rate.

How did I determine that the IRR is 16.5 percent? I
used my financial calculator. How does the calculator
find the IRR? A trial-and-error process is used to solve
for the IRR, whether you do it with a financial calculator or with a spreadsheet. The trial-and-error routine
(algorithm) is programmed into calculators and spreadsheet programs. Basically, you start with a feasible discount rate and then the rate is adjusted in the right
direction until the answer comes out just right. The
electronic process is so fast that you think it is just one
computation, but it isn't.

Figure 19.3 demonstrates that the IRR for the
investment is 16.5 percent. The 16.5 percent rate is
correct because the total capital recovered equals the
$100,000 entry cost. To sum up briefly, the company
would invest $100,000 today, to start the investment.
One year later it receives an after-tax return of
$62,689. From this, the company takes out, or dis-
counts, 16.5 percent, which for year one is $16,500.
This amount is deducted from the cash return, and
the $46,189 remainder is the capital recovery for
year one.

The company's capital investment is reduced by
this capital recovery amount. So the company would
have only $53,811 invested during the second year.
For both years combined, the total capital recovered
is exactly equal to the $100,000 entry cost. Therefore,
the 16.5 percent annual rate of earnings is
correct.

As a rule, the business should favor investments
with higher IRRs in preference to investments with
lower IRRs and should not accept any investment that
has an IRR less than the company's hurdle rate, that is,
its after-tax weighted-average cost-of-capital rate.
Putting this another way, a business should not accept
an investment that has a negative net present value.
This is the theory.

Making capital investment decisions is very complex and usually involves many other nonquantitative
or qualitative factors that are difficult to capture in the
analysis. A company may go ahead with an investment that has a low IRR because of political pressures
or to accomplish social objectives beyond the profit
motive. The company may make a large capital
investment even if the numbers don't justify the decision to forestall competitors from entering its market,
for example. Long-run capital investment decisions
are, at bottom, really survival decisions—the company
may have to make huge capital investments to
upgrade, automate, or expand; if they don't, they
may die.

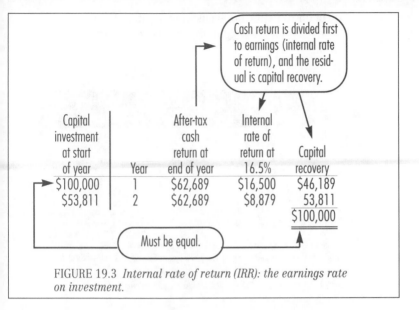

FIGURE 19.3 *Internal rate of return (IRR): the earnings rate on investment.*

 CASH REGISTERS INVESTMENT EXAMPLE REVISITED

One limitation of the previous discussion in this chapter is that we do not address the question of depreciation. The earlier examples assume that the future cash returns are already on an after-tax basis and that the correct amount of income tax is deducted. Income tax depends on which depreciation method is used. Most business capital investments are in depreciable assets. Thus, the depreciation factor is an important element in business capital investment analysis.

A good example is the one discussed in the previous chapter: the investment in the new cash registers. Please refer to Figure 18.2; notice that the capital recovery amounts each year differ from the depreciation deductions for income tax that year. Depreciation deductions are made according to an accelerated method or the straight-line method of allocation. In contrast, capital recovery depends on the stream of future cash returns from the investment.

The disparity year by year between the capital recovery amount and the depreciation amount makes it necessary to do two separate PV computations, which are explained as follows (see Figure 18.2 for data):

1. Pretend that the before-tax cash returns from the investment are entirely taxable and deduct 34 percent (the income tax rate) from the returns. This step ignores the depreciation deduction, which is taken into account in the second step. Interest is also deductible, so this step also overstates income tax for a second reason, but this part of the overstatement is adjusted for by putting the interest

rate on the after-tax basis in computing the company's after-tax weighted-average cost-of-capital rate.

Year	Before-tax returns	Less tax @ 34%	After-tax returns
1	$78,927	$26,835	$52,092
2	78,927	26,835	52,092
3	78,927	26,835	52,092
4	78,927	26,835	52,092
5	78,927	26,835	52,092
Present value @ 11.848% discount rate			$188,488*

*You can solve for this amount on a financial calculator by entering N = 5, PMT = $52,092, INT = 11.848%, and then pushing the PV key. Make sure that the calculation is set for end-of-period payments and that the ending value (FV) is set equal to $0. The FV key is used to enter the terminal value of the investment. Computer spreadsheet programs include the PV, as well as many other financial functions.

This step provides an intermediate answer; income tax is overstated because the depreciation deduction has not yet been considered, which is done in the next step.

2. Next, the present value of the depreciation tax *savings* (as they are called) is computed. In this example, the straight-line depreciation method is used; the company deducts $50,000 depreciation each year. This reduces taxable income each year and thus reduces income tax $17,000 each year: $50,000 × 34% tax rate = $17,000.

Year	Depreciation	Tax savings @ 34%
1	$50,000	$17,000
2	50,000	17,000
3	50,000	17,000
4	50,000	17,000
5	50,000	17,000
Present value @ 11.848% discount rate		$61,512

Adding together the two present values gives: $188,488 + $61,512 = $250,000. The $250,000 present value exactly equals the entry cost of the investment. Therefore, the IRR for this investment project is 11.848 percent, which is the company's after-tax weighted-average cost-of-capital rate. (Figure 18.2 also demonstrates that the company earns exactly its cost-of-capital rate in a different manner.)

REGARDING THE COST-OF-CAPITAL PARAMETERS

One brief comment here on the cost-of-capital parameters. Most discourses on business capital investment analysis assume a constant mix, or ratio, of debt and equity. And the cost of each source of capital is held constant. Also, the income tax rate is held constant. Before spreadsheets came along, there were very practical reasons for this: to avoid having to use more than one cost-of-capital rate or discount rate in the analysis. Today, this is no longer necessary.

If the situation calls for it, the manager should change the mix of debt and equity from one period to the next, or change the interest rate and/or ROE rate from period to period. Each period could be assigned its own cost-of-capital rate, in other words. Sometimes this is necessary in the analysis. For instance, a capital investment may be of a *direct financing* variety, in which a specific loan is secured that is tied to this one and only one investment.

One example of direct financing is when a business leases its products instead of selling them. It may use the assets being leased as collateral for the debt. In any case, the company commits to a definite payoff schedule on the loan. The mix or ratio of debt-to-equity capital invested in the lease will differ period to period. Also, the interest rate on the lease loan as well as the ROE goal for the lease investment generally are different from the company's main line of business.

END POINT

This chapter presents a succinct survey of basic mathematical tools for analyzing business capital investments. The generic term of these tools is *discounted cash flow* (DCF). A series of future cash returns is discounted to calculate the present value (PV) or net present value (NPV) of the investment. Alternatively, the internal rate of return (IRR) that the future returns would yield is determined. Instead of starting with a predicted stream of future cash returns, the analysis may begin with the entry cost of the investment and determine the one or more future cash returns that would have to be received from the investment to meet the cost-of-capital requirements for the investment.

The criterion for the mathematical tools of analysis is the *after-tax weighted-average cost of capital,* which is used as the discount rate to determine PV and NPV or as the yardstick for comparison with the IRR. This is often called the hurdle rate; it is based on the company's mix of debt and equity capital and the cost of each, as well as the company's income tax rate.

For capital investment analysis, both the spreadsheet tool and the mathematical tools rest on the same premise: the time value of money. The mathematical tools concentrate on one number, such as PV or IRR. Other aspects of the investment such as the amount of capital invested and the amount of earnings period by period are excluded from attention.

Spreadsheets are a practical and efficient tool for analyzing and displaying all relevant information for management decision making, as well as for management control after the decision has been made. Spreadsheet programs include the financial mathematical tools; these are included as functions in the program, which are called up by name. This and the preceding chapter, taken together, offer a complete menu of analysis tools for the business manager to choose from for capital investment analysis.

Glossary of Key Terms, with Management Commentary

(*Note:* **Bold** indicates terms defined in the Glossary.)

accounting system   The forms and procedures used to facilitate and record transactions and operations, and the accounts and documents used to store information for the preparation of **financial statements,** tax returns, and **management control** reports. See also **internal (accounting) controls.**

accounts receivable turnover ratio   See **receivable/revenue ratio.**

accrueds/interest expense ratio   Interest payable at the end of the period divided by the total interest expense for the period. A certain amount of interest expense is unpaid at the end of the period. A change in the interest payable **operating liability** affects **cash flow from profit.**

accrueds/operating expenses ratio   Accrued expenses payable at the end of the period divided by total operating expenses for the period, excluding cost of goods sold, **depreciation,** interest, and income tax expenses because these four expenses do not involve this particular **operating liability.** Expressed as weeks of operating expenses. Depends on the average time between when the business records certain operating expenses and when they are later paid. A change in the accrued expenses operating liability affects **cash flow from profit.**

acid test ratio   See **quick ratio.**

asset turnover ratio   A broad-gauge measure of the sales revenue productivity of assets. In this book, this ratio equals annual sales revenue divided by **net operating assets;** short-term non-interest-bearing **operating liabilities** are deducted from total assets.

Although a useful ratio, the more critical test is not sales but **profit** earned on assets measured by the **return on assets (ROA)** ratio. More specific asset and liability **operating ratios** are needed for management decision making and control.

balance sheet   Better titled the statement of financial condition. This **financial statement** summarizes the assets, liabilities, and owners' equity of the business at a moment in time. Prepared at the end of each profit period and whenever else needed. Presents the cumulative results of profit-making operations and investment and financing transactions. One of the three primary financial statements of business.

bottom-line profit   See **net income.**

breakeven (point or **volume)**   The annual sales volume level at which total **contribution margin** equals total annual **fixed expenses.** Only a point of reference, not the goal of business. Computed by dividing total fixed expenses by the contribution margin profit per unit. Breakeven is useful for three purposes: (1) actual sales volume is compared against it to measure the **margin of safety,** (2) it serves as the baseline point of reference to determine **operating profit,** and (3) it can be used to analyze the effects of **operating leverage.**

budgeting   A financial planning and control system based on sales forecasts, as well as capital expenditures and capital sources forecasts. Can be very general or exceedingly detailed, informal or very formal. Objectives are established and actual performance is compared against these goals to determine achievements and variances. There is much debate on the incentive and other behavior aspects of budgeting.

capacity   Most often thought of as the maximum annual production output of a manufacturer. The concept applies with equal relevance to sales volume potential for retailers and service businesses. Capacity is provided by the **fixed costs** of the period, which should be translated into how much capacity is made available. If actual production output is substantially less than manufacturing capacity, the appropriate fraction of total fixed **manufacturing overhead costs** should be charged off to the period and not included (absorbed) in **product cost.**

capital investment   The term *investment* means that money put in the venture is expected to be recovered (restored or reclaimed) through future **returns** and that there will be earnings, income, or profit on the capital until the capital has been fully recovered. The business taken as a whole is a capital investment project; capital is invested in **net operating assets.** As capital is recovered, it is reinvested by the business to remain a going concern. Capital investments in specific assets by business involve the comparison of alternatives, which is called *capital budgeting* in the finance field. *Budgeting* here refers to the allocation of scarce capital resources.

capital investment analysis   The basic purpose is to determine the income, earnings, or gain relative to the amount of capital invested, and is usually expressed as a **return on investment (ROI)** percentage per period. The two basic tools for capital investment analysis are: (1) the more recent **spreadsheet** approach and (2) the more traditional mathematical approach based on key equations for determining **present value** and **internal rate of return (IRR)**. See also **net present value (NPV), weighted-average cost of capital (hurdle rate), returns, capital recovery,** and **return on equity (ROE).**

capital recovery   The first priority on the **returns** from a **capital investment** is to recover the initial amount of capital invested—there is no profit, income, or earnings on the investment unless the original amount of capital invested is recovered. Capital recovery means the recapture or regaining of the initial capital invested over the life of the investment. In brief, this means the return of capital. In addition, the future returns have to be enough to provide for earnings or return on capital. The **spreadsheet** tool for **capital investment analysis** sorts out how much capital is recovered each period, whereas the mathematical method of analysis does not, which is a major disadvantage of this equation-based tool.

capital turnover   The cycle of investing capital and then recovering capital either over the short run, such as inventory bought and then sold, or over the longer run, such as fixed assets that are bought and then used many years. Also refers to the cycle of raising capital and returning capital to its sources, such as borrowing and later repaying a short-term note payable or issuing capital stock that is not retired for many years.

capitalization structure   Refers to the mix and proportions of interest-bearing debt versus equity capital sources that are used to finance the **net operating assets** of a business. Also includes the variations and modifications to basic debt and equity instruments such as stock options and convertible features on debt. Using debt capital has a **financial leverage** effect on **net income.**

cash flow   At once an obvious yet elusive concept. Obviously, it refers to cash inflows and outflows during a period. Yet the specific sources and uses of cash flows are not clear from this general term. Frequently used as a shorthand phrase for **cash flow from profit.** The **cash flow statement** classifies **cash flows** into three fundamentally different types.

cash flow analysis   Determining differences in **cash flow from profit** caused by changes in profit factors, such as sales volume and sales price increases and decreases. Cash flow from profit depends heavily on which particular profit factors change. Some changes have much more favorable results than other changes, and managers must be clear on these differences.

cash flow from profit   Equals **net income** for the period adjusted for changes in short-term **operating assets** and **liabilities** during the period; also, **depreciation** expense is added back to net income (as well as any other noncash outlay expense). Labeled "cash flow from operating activities" in the external **cash flow statement** because revenue and expenses are the profit-making operations of the business. Can be less than **profit** for the period, and even negative in extreme cases. Also called **free cash flow** to emphasize that this source of cash is free from need of borrowing money, issuing capital stock shares, or selling assets.

cash flow statement   Exactly what its name implies, it summarizes cash inflows and outflows for a period according to threefold classification: (1) **cash flow from profit** (operating activities), (2) investing and disinvesting activities, and (3) financing activities. One of the three primary **financial statements** of business. This financial statement can help to detect possible fraud because such schemes often require the overstatement of accounts receivable or inventory. Increases in these two **operating assets** are reported in the cash flow statement and should be scrutinized closely by managers.

cash/sales relationship   Equals cash balance at the end of the period divided by total sales revenue for the period, usually expressed as weeks of sales. A fascinating comparison, because these are two of the most important numbers in **financial statements.** Clearly, a business needs an adequate day-to-day working cash balance to serve as a buffer against unexpected delays in cash receipts and unexpected demands for cash payments. *Note:* There is no general agreement or benchmark regarding how large the cash balance should be relative to annual sales revenue.

contribution margin (profit)   Equals sales revenue minus cost of goods sold and all variable operating expenses, but before fixed operating expenses are deducted. Profit down to this point contributes toward covering fixed operating expenses, and interest and income tax expenses as well. On a per-unit basis, contribution margin equals sales price less unit **product cost** and less variable operating expenses per unit. An exceedingly important intermediate measure of profit that is used throughout the analysis of profit performance.

cost (expense) allocation   Some costs are indirect from specific products and sales activity; there is no obvious basis for matching up these costs with sales revenue. In contrast, direct costs can be coupled with their corresponding sales revenue. Indirect costs may be allocated; the costs can be apportioned to specific products and sales revenue sources by some method. Any allocation of indirect costs should be taken with a grain of salt. Cost allocation is not done primarily for management decision making and control.

cost of capital   Refers generally to the need to pay interest on debt capital and to earn at least an adequate **net income** on equity capital. See **weighted-average cost of capital** and **opportunity cost of capital.**

current ratio   Calculated to assess the short-term solvency or debt-paying ability of a business; equals total current assets divided by total current liabilities. However, it's not necessarily a good predictor of short-term solvency. Some businesses remain quite solvent with a low current ratio, and others could be in trouble with an apparent high current ratio.

depreciation (expense)   Usually discussed in two contexts: (1) the allocation of fixed asset cost over the useful lives of these **operating assets** and (2) a noncash outlay expense that is added back to **net income** in computing **cash flow from profit.** A third important aspect of depreciation is that the original capital invested in fixed assets is recovered year by year through sales revenue; in this way, fixed assets are gradually sold off to customers. In pure theory, the **capital recovery** pattern of fixed assets should determine depreciation expense recorded each period. In actual practice, arbitrary allocation methods are used that are heavily influenced by the income tax code.

depreciation/fixed assets relationship   Annual **depreciation** expense expressed as a percent of original cost of depreciable fixed assets (which excludes land). Depends on mix of short-lived and long-lived fixed assets used by business, and the choice between accelerated versus straight-line depreciation methods. A significant change in this percentage may have major impact on **profit** performance period to period.

discounted cash flow   A **capital investment analysis** technique that "discounts" or deflates future cash **returns** by taking out (removing) the amounts of earnings each period on the investment. The amount remaining after discounting out earnings is the total **capital recovery** from the future returns. *Note:*   If the discount rate is not exactly equal to the actual earnings rate, which is called the **internal rate of return (IRR),** there will be either a positive or negative **net present value.**

earnings per share (EPS)   Equals **net income (bottom-line profit)** for a period divided by the number of equity (capital stock) shares of business. In other words, **net income** is put on per-share basis. EPS is divided into market value of stock shares to calculate **price/earnings (P/E) ratio.**

earnings before (income) tax   Sales revenue for a period less cost-of-goods-sold expense, variable and fixed operating expenses, and interest expense, but before deducting income tax expense. (*Note:*   Other taxes such as social security taxes paid by employer and property taxes are included in operating expenses.) May not equal taxable income for the year because different accounting methods may be used for income tax.

expense behavior   Focuses on the factors that drive and determine the total amount of an expense for a period—in particular, whether the expense varies with sales volume or sales revenue, or the expense is relatively fixed and insensitive to the sales level over the short run. Variable versus **fixed expenses** is a critical distinction throughout **profit** performance analysis.

external financial statements   The **financial statements** prepared quarterly and annually that are presented in a financial report distributed outside the business to stockholders and creditors. Prepared according to generally accepted accounting principles (GAAP) that govern the measurement of net income and the presentation of financial condition and cash flows, and that require other disclosures. **Internal financial statements,** although based on the same **profit** measurement accounting methods, are classified differently and should report more information for management decision making and control.

financial leverage   Refers to the use of debt to finance part of the total capital invested in the **net operating assets** of a business. The equity capital of the business serves as the lever for securing debt capital—hopefully, at interest rates lower than the **return on assets (ROA)** that the business can earn. The financial leverage gain (or loss) equals the difference between its ROA and average interest rate times the amount of debt, which causes amplified swing in **net income** and **ROE.** The term also applies in general to any investor who uses debt for part of total capital invested.

financial statement   *Financial* means having to do with monetary value and economic wealth. *Statement* means a formal report and presentation. Sometimes called simply *financials.* Businesses prepare three primary financial statements: **balance sheet, cash flow statement,** and **income statement.**

fixed expense or **cost**   An expense or cost that remains the same total amount over the short run and does not vary with changes in sales volume or sales revenue. Over the longer run, however, these expenses and costs are raised or lowered as the business grows or declines. Fixed operating costs provide the **capacity** to carry on operations and make sales. (Fixed manufacturing costs provide production capacity.) Fixed expenses are the key pivot in analysis of **profit** behavior, especially in **operating leverage** analysis and determining **breakeven.**

free cash flow   Generally, the same as **cash flow from profit.** A business is free to do what it wants with this cash flow. However, a business usually has many ongoing commitments and demands on this cash flow, so business may not be all that free to do what it wants with the cash.

gross profit or **margin**   Equals sales revenue for a period less total cost of goods sold for the period; equals **profit** before operating expenses and interest and income tax expenses are deducted. Generally reported in the external **income statement** and should always be reported in the internal management income statement. This profit measure doesn't apply to service businesses that don't sell products.

income statement   The **financial statement** that summarizes sales revenue and expenses for a period, and reports one or more **profit** lines for the period. One of the three primary financial statements of business. The **bottom-line profit** is titled **net income** or net earnings by most businesses. External income statements disclose far less information compared with internal income statements for managers, but both should be based on the same profit accounting principles and methods. The key point is that profit is not known until accountants record sales revenue and expenses (as well as extraordinary gains and losses in period). Profit number depends on the reliability of the **accounting system** and choice of accounting methods.

internal (accounting) controls   Forms and procedures, beyond what would be required for the record-keeping and reporting functions of accounting, that are designed to deter and detect errors and fraud (a broad term covering embezzlement, employee theft, shoplifting, etc.). Two common internal control examples are requiring the signature of one or more persons higher in the organization to approve a transaction and giving customers printed receipts. Other examples are conducting searches at entry and exit points, surveillance cameras, and surprise counts of inventory. Internal controls should be cost effective; the cost of the control should be less than that of the loss prevented.

internal (management) financial statements   The **financial statements** prepared for use by managers to help them carry out their decision-making and control functions. Much of the detailed information in these statements is confidential and the business does not want its competitors to know it. Internal financial statements should not be limited or constrained by external financial reporting practices. **External financial statements** sit at the top of the pyramid, under which are the more detailed internal financial statements and other accounting reports to managers.

internal rate of return (IRR)   The exact discount rate that makes the **present value (PV)** of future cash **returns** from a **capital investment** equal to the initial capital amount invested. If IRR is higher than the company's **weighted-average cost of capital (hurdle rate),** the investment is an attractive opportunity; if less, the investment is substandard from the cost-of-capital point of view.

inventory turnover ratio   See **inventory/cost-of-goods-sold ratio.**

inventory/cost-of-goods-sold ratio   Equals ending inventory divided by total cost-of-goods-sold expense for the period; usually expressed as weeks of sales held in ending inventory. Depends on how long products are held in stock before sale. Reciprocal is the inventory turnover ratio. Ratio should be closely monitored by managers. Changes in inventory can have major impact on **cash flow from profit.**

management control   The follow-through on decisions for the purpose of achieving goals according to an established timetable. Includes virtually everything managers do toward this broad purpose. Depends on reports that track actual performance and which compare actual results against objectives and targets— called *feedback* information. Management control requires keeping close watch on everything.

manufacturing overhead costs   *Overhead* means indirect, in contrast with direct materials and direct labor costs of manufacturing products. Includes both variable manufacturing costs such as energy charges that vary with total output and fixed manufacturing costs that do not vary with actual output over the short run. Fixed manufacturing costs provide production **capacity,** which may not be fully used during the year. Some idle capacity is normal; thus, some of total annual fixed manufacturing overhead cost is absorbed in the **product cost** of the units manufactured during the year.

margin of safety   Excess of actual sales volume over **breakeven** sales volume, often expressed as a percent. Depends mainly on **contribution margin** per unit and keeping **fixed costs** of **capacity** consistent with actual sales volume. Reported only internally to managers; not disclosed in **external financial statements.**

net income   Sales revenue for the period less all expenses for period; also includes any extraordinary gains and losses for the period. Everything is taken into account to arrive at net income, which is popularly called *the bottom line.* Depends on the reliability of the **accounting system** and choice of accounting methods to measure revenue and expenses. Used in computing **return on equity (ROE)** and **earnings per share (EPS).** Clearly, the single most important number in business **financial statements.**

net income plus depreciation   A not entirely satisfactory shortcut for computing **cash flow from profit;** ignores changes in **operating assets** and **operating liabilities** that also have impacts on **cash flow** from profit-making operations. At best, an intermediate, "quick-and-dirty" approximation. Use with caution!

net operating assets   The total assets used in operating the business less accounts payable, accrued expenses payable, and income tax payable (which are called **operating liabilities** because they are generated spontaneously in the operations of the business). Net operating assets equal the total amount of capital that must be raised from interest-bearing debt and equity sources of capital. See also **return on assets (ROA)** and **return on equity (ROE).**

net present value (NPV)   Equals the **present value (PV)** of a **capital investment** minus the initial amount of capital invested. A positive NPV signals an attractive capital investment opportunity; a negative NPV means that the investment is substandard. **Internal rate of return (IRR)** is the discount rate that makes NPV equal to zero.

operating assets Assets used in the profit-making operations of business. Includes cash, accounts receivable from making sales on credit, inventory for businesses that sell products, prepaid expenses, and various fixed assets. Nonoperating assets (little discussed in this book) are other assets held by the business as a passive investor or assets not directly a part of the mainstream activities of business.

operating earnings or **profit** Equals sales revenue less cost-of-goods-sold expense and less all variable and fixed operating expenses for the period, but before interest and income tax expenses are deducted. Also called *earnings before interest and tax* (EBIT), especially in finance literature. Operating earnings are divided by **net operating assets** to determine **return on assets (ROA),** which is an extremely important **capital investment** performance measure. Operating earnings must be enough to cover interest on debt and earn a satisfactory **return on equity (ROE).**

operating leverage A relatively small percentage increase or decrease in sales volume causes a much larger percentage increase or decrease in **operating earnings**—frequently by two or three times. So sales volume changes have a lever effect on operating earnings. Should be called *sales volume leverage,* but in practice is called *operating leverage.*

operating liabilities Refers to the short-term liabilities generated spontaneously in the profit-making of business. Basically three types: accounts payable from inventory purchases and expenses, accrued expenses for unpaid amounts, and income tax payable. None are interest bearing, although if not paid on time business may be assessed a late payment penalty in the form of an interest charge. Being noninterest in nature, operating liabilities are deducted from total **operating assets** to determine **net operating assets** of business.

operating ratio The umbrella term for the several different ratios between either sales revenue or an expense (the profit-making operations of the business) and its corresponding asset or liability. These ratios are like X rays that show the skeleton of the business. Essential connections between the **income statement** items and **balance sheet** items are specified in these ratios. Expressed as so many weeks of revenue or expense. **Cash flow from profit** depends on controlling these ratios.

opportunity cost of capital A fundamental concept in economic theory and business finance referring to the **return on assets (ROA)** or **return on equity**

(ROE) that could be earned from the best alternative use of the capital employed by the business. A key point is that capital invested in one place could be invested someplace else; the earnings rate on the best investment alternative should be used as a benchmark for judging the **capital investment** performance of the business.

overhead   Refers to indirect operating expenses and indirect manufacturing costs, most of which are also fixed. *Indirect* means that the expense or cost cannot be matched or coupled in any obvious or objective manner with particular products, specific revenue sources, or an organizational unit. See also **fixed costs.**

payable/inventory ratio   Equals ending accounts payable from inventory purchases divided by ending inventory. Depends on credit terms offered by suppliers and actual payment practices of the business. Usually expressed as weeks of inventory purchases unpaid. Changes in the accounts payable **operating liability** can have a major impact on **cash flow from profit.**

payable/operating expenses ratio   Equals accounts payable for unpaid expenses at the end of the period divided by total operating expenses for the period, excluding cost of goods sold, **depreciation,** interest, and income tax expenses, which do not involve the accounts payable account. Depends on how long the business waits to pay for certain operating expenses after they have been recorded. Usually expressed as weeks of operating expenses in ending accounts payable. Changes in the accounts payable **operating liability** can have a major impact on **cash flow from profit.**

prepaids/operating expenses ratio   Equals prepaid expenses at the end of the period divided by total operating expenses for the period, excluding cost-of-goods-sold expense, **depreciation,** interest, and income tax expenses, which do not involve the prepaid expenses account. Depends on how long in advance the business has to prepay for certain items before the costs are charged off to expense. Usually expressed as weeks of operating expenses in ending prepaid expenses. Usually not as significant as accounts receivable and inventory, but business has to invest a certain amount of capital in these prepaid items. A change in the prepaid expenses **operating asset** affects **cash flow from profit.**

present value (PV)   The result from discounting the future cash **returns** from a **capital investment.** The discount rate is the **weighted-average cost of capital** for the business. If PV is more than the initial amount of capital that would have to be invested, then the investment is attractive; if less, better alternatives should be looked for. In other words, if PV is more than the initial cash outlay to enter the investment, then the earnings rate or **internal rate of return (IRR)** from the investment is higher than the discount rate and the **net present value (NPV)** is positive. If PV is less, then the IRR is less than the discount rate and the NPV is negative.

price/earnings (P/E) ratio Current market price of equity (capital stock) shares divided by **earnings per share (EPS).** A low P/E may signal an undervalued stock or a pessimistic forecast by investors. A high P/E may reveal an overvalued stock or an optimistic forecast by investors. *Caution:* The average P/E ratio for the stock market as a whole varies considerably over time.

product cost Equals purchase cost for retailers and wholesalers (distributors). In contrast, a manufacturer has to accumulate three different types of production costs to determine product cost: direct materials, direct labor, and, **manufacturing overhead.** Overhead means indirect and, thus, these costs must be allocated to different products. The cost of products (goods) sold is deducted from sales revenue to determine **gross profit** (or **margin**), the first profit line reported in the **income statement.**

profit The general term *profit* is not all that well defined; it may mean gains less losses, or inflows less outflows, or some other kinds of increases minus decreases. In business, the term means revenue (or other sources of operating income) minus expenses for a certain period of time. In the **income statement,** the final or bottom line of profit is called **net income,** which equals sales revenue (plus any extraordinary gains) less all expenses (and less any extraordinary losses) over the period. In addition to the net income, the internal management income statement of the business should report several other important profit lines: **gross profit (margin), contribution margin (profit),** operating profit (earnings), and profit (earnings) before income tax.

quality trade-off analysis Sometimes overlooked and not an explicit factor in analyzing changes in sales prices, **product costs,** and variable and **fixed operating costs.** Increases and decreases in these key profit factors often involve trade-offs with the quality of the product and service sold to customers. Quality changes can have a major impact on sales volume. Quality is an elusive measure, but managers should keep the quality factor in mind at all times.

quick ratio   Equals total of cash, accounts receivable, and marketable securities (if any) divided by total current liabilities. If all short-term creditors pounce on a business and do not allow rollover of the debts owed them by the business, this ratio indicates whether the cash and near-cash assets of the business are enough to pay off its short-term current liabilities. An extreme or acid test not likely to be imposed on a going business. Much more relevant in involuntary liquidation and bankruptcy workout situations.

receivable/revenue ratio   Equals accounts receivable at the end of the period divided by total credit sales revenue for the period; usually expressed as weeks of revenue in ending receivables. Depends on credit terms offered to customers and the actual collection experience of business. Reciprocal is the accounts receivable turnover ratio. A change in the accounts receivable **operating asset** can have a major impact on **cash flow from profit.**

return on assets (ROA)   Equals **operating earnings** (before interest and income tax) divided by the **net operating assets** used to generate the earnings. ROA is a key test of whether a business is earning enough to cover its cost-of-capital requirements. ROA is the essential starting point for determining **financial leverage** gain (or loss).

return on equity (ROE)   Equals **net income** (after deducting interest and income tax expenses) divided by total book value of owners' equity; usually expressed as a percent. Owners' equity includes both capital stock and retained earnings. ROE is the bottom-line **return on investment (ROI)** measure for the owners' equity capital invested in the business. ROE is a key component in determining the **weighted-average cost of capital.** Actual ROE performance should be compared with the **opportunity cost of capital.** Should be higher than the interest rate on debt because the owners take more risk.

return on investment (ROI)   The broad, generic term for measuring income, profit, or gain, or earnings on **capital investment** over one or more periods; expressed as a percent of the amount of invested capital during the period. The business as a whole is a **capital investment** project; the most relevant ROI ratios for business are **return on assets (ROA)** and **return on equity (ROE).** A specific capital investment can be analyzed to determine its **internal rate of return (IRR),** which is compared with the company's **weighted-average cost of capital (hurdle rate).**

returns (from a **capital investment**)   Refers to the timetable of future cash flows that are forecast to be received from a capital investment. (An investment might have negative net cash flow in one or more of the future periods.) The returns are discounted to determine the **present value (PV)** or to solve for the **internal rate of return (IRR)** of the investment. Alternatively, returns can be analyzed using the **spreadsheet** tool, which sorts out **capital recovery,** distributions to capital sources, and income tax payments period by period. *Caution: Return* is also used in **return on investment (ROI);** it means the percent of earnings on the amount of capital invested, not the stream of future cash flows from investment.

sales mix   The relative size, proportion, or percent of sales volume of each product or product line to total sales volume or total sales revenue. Usually different products (or product lines) have different profit margins, so shifts in sales mix are very important in profit analysis.

sales price analysis   Determining the impacts on **profit** and **cash flow from profit** from changes in sales price, either by holding all other profit factors constant or by making trade-offs between sales price and one or more other profit factors. Sales price is one of the few most fundamental determinants of profit.

sales-revenue-driven (dependent) operating expenses   Those operating expenses that are very sensitive to and vary in close proportion to changes in total sales revenue (total dollars). Examples are sales commissions based on sales revenue, credit card discount expenses, and rent expense and franchise fees based on total sales revenue. Not disclosed separately in external **income statements** but essential for management decision-making analysis. Compare with **sales-volume-driven operating expenses.**

sales volume analysis   Determining the impacts on **profit** and **cash flow from profit** from changes in sales volume, either by holding all other profit factors constant or by making trade-offs between sales volume and one or more other profit factors. Sales volume is one of few most fundamental determinants of profit. See also **operating leverage.**

sales-volume-driven (dependent) operating expenses
Those operating expenses that are very sensitive to and that vary in close proportion to changes in sales volume (quantity of products sold). Examples include many delivery costs, packaging costs, and other costs that depend mainly on the number of products sold or the number of customers served. *Note:* Cost-of-goods-sold expense is dependent on sales volume, but it is such a dominant expense for product businesses that it is always accounted for and

reported separately to determine **gross profit.** Variable operating expenses are reported below the gross profit line. Not disclosed in the external **income statement** but essential for management decision-making analysis. Compare with **sales-revenue-driven operating expenses.**

sales/fixed assets relationship   Equals annual sales revenue divided by the original cost of property, plant, and equipment (fixed assets) used by business. Measures how much sales revenue per year is generated for each dollar originally invested in fixed assets. Depends on whether the business is capital intensive or not, i.e., whether a lot of fixed assets are needed for making sales or not. The older the fixed assets, the less useful this comparison becomes because sales revenue is stated in current dollars but fixed assets are stated on a historical cost basis.

solvency ratio   Any ratio used to test and predict the ability of a business to pay its liabilities as they fall due. These ratios do not indicate the willingness of the business to pay on time without evasive tactics for delaying payment, or the intent to renegotiate payment terms or roll over the debt. See **current ratio** and **quick ratio.**

spreadsheet analysis of capital investments   The newer tool of analysis that has key advantages over the traditional mathematical methods for analyzing **capital investments.** The math methods are limited in scope and do not display all relevant data and information period by period for the capital investment. The **spreadsheet** method breaks out the distribution of each period's return between **capital recovery** and the payouts to income tax and sources of capital. The assumptions behind the analysis are much clearer in the period-by-period spreadsheet printout.

spreadsheet (computer programs)   Spreadsheet programs for personal computers are the successor to the worksheets used for many decades to organize and analyze data. Data, information, and titles are entered into *cells,* which is like a pigeonhole in an old-fashioned rolltop desk; it is addressed by its column and row intersection. Spreadsheet programs offer one main advantage: A long series of changes and computations can be redone or reworked literally in a matter of seconds. This power is especially useful in management decision-making analysis. The relationship and dependency of one cell with one or more other cells must be specified exactly and completely by entering formulas in the appropriate cells.

sunk cost   Could conceivably refer to the book value of any asset because the acquisition of most assets cannot be undone or reversed. Once the asset has been bought or acquired, its cost is irretrievable. So its book value is *sunk.* Usually the term has a narrower meaning: an asset that cannot be converted into cash through the normal operating cycle of the business. Examples are inventory items that cannot be sold, receivables that cannot be collected, and fixed assets that are no longer usable. The book value of such assets should be written off to expense; their normal book values are irrelevant and should be disregarded in making decisions.

tax payable/income tax ratio   Equals unpaid income tax at the end of the period divided by the total income tax expense for the period. The federal income tax law calls for annual business income tax to be paid by year-end, but some fraction is typically unpaid at year-end. A change in income tax payable **operating liability** affects **cash flow from profit.**

trade-off analysis   Determining the **profit** and **cash flow** effects caused by decreasing one key profit factor (such as sales price) and simultaneously increasing one or more of the other key profit factors (such as sales volume). A very common decision situation facing business managers.

trading on the equity   See **financial leverage.**

variable expense   An expense that changes in proportion with changes in sales volume or sales revenue. See **sales-revenue-driven operating expenses** and **sales-volume-driven operating expenses.**

weighted-average cost of capital (hurdle rate)   *Weighted* because it is based on the company's **capitalization structure** (mix of debt and equity capital); depends on interest rate(s) on debt, income tax rate, and **return on equity (ROE)** goal. Also called the *hurdle rate* because the business should earn at least this (minimum) **return on assets (ROA)** rate on its **net operating assets.** Used as discount rate to determine **present value (PV)** of specific investments.

Topical Guide to Figures